CREATED
for His
GLORY

GOD'S PURPOSE FOR
REDEEMING YOUR LIFE

JIM BERG

BJU PRESS
GREENVILLE, SOUTH CAROLINA

Library of Congress Cataloging-in-Publication Data

Berg, Jim 1952-

    Created for His glory : God's purpose for redeeming your life / Jim Berg.

    p.   cm.

    Includes bibliographical references and index.

    ISBN 1-57924-809-8 (softbound : alk. paper)

    1. Christian life.   I. Title

BV4501.3.847   2002

248.4—dc21   2002011072

Cover images: Background sky, EyeWire, Inc.; clouds, PhotoDisc, Inc.

NOTE: The fact that materials produced by other publishers may be referred to in this volume does not constitute an endorsement by Bob Jones University Press of the content or theological position of materials produced by such publishers. The position of Bob Jones University Press, and of the University itself, is well known. Any references and ancillary materials are listed as an aid to the reader and in an attempt to maintain the accepted academic standards of the publishing industry.

All Scripture is quoted from the Authorized King James Version.

Created for His Glory: God's Purpose for Redeeming Your Life

Design by Chris Hartzler
Composition by Kelley Moore

ISBN 1-57924-809-8

15 14 13 12 11 10 9 8 7 6 5 4 3 2 1

*To Patty, my beloved wife—the most God-loving,
Word-filled, ministry-minded person I know*

TABLE OF CONTENTS

FOREWORD   vii

PREFACE   ix

ACKNOWLEDGMENTS   xii

Chapter 1   Seeing the Invisible   1

PART ONE: REJOICING IN THE GRAND
             REALITY OF GOD   21
Chapter 2   The Reality of God's Supremacy   23
Chapter 3   The Reality of the Father's Sovereignty   43
Chapter 4   The Reality of Christ's Sufficiency   65
Chapter 5   The Reality of the Spirit's Security   93

PART TWO: EXPERIENCING THE GRAND
             REALITY OF GOD   113
Chapter 6   Relishing the Assurance   115
Chapter 7   Restoring the Unity   139
Chapter 8   Rejecting the Fantasy   163
Chapter 9   Responding to the Spirit   185

PART THREE: DISPLAYING THE GRAND
             REALITY OF GOD   209
Chapter 10   Living in the Fear of God   211
Chapter 11   Ruling in the Fear of God   233
Chapter 12   Submitting in the Fear of God   253
Chapter 13   'Tis Mystery All   273

EPILOGUE

APPENDIX A: REPRODUCIBLE STUDY SHEETS
Five Significant Statements/Take Time to Reflect   291

APPENDIX B: SUPPLEMENTAL ARTICLE
Salvation: Divine Determination or Human Responsibility
  by Layton Talbert   295

APPENDIX C: HOW TO USE THIS BOOK WHEN
            WORKING WITH OTHERS   313

BIBLIOGRAPHY   319

SCRIPTURAL INDEX   323

TOPICAL INDEX   331

FOREWORD

I first met Jim Berg in the early 1970s when we were undergraduate students at Bob Jones University. Now three decades later our offices are next to each other as we serve in administrative capacities. His love and enthusiasm for God and His Word and His work were as evident then as they are now, although his own maturation in the Faith has deepened and refined his life and thought. If you have ever heard him speak in person, that same infectious enthusiasm and desire to communicate sound forth from every page of this book.

Using Paul's "rich" letter to the Ephesians as his base, Jim wants believers to know the "wealth" that is theirs as a member of God's family. Not only is the Christian being *Changed into His Image* but he has also been *Created for His Glory*! And when a believer comes to grips with these "heavenly realities," his attitudes and actions will radically change.

Jim is a well-equipped guide to lead us from the humdrum, defeated wastelands where most Christians dwell to the fresh and invigorating air of walking in "the heavenlies." For years he has taught classes at the university level on leadership and counseling; he regularly conducts weekend seminars in churches all across America on these issues; and his daily responsibility is to administer discipline to college-age youth. So from all of this personal interaction he knows that what God says in His Word "works"!

With a combination of sound exposition and personal illustrations, Jim gets to the heart of each matter and lays bare our usual superficial thinking. There are no simplistic formulas for success here—only the "simpleness" of choosing to follow God's way. Jim's only desire is for us to realize God's "marvelous redemptive work on our behalf through Jesus Christ, and how those truths must filter down into our daily lives." The book is enhanced by the concluding application questions for each chapter, where the reader comes face to face with how he will put this material to use.

Good books point the reader beyond their pages to a higher plane. As you read *Created for His Glory*, you will decrease and Jesus Christ will increase. Perhaps you will even find yourself on your knees with tears of confession and joy and thanksgiving as you understand a little more clearly all that God has done for you. And perhaps even this side of heaven you will find yourself "lost in wonder, love, and praise" as you contemplate God's purpose for redeeming your life. I hope that many in our day will hear that child's voice of old, "Take up and read, take up and read"—and if you obey, you will be the better for it!

Dr. Royce Short

Dean, Bob Jones University
  School of Religion
Greenville, South Carolina

PREFACE

Vibrant Christianity

The burden for this book has grown out of the opportunities God has given Patty and me to minister in couples retreats and family conferences in hundreds of churches over the past twenty years.

We have been encouraged as we have met numbers of God's people who testify of the satisfaction and delight they have found in their walk with God. We are saddened, however, to have come upon countless others whose driven lives are filled with guilt, failure, heartache, and trouble. Just as pitiful are others whose lives are filled with restlessness, joylessness, and energy-draining activities. The experience of most believers in the church today is a far cry from the abundant life Jesus promised in John 10:10. This is no new phenomenon, however. Tozer observed in the last generation,

> Among the many who profess the Christian faith *scarcely one in a thousand*[1] reveals any passionate thirst for God.[2]

While pondering this sad condition and while preparing a series of messages on the family for a summer conference in my own church, I turned once again to Ephesians 5 to consider what God says to husbands and wives. I was struck afresh with the fact that this teaching about the home does not come until midway through the *fifth* chapter of the book. Before it are four and a half chapters of instruction about something else! Not until Paul finishes with that "something else" does he even begin to say anything about Christian families.

A serious reflection upon the opening chapters of the book reveals that God is intending for Christian families to be built upon a foundation

---

[1]Throughout this book all italics are mine unless specifically noted. Anytime words are [bracketed] in a Scripture text, it means I have added some words to further explain the meaning of the verse.

[2]A. W. Tozer, *The Root of the Righteous* (Camp Hill, Pa.: Christian Publications, 1955), 56. Please note that citing an author in this book does not imply endorsement of the positions he has taken theologically and ecclesiastically in other matters. There is much that is correct theologically, and thus helpful, in the works cited; but like any book, including this one you are reading, they must be read with an open Bible before you.

of vibrant Christianity! When we jump into Ephesians 5 and ignore the truths of the first four chapters, we are like builders trying to construct a house without a solid foundation. <u>Strong Christian homes cannot be built out of weak Christians</u>. The condition of every Christian home is an exact reflection of its understanding and practice of Christian doctrine—the bedrock of vibrant Christian living.

This book is not primarily about building strong Christian homes, however, though the emphasis of this study is the foundation of any solid believing family. This study is, rather, a look at those basic truths of the Faith that built the solid, joyful Christianity of the first century—the kinds of truths that Paul covered in the opening chapters of Ephesians.

Neither is this book a study in the Epistle of Ephesians, per se. It is, however, a study of its major themes. Ephesians has been called the crowning Epistle of the New Testament. In it are contained all of the essential doctrines of the Faith in their most basic, yet their most majestic, presentation. Meditation upon its themes will give us the sense of transcendence—the ability to see the things that stand above our physical existence—which we so desperately need if we are to have an impact for God in "this present evil world."[3]

While *Changed into His Image: God's Plan for Transforming Your Life*, my previous book, dealt with the essential elements of biblical change in a believer's life, this volume deals with the Christian life in even broader strokes. *Created for His Glory: God's Purpose for Redeeming Your Life* takes up God's ultimate plans for us, His marvelous redemptive work on our behalf through Jesus Christ and how those truths must filter down into our daily lives.[4] My desire is that God will open your eyes to the beauty and wonder of your salvation.

Join me as we survey the things God has done for us "in the heavenlies." If your life is filled with doubt, restlessness, despair, failure, or

---

[3]Galatians 1:4.

[4]Though the book you hold in your hands can be read and studied without an understanding of the truths presented in *Changed into His Image* (Greenville, S.C.: Bob Jones University Press, 1999), you will profit more from this study if you have read and studied the previous work.

boredom—or if you are helping other believers whose lives are described by those terms—this study is for you.

Some readers may find this study somewhat challenging because it deals with topics unfamiliar to many modern believers. Those who have studied *Changed into His Image* will find it just another step toward a fuller understanding of spiritual things. We must all keep in mind as we go through this study together that the epistles of the New Testament were not written as apostolic literary exercises or merely dry collections of theological data. They were written with pastoral intent to congregations largely composed of first-century "blue-collar workers." They are inspired accounts of how Spirit-filled members of the church can live to the glory of God in a sin-cursed world.

They were intended to be thoroughly understood by *common* people and rigorously practiced in the power of God's Spirit to the glory of Jesus Christ. Therefore, what we are going to study together is not optional window-dressing for those who wish to become some kind of super-saint. They are essential elements to be understood and lived in the milieu of daily life in order to satisfy our thirsty souls and to demonstrate to a lost world that all of us were *Created for His Glory*.

ACKNOWLEDGMENTS

In a Shakespearean play or an opera, the curtain calls come at the end of the performance. In a book they come before the play even starts. I am happy, therefore, to hold the curtain back and shine the spotlight on the many others who have made this production possible. I have relied upon the spiritual judgment and biblical knowledge of several men as these chapters unfolded and wish to recognize them first.

I extend my deepest thanks to my closest friend, Dr. Ken Collier, director of THE WILDS, for his constant personal encouragement throughout the writing of this project. He has always listened attentively—as only committed friends would do—as I rambled on about what I was developing for the next chapter or section. His life and feedback have been a constant encouragement to me.

Dr. Jim Newcomer, former staff member of mine and now a senior pastor, meticulously examined the manuscript, giving me blow-by-blow feedback about how the material would read to his people. His biblical insight, encouragement, and friendship are deeply appreciated.

My own pastor, Dr. John Vaughn, combed through the manuscript, offering excellent editorial and theological advice. He has also invited me to preach through the book each summer for the past three years as I developed the material. These weeklong seminars gave me opportunity to fine-tune its message while committing it to writing. The people of Faith Baptist Church in Greenville, South Carolina, were especially encouraging while I "practiced" on them.

Though these three men had the most personal involvement in the project, I do not want to minimize the vital contribution made by several of my personal friends and ministry partners at Bob Jones University. The insightful suggestions of Dr. Bruce McAllister, Dr. Royce Short, Dr. Stephen Hankins, and Dr. Randy Leedy have been woven into the fabric of this work. I have profited from the "iron sharpening iron" effect of their lives upon mine—not only as it relates to this manuscript but also as our lives intersect each other at BJU.

Once again, the editorial and production staff of Bob Jones University Press win my highest commendation. Suzette Jordan, who edited the

ACKNOWLEDGMENTS

manuscript, wins the gold for her Olympian effort to put my writing into polished form. The many men and women in the printing division of BJU Press take every project as a personal statement of their dedication to Jesus Christ and demonstrate that dedication in the quality of their work—as you can see for yourself. I esteem them highly for their work's sake. They are unseen but definitely not unappreciated.

Last but not least I thank my wife, Patty, for her patience and input throughout this project. The book is dedicated to her because it really is the product of our study and our lives together. I can testify that she seeks to know God with a fervor rarely seen in God's people today. I am not exaggerating when I say that the work of the Spirit of God in her has produced the most God-loving, Word-filled, ministry-minded disciple-maker I know. Her price is far above rubies.

CHAPTER ONE

SEEING THE INVISIBLE

WHAT YOU DON'T SEE *CAN* HURT YOU

Things you cannot see often make a big difference in your life. A skateboard left on the stairway you are descending—invisible in the middle of the night—can have a big impact upon your life. Invisible bacteria in your chicken salad sandwich at lunch can rearrange your whole afternoon. An undetected computer virus can set you back hours or days when it attacks your home computer or office network. A buildup of cholesterol or plaque in your arteries or a growing mass of cancerous tissue can dictate significant changes in your life in the days to come.

These scenarios are familiar to us, and responsible people take adequate measures to shield themselves from these unseen menaces in the physical world. Far more crucial, however, are the issues of the unseen spiritual dimension since choices in the spiritual realm can be eternally consequential. In addition, living in light of the unseen spiritual realm can add joy and peace to everything that happens in the physical realm—both good and calamitous.

Take for example the apostle Paul's experiences in jail. In Philippi he was arrested for "disturbing the peace" when he exorcised a demon from a fortune-telling girl and thereby enraged her profit-making masters. Though beaten bloody by scourging and thrust into pain-racking stocks, Paul and his companion, Silas, saw beyond the physical realm and "prayed, and sang praises unto God."[1] The happy result was that later that evening their jailer fell to his knees—instead of falling on his

---

[1] Acts 16:25.

sword—and begged them to show him the way of salvation. Though pain normally galvanizes a man's attention toward his physical circumstances, *the apostles' attention was centered in an unseen realm.* It made all the difference in the world—especially for a certain jailer and his family.

An event in the prophet Elisha's life also shows us the difference that "seeing the invisible" makes. The Syrian king had tried to make repeated guerrilla raids upon Israel. God, however, continually revealed the Syrian plans to Elisha, who in turn relayed them to the king of Israel. Of course, after several foiled raids the king of Syria was understandably frustrated and thought he had a traitor in the camp. Finally, word reached him that Elisha was the problem. The Syrian king set off immediately to Dothan to stop Elisha's interference. During the night, he surrounded Elisha's hometown. The Scriptures pick up the narrative in II Kings 6:15-17.

> And when the servant of the man of God was risen early, and gone forth, behold, [the Syrian army] compassed the city both with horses and chariots. And his servant said unto [Elisha], Alas, my master! [what] shall we do? And [Elisha] answered, Fear not: for they that be with us are more than they that be with them. And Elisha prayed, and said, Lord, I pray thee, open his eyes, that he may see. And the Lord opened the eyes of the young man; and he saw: and, behold, the mountain was full of horses and chariots of fire round about Elisha.

What a comfort those *invisible* hosts must have been to Elisha's servant at that time! Of course, God does not in this dispensation of time open physical eyes to see the spiritual realm as He did for Elisha's servant. Instead, He has given us something better! He has permanently revealed everything He wants us to know about the spiritual realm in His inspired Word.[2] His revelation of the unseen world through the Word is an immense blessing to us, His creatures, because *blindness in either realm is a serious handicap.* Let's look at why blindness is so serious.

---

[2]II Peter 1:3.

LIFE IS MORE DANGEROUS WHEN YOU CAN'T SEE

Through the years we have had several students at Bob Jones University who were legally blind. As a whole they have been a great blessing to the student body. Instead of the stubborn, self-reliant determination so characteristic of unbelievers with serious limitations, these wonderful young people possessed a quiet confidence in God's sufficiency for them. As a result, their testimonies inspired others with lesser limitations to endure by "seeing him who is invisible."[3]

Though their spiritual lives evidence God's power, physical life is more dangerous for them than it is for sighted students. They must move slowly to avoid obstacles and must concentrate on their surroundings to maintain their bearings. A blind student on campus cannot see a careless cyclist coming down the street. He cannot see the book bag left unattended on the hallway floor. He cannot read "Slippery When Wet" or "Watch Your Step" signs. There are many hidden dangers for him.

Life is certainly more dangerous for the physically blind, but it is hazardous for the spiritually blind as well. Proverbs 22:3, 5 address this issue.

> A prudent man forseeth [sees] the evil, and hideth himself: but the simple [the spiritually imperceptive] pass on, and are punished. . . . Thorns and snares are in the way of the froward.

The above verses teach that a man with spiritual perception can see the difficulties ahead and prudently avoid them, but the path of the spiritually blind will be filled with hidden traps. What seem to them like momentary indulgences in innocent pleasures become life-dominating habits that hold them in ever-constricting traps. Sadly, they never see the calamity coming, and many do not even recognize the entrapment, even while held in its cords.

The Scriptures are full of warnings to the spiritually blind. Proverbs 14:12 says, "There is a way which seemeth right unto a man, but the end thereof are the ways of death." The simple, or unwary, man in Proverbs 7, who is naive about the consequences of following the

---

[3]Hebrews 11:27.

harlot's advances, "goeth after her straightway, as an ox goeth to the slaughter, or as a fool to the correction of the stocks; till a dart strike through his liver; as a bird hasteth to the snare, and knoweth not that it is for his life."[4] The fact that he "knoweth not"—that he is spiritually insensible—has devastating results for him.

Lessons from a Medicine Cabinet

Spiritual blindness in many believers is most evident in how easily they are influenced by this world. Worldliness—taking our cues from the world as to what is important in life—is of serious concern to God. Too many Christians "play" with the world as unruly children play in the forbidden medicine cabinet in the bathroom of their home. These unsuspecting and disobedient youngsters may pop pills and smear ointments on each other with no knowledge of the danger involved. They just know they are having fun, and that is all that matters to them.

Spiritually insensible believers "pop" this or that movie or concert or "smear on" this or that mind-numbing experience with no thought of its toxicity or potency. Too many believers merely ask themselves, "Is the drug in the medicine cabinet *legal?*" They want to know only if the Bible directly forbids a certain activity. If not, they assume they can indulge in it and claim it as their Christian liberty.

Think with me about this approach with your doctor. Suppose you ask your physician, "Doc, is it *legal* for me to take ibuprofen[5] for my headache?" Or, "Is it within my *liberties* to consume this drug?" He would think your question to be quite strange since the important issues are more involved than just whether ibuprofen is a legal drug. *The fact that the law does not forbid a drug's use does not mean that one should take it.*

Your doctor has many questions to ask before he can give you a helpful answer. "How much are you planning to take?" "How often are you planning to take it?" "What other medications are you taking?" "What might be causing your pain for which the ibuprofen will only alleviate the symptoms?" "How long have you had the headaches?" "How long

---

[4]Proverbs 7:22-23.

[5]Ibuprofen is a nonsteroidal anti-inflammatory drug (NSAID) used to reduce inflammation, relieve minor pains, and reduce fever. Its most common brand names are Advil and Motrin.

were you planning to take the medication?" "What is your general physical condition?" "What other problems are you having besides the one for which you wish to take this medication?" And the list could go on and on.

He knows that a headache from a sinus infection may need an antibiotic to deal with the infection rather than a painkiller to alleviate the discomfort. A headache from muscular tension may show a need for exercise instead of something to dull the pain. The pain may be a signal that something else is drastically wrong and needs attention.

The same is true for involvement in the worldly culture around us. Asking if the *content* of the song, movie, sporting event, vacation excursion, or computer game is spiritually "legal" is only a small fraction of the issue. Even if something is not directly forbidden in the Word by command or principle, the believer must ask himself many more questions before he decides whether he should partake.

He must consider, "How much of this kind of thing am I already filling my life with?" "What is being neglected in my life while I partake?" "What other kinds of entertainment and recreation am I already involved with?" "Why am I indulging in the first place? Is my soul restless for entertainment because I am so spiritually empty?" "Should I be handling the restlessness, loneliness, or emptiness another way?" "If I am merely trying to unwind, is this the primary way God teaches me to handle stress?" "Would this activity be all right if I, indeed, handled pressure God's way?" "Whom will I be affecting—and in what way— by my example?" The list of questions goes on and on.

Just as a physician needs to know physiology and pharmacology to answer the question about ibuprofen, a Christian needs to know his Bible well before he can determine whether he should partake of some element in our culture. The truth to be learned about making right choices is this:

> You cannot make the right choices in the visible world unless you are spending much time in the invisible world.

A believer dare not indulge by default in what the world has to offer! If he is spiritually insensible to the effects of the world, his spiritual life will be in danger. He must know his Bible, and he must be viewing it through illuminated eyes. His ignorance of spiritual issues will be disastrous to his heart.

LIFE IS MORE DISCOURAGING WHEN YOU CAN'T SEE

It is also important to note that life can be far more *discouraging* for the blind. As the difficulties and dangers increase, so do the temptations to be discouraged. The blind student must often expend more energy to accomplish the same things a sighted student does. He may feel left out and isolated from others. Because he doesn't see everything everyone else sees, he misses the humor in many situations. Sighted people don't fully understand him, and life can become very discouraging.

In a similar fashion, spiritual blindness in believers can be very discouraging. The apostle Peter addresses this when challenging believers to be diligent about growing in their spiritual lives. He says, "But he that lacketh these things is blind, and cannot see afar off, and hath forgotten that he was purged from his old sins."[6] A spiritually stunted believer can't "see" well and may even have serious doubts about whether he has even been saved. There is not a trail of illuminated truth that marks his spiritual progress. He cannot point to repeated times when God Himself has intersected His life through the Word and has spoken through it to him. The relationship with God is so distant, he wonders if it even exists. The discouragement sets in, and he spirals downward to despair.

Because of its growing prevalence in our society today, I want to extend our discussion of this second aspect of spiritual blindness—"life is more discouraging when you cannot see"—and look more closely at the phenomenon we call despair.

Darkness and Despair

Despair is always the inevitable result of *life without light*. There are times when some Christians have come into what the Puritans called "the dark night of the soul." God seems to hide His face though the believer has been seriously seeking God.

Job experienced it while suffering many other afflictions. He knew God was present, but Job was "kept in the dark" for several months. Job

---

[6]II Peter 1:9.

began his time of suffering with triumphant declarations of God's purposes and faithfulness, but as the suffering and darkness wore on, Job began to lose heart. Nothing seemed to help. All he could do was cry out for God to show Himself. In due time, God answered Job and intervened with a revelation about Himself that breathed fresh light into Job's weary heart. This kind of darkness falls when God "withdraws himself in order to make us appreciate him more so that we diligently seek for him as we would seek for a lost precious treasure."[7]

It is not my purpose at this point to deal with the specifics of this particular kind of "darkness." The focus of our study will be directed more at those who experience despair when the light of God is shut off *because of their own spiritual neglect.*

More and more believers are tasting the same despair the world lives in because they have chosen to "walk . . . as other Gentiles walk, in the [emptiness] of their mind."[8] I believe as the days draw closer to the coming of the Lord, and as individuals and societies increasingly ignore and defy God, we are going to see an unprecedented rise in despair.

The bottom line truth is that *life is not supposed to work without God at the center.*[9] Those who try to do so—even Christians—can maintain only an artificial facade of hope and satisfaction. The grim reality is that the emptiness of life without God at the center pushes itself to the consciousness once again when the music stops, the drugs wear off, the eroticism fails, the fashions grow old, the relationships disappoint, the accomplishments fade, and the thrills subside. They are left to themselves, and the emptiness for most people is too much. Instead of crying out to God for light, however, they dive back into their activities,

---

[7]John Owen, *The Glory of Christ* (Carlisle, Pa.: The Banner of Truth Trust, 1994), 109-10.

[8]Ephesians 4:17.

[9]By "God at the center" I mean that He is acknowledged, served, and worshiped as the central passion of a man's life. It is the attitude embodied in such Old Testament passages as Deuteronomy 6:5, "And thou shalt love the Lord thy God with all thine heart, and with all thy soul, and with all thy might." It is having "no other gods before [Him]" (Exodus 20:3). It is to "know therefore this day, and consider it in thine heart, that the Lord he is God in heaven above, and upon the earth beneath: there is none else" (Deuteronomy 4:39). The New Testament takes this further and introduces Jesus Christ as the central focus of the believer's attention as we shall see in the chapters ahead.

mainlining the anesthesia of their endless pursuits to dull the pain of their empty souls. Such is the picture of man without God at the center—even believing man who isn't seeing God in new and fresh illuminated truths through the Spirit of God.

Reflection – Illumination = Despair

When I deal with a despairing individual—Christian or non-Christian—I know that I am dealing with a person who has spent some time in recent days *reflecting*. He has allowed himself to *think* much about the way his life has not turned out the way he expected. He is thinking about how pointless things are. He has *reflection minus illumination*. By the phrase "minus illumination" I mean that he has not been "seeing the invisible." There has been little or no illuminated truth penetrating his soul. God is not the biggest concern of his life. He has been existing with little or no personal relationship with Jesus Christ.

But spiritually insensible people don't "see" this. They think other things are the problem. When they despair, rather than acknowledging the poverty of their relationship with Jesus Christ, they seek to medicate the "down" feelings[10] or distract themselves with activity. We have seen this phenomenon in several ways during our modern times but have "misdiagnosed" the cause. I want to look at some of these circumstances.

Midlife Crisis—One of the more common manifestations of modern despair is the cluster of behaviors and attitudes our culture calls "midlife crisis." I certainly don't want to legitimize a psychological view of this phenomenon. Rather, by addressing it here, I want us to see that if we understood our Bibles better, nothing in this "crisis" would surprise us.

Here is a man, usually in his mid- to late-forties, who in disturbing moments of *reflection* begins to realize that he has not "left his footprints on the sands of time" as he had envisioned he would when he was in his twenties. He hasn't advanced in his work as he had hoped. His marriage hasn't yielded the satisfaction he had anticipated. His children have deeply disappointed him, and so forth. Perhaps a physical limitation—heart surgery, hip replacement, back injury, endocrine malfunc-

---

[10]Low spirits are not, in themselves, unspiritual. I am speaking here only of those feelings that are *caused* by the hopelessness of the despairing individual who is reflecting on a life that has been lived only half-heartedly for God.

tions, or other malady—may jolt him into the reality that he isn't getting any younger and that his stamina is gone. Though he would like to start life over again, he knows that even if he had the opportunity, he doesn't have the strength or the time. Perhaps he has even been a Christian all of his adult years. He may even have graduated from a Bible college. But he must confess that he has little thirst for God.

As a whole, nothing is turning out the way he planned. All the things he thought would have to be in place to make life worthwhile have evaporated with little hope of a second chance at any of them. He looks back at all the years, and everything seems so pointless. The more he *reflects*, the more he despairs. He may even grow angry with God or look around and blame his "insensitive" wife or his "ungrateful" children or his "stingy" employer for his failures. He may start telling himself that no one deserves to live like this. Hasn't he sacrificed for others—even God—all these years and isn't he entitled to a little enjoyment out of the whole thing? His heart now begins to fill with bitterness, and the temptations of the world around him grow stronger.

Indulgence in an affair or pornography may give him a temporary eroticized high. He may turn to gambling or extreme sports, or he may leave his wife and home entirely to "find" himself. His doctor, noting his depression during an annual checkup, may offer him a prescription to help neutralize his low times.[11]

Though at times he has asked God to help him and may have tried not to disobey God too much, God has not been his first concern. He has not pursued God with all his heart, soul, and strength.[12] God has made it clear, however, that *mediocre Christianity is not supposed to work.*

---

[11]Of course, I am not speaking here of medications to correct a known endocrine or organic malfunction such as hypothyroidism, and so forth. I am speaking here entirely of psychotropic drugs that are given not to treat a truly organic etiology but to treat an affective symptom of discomfort. The discomfort certainly is real, but the cause *in this case* is in the person's handling of life as described in this chapter, not some organic disorder. Furthermore, it is crucial to understand that though some physical illness may cause us to feel down at times and *tempt* us to think thoughts of hopelessness and self-pity, no physical malady *causes* us to say hopeless and self-pitying words and statements—thoughts—to ourselves. Every thought we have comes from our heart and reveals the heart. The enemy of our soul is never a "low spirit" in itself. The enemy is "unbelief"—handling life without God as our central Hope.

[12]Luke 10:27.

The words of David, though pleasant sounding at times to our man in crisis, have never been the consistent reality of his life: "As the [deer] panteth after the water brooks, so panteth my soul after thee, O God. My soul thirsteth for God, for the living God."[13]

He cannot say that Paul's testimony has ever been his experience either. The apostle recounted, "I count all things but loss for the excellency of the knowledge of Christ Jesus my Lord: for whom I have suffered the loss of all things, and do count them but dung, that I may win Christ."[14]

In contrast, our man in crisis has always stopped some distance away from such drastic pursuit of spiritual things. He has done enough to get by—enough to maintain some degree of calmness in his conscience and some degree of testimony before other Christians. He would have to confess, however, that he hasn't taken seriously the teaching of our Lord that the "corn of wheat [must] fall into the ground and die, [or] it abideth alone."[15] He has settled for a "respectable" Christian life. From the biblical viewpoint, however, he is "lukewarm,"[16] "double minded,"[17] and a man trying to "serve two masters."[18]

He never wanted to do anything too radical with his spiritual life or think too long about what God might want out of him. Instead he danced around the edges of total abandonment to God, concerned only about his immediate happiness and his public image. He avoided the hard thoughts about what God might ask of him.

So our society calls this a "midlife crisis," and by giving it a psychological name, it effectively masks again the real dilemma—man without God at the center, man in despair.

As a Christian community we have failed to see that this believer, like the unbelieving world around him, is walking "in the vanity of [his] mind, having the understanding darkened, being alienated [i.e., dis-

---

[13]Psalm 42:1-2.
[14]Philippians 3:8.
[15]John 12:24.
[16]Revelation 3:15-20.
[17]James 1:8.
[18]Matthew 6:24.

tant] from the life of God through the ignorance that is in [him], *because of the blindness of [his] heart.*"[19] What a tragedy that it should take place, for the Scriptures are full of warnings against mediocre Christianity. But this isn't the first time we have misdiagnosed the despair of people around us. We missed it in the sixties with the hippies, as well.

Flower Children—The last time our society saw wholesale despair was in the 1960s when many college students of the day started *reflecting*. They thought upon the condition of their world. They asked the painful questions about life and concluded, "What's the point?" Their conclusion was valid—there was no point. There was no point in the Vietnam War. It didn't seem to have a righteous beginning or a noble end. They saw no point in higher education. It had not kept its promises of a better world. There seemed to be no point in pursuing a career. Why should they work for forty years like their fathers, who retired only to do nothing? They concluded they could do nothing now and avoid the forty years of agony. So they did.

Some tried to deaden the emptiness with free sex and mind-numbing drugs. Others sought meaning by throwing their lives into causes of injustice, while still others isolated themselves into communes trying to find peace and trying to "find" themselves. Each group sang songs advertising the psychedelic trips, protesting the injustice, or testifying of the despair and "pointlessness."

The same mood of the flower children is fostered today through a post-modern philosophy that says, "Objective truth doesn't exist. It is created by groups of people and is valid only for them in their own culture." This worldview puts each individual squarely in the center of his own world, leaving others on the fringes and leaving God out entirely. This self-absorbed thinking will lead to even greater emptiness, moral destruction, and social decline than was ever produced in the hippie movement of the sixties. Despair will be epidemic in the days ahead.

Extreme Everything—As despair becomes more prevalent, we can also expect all of the possible anesthesias for the pain of emptiness to increase as well. We will see a rise in extreme drug therapies. Television

---

[19]Ephesians 4:17-18.

and movie content will feature increasingly extreme programming in the name of "reality shows." We will see extreme sports and adventures rise to unprecedented heights as people rebel against the limitations placed upon them by their own bodies and by nature itself and as they seek some new means to experience a rush. Increasingly kinky sexual exploits both inside and outside of marriage will hold out a promise of extreme pleasure for deadened souls but will leave the participants only more deeply mired in their despair.

I saw an example of this during the summer of 2000 while I was writing this opening chapter. I was on vacation during the Republican National Convention and occasionally turned on the television to see how the events were unfolding. One afternoon when I tuned in, expecting to see convention highlights, I saw instead an interview with a man named Ted—not his real name. Unlike the man we saw in midlife crisis who had not achieved his goals, Ted *had* accomplished everything he set out to do. He was a star teacher in a large public high school. He was fired when he announced to his students that he had felt all of his life that he was born the wrong gender and that now he was going to go through a sex change operation and live as a woman. In the interview, Ted, now renamed Trisha—not his real assumed name either—told his story.[20]

He said that throughout his growing-up years he had raced motorcycles, climbed mountains, and rafted whitewater. He said, however— and this is important—that adventure had a "hollow ring" to it. He had been at the point of suicide many times. He said, "I buried myself in trying to be a success . . . but it just wasn't enough." He was depressed and knew something was wrong but couldn't put his finger on it. He tried cross-dressing and finally came to the conclusion through therapy that he was born the wrong gender.

---

[20]I refer to Ted as "he" even though in the interview he was addressing the audience as a woman. No surgical sex change can undo the fact that God made him a man—despite his feelings to the contrary. It is also unloving to refer to Ted as "it" as if there were some confusion about whether Ted is a man or a woman. Though calling him "it" may produce a few laughs among the brethren, it is uncharitable and insensitive. God is not confused about what gender Ted is, and neither should we be confused about his identity. He is, furthermore, a soul for whom Christ died, and he desperately needs the gospel just like the rest of the world. We must not in any way be a stumbling block to the gospel to the Teds of this world.

He was quite excited about his "solution" and was riding on the crest of a wave of public recognition as a trailblazer for his cause of gender-transition. The real danger for Ted was that this time he *really* thought he had isolated his problem and had solved it. When the despair sets in again, he has nothing left to try—except suicide.

Indeed, many like Ted have come to this point and have ended their lives. Some have left a note saying that even though they were finally "true to themselves," life was not worth living because others still rejected them. And society will be blamed for being homophobic or unloving.

The sad reality is that the "Teds" of our day have missed the real reason for the emptiness of life. It is not due to rejection by the heterosexual world—although we must admit that many "straights," while rightly speaking against sinful "alternative" lifestyles, are certainly unloving. The real problem is the emptiness of a soul estranged from its thirst-quenching Creator—a soul that is not "seeing the unseen."

Ted Isn't the Only One with a Problem

Sadder still is that many *believers* do not have much more hope or peace or joy than Ted. These brethren will go to their grave defending their salvation, but they have little enjoyment of it in this life. They have very little light from God in their souls, and they have no idea why their life is so empty. Inwardly, they feel cheated and betrayed by a Christianity that hasn't delivered.

A. W. Tozer put his finger on the problem when he said, "The difference between a great Christian life and any other kind lies in the quality of our religious concepts."[21] Our "religious concepts"—our knowledge of God and His ways—are too shallow today. We aren't spending much time "in the heavenlies," as Paul describes in Ephesians 1. Even those believers who are familiar with at least some of the major responsibilities outlined in Ephesians 4-6 are not at home in chapters 1-3. Think with me for a few moments about the letter to the Ephesians.

---

[21]A. W. Tozer, *The Pursuit of Man* (Camp Hill, Pa.: Christian Publications, 1950), 3.

Chapters 1-3 of Ephesians have often been called "The Wealth of the Believer." These three chapters do not contain a single command! They are packed, however, with propositional statements about the person and work of Jesus Christ—the one who *is* at the center of the universe! It is ignorance of these doctrines that has led to the failure of most believers today to fulfill the sixty-five commands of chapters 4-6, often called "The Walk and Warfare of the Believer."

Those who have taken the time to meditate upon Ephesians have been richly rewarded. John Bunyan was inspired to write *The Pilgrim's Progress* through his study of Ephesians. Another called it "God's Handbook of the Universe." While that may sound too lofty for us, we must remember that Ephesians was not written to seminarians or Bible college students. It was written to a church of first-generation Christians saved out of the pagan worship of the goddess Diana. Many of the number in that church were slaves. They took seriously Paul's words, and in spite of their non-Christian backgrounds God molded them into a church commended by Jesus Christ Himself for their "works, and . . . labour, and . . . [endurance]."[22] They had no time for false teachers and did not faint when the fires of persecution hit. All of that was possible because they spent time "in the heavenlies" as we shall do in this study together. *They proved that the quality of what you see "in the heavenlies" determines the quality of what others see in your life.* So you see, "what you don't see *can* hurt you, but . . . ."

WHAT YOU *COULD* SEE WILL AMAZE YOU

Let's take a look at where we are headed in this book. Part One of this study will begin by looking at who God is. This is how Paul began his Ephesian letter. I call it "Rejoicing in the Grand Reality of God." In the first chapter of Ephesians Paul looks at several important realities that he calls "spiritual blessings in heavenly places." They are truths that were at the forefront of his mind while he was imprisoned and must be dominant parts of our worldview as well if we are to have the kind of rejoicing heart that Paul had in times of trouble. We must "see" them with spiritual illumination. Insensibility and blindness to them will be disastrous.

---

[22]Revelation 2:2-3.

Next, in Part Two, "Experiencing the Grand Reality of God," we will discuss how those overarching truths about who God is are to be translated into various broad issues of our daily lives. We will see how these truths apply to the matters of personal joy and security in the Lord, our ability to resist temptation, and our ability to get along with other believers as we walk in the Spirit. God gave us Ephesians so that we can understand these issues, rejoice in their beauty, and "walk worthy" of the salvation He has given us.

Lastly, in Part Three we will see how what we have learned about God becomes the foundation for the "fear of the Lord." We will also see how the fear of God is the energizing and guiding force behind the fulfillment of our daily living at home, at work, and in society in general.

My burden in this study is twofold. I wish for it to be *prescriptive*—attempting to solve problems that already exist within the Church. But I wish it to be *polemic* as well—attempting to lay a theocentric, or God-centered, foundation for Christian living that will withstand the coming storms that will pummel the believer's faith in the twenty-first century. We will encounter in our study theological terms such as transcendence, supremacy, sufficiency, adoption, and atonement. These are not "highbrow" words to be avoided but rich truths to be understood and relished as we reflect upon the wonderful things our God has done for us!

Dangerous Days Are Here!

The freedoms to live and proclaim the faith of the Bible are under vicious attack today, and many within the church are not "ready always to give an answer . . . of the hope that is in [them]."[23] The exclusiveness of Christianity will not be tolerated much longer in our world. Inclusivism will finally become the dominant belief of our increasingly post-Christian, pluralistic culture, and the heat will be on.

Dangerous days—the "perilous times" of the "last days"[24]—are upon us, and we must be clear about the essentials we must believe and be willing to die for. This is the time when Christians must "gird up the loins

---

[23]I Peter 3:15.
[24]II Timothy 3:1.

15

of [their] mind"[25] and "continue . . . in the things which [they have] learned."[26] It is the time to leave our "tourist mode" of Christianity—living on earth as if our sole purpose is to visit all the interesting sites and collect all the souvenirs—and put ourselves into "warfare mode"—living on the alert as soldiers on assignment in occupied territory.

As the situation darkens here, our vision of "the heavenlies" must become clearer. We must "see" some things we aren't presently "seeing." As we study together, ask God to open your eyes to the Grand Reality of Himself! Beg Him to allow you to "see the unseen." It will make all the difference in the world for you and those whose lives you touch in the "dangerous days" ahead. What He will allow you to see with illuminated eyes will indeed amaze you!

TAKE TIME TO REFLECT[27]

1. Since the Holy Spirit has revealed what God is like in the Bible, how regularly are you studying the Word and looking for God in the Scriptures?

2. Since only the "pure in heart" see God (Matthew 5:8), how diligent are you about staying in fellowship with God and not allowing sin to pollute your relationship with Him?

3. As you study, are you praying specifically for God to illuminate your own heart?

4. As you teach your children/disciples, are you praying specifically for God to illuminate their hearts?

5. When is the last time God truly illuminated your heart to something about Himself in the Word and you "relished" the truth because God opened your eyes? What life-changing truth did He illuminate in His Word?

---

[25] I Peter 1:13.

[26] II Timothy 3:14.

[27] Each chapter will close with application questions like these. Take some time to reflect on them, asking God to make His truth operative in your life. Photocopy from Appendix A the study sheet entitled Five Significant Statements/Take Time to Reflect for each chapter, and write out your answers so that you can later review the things you have learned (Proverbs 10:14) and share them with others. For an extended discussion of ways to use this book, both in personal and in group study, see "How to Use This Book When Working with Others" in Appendix C.

A WORD TO DISCIPLE-MAKERS

Sorrow vs. Despair

As you try to help those in our day who are despairing, please understand the difference between "sorrow" and "despair." *Sorrow is the taste of death that permeates everything upon a fallen planet.* It is the emotion of loss—the awareness that something has gone bad and isn't the way it was meant to be. It is the reminder that an essential of life is missing. It is the echo within our hearts that we were made for something better. It is what Paul is speaking of when he says,

> For we know that the whole creation groaneth and travaileth in pain together until now. And not only [does the creation groan], but ourselves also, which have the firstfruits of the Spirit, even we ourselves groan within ourselves, waiting for the [final] adoption, [that is] the redemption of our body (Romans 8:22-23).

> For we that are in this tabernacle [i.e., this temporary body] do groan, being burdened: not for that we would be unclothed, but clothed upon, that mortality might be swallowed up of life (II Corinthians 5:4).

When we lose a loved one, when we lose a cherished possession or opportunity, or when we lose our physical well-being because of disease or a cycle of life, we sense that loss in an emotion called sorrow. It is a legitimate pain of the soul—a grief—that reminds us something is missing. It is a time not to numb the sorrow with medications, accomplishments, dependent relationships, or incessant activities; it is a reminder to look away from this temporal world and turn our face to God for help. Sorrow wells up when we *think* about the loss and can be legitimately alleviated only by embracing the eternally satisfying reality of fellowship with Jesus Christ.

This sorrow of which I am speaking is what Jesus experienced in the garden when He contemplated the coming loss of fellowship with His Father when He became the sacrificial lamb for the sins of the world.

> And he took with him Peter and the two sons of Zebedee, and began to be sorrowful and very heavy. Then saith he unto them, My soul is exceeding sorrowful, even unto death: tarry ye here, and watch with me (Matthew 26:37-38).

Jesus is not depressed here; He is not despairing. Depression and de-spair are accompanied by hopelessness, disinterest, and often self-pity. Jesus is experiencing sorrow—the emotion of loss that comes with our awareness that things aren't the way they were intended from the be-ginning. It is not a sinful emotion. On the contrary, it is a legitimate emotion for anyone who is truly reflecting about life on a fallen planet. This is why it is often the characteristic emotion of those who are more contemplative. Its heaviness grows as we *think* about the true nature of things in a fallen world. Those who never think seldom feel its weight. Indeed, this is exactly why many try not to think about life and its prospects—the weight of sorrow seems to them to be too heavy to bear.

Those who sorrow, however, must beware since sorrow turns to despair when there seems to be no end, purpose, or remedy to the sorrow. When sorrow is laced with self-pity—when the thoughts are turned in-ward in wound licking or are turned outward in finger pointing—sor-row becomes corrupted with the poison of the flesh, and despair is the result. *When a man does not seek God in his sorrow, God intends for him to despair.* God's plan is that the soul should sense its poverty and in-completeness and turn not to itself in self-pity or turn on others in ac-cusation but turn to God in dependence.

That turn toward God in dependence is the secret of how a fallen crea-ture can joyfully and peacefully live with himself and others on a fallen planet. That dependent turn is called faith—"the gaze of a soul upon a saving God."[28] It confesses its own incompleteness and neediness, and at the same time, affirms that God is the worthy Completer and only Fountain of joy and peace.

This is why turning to any part of the creation—which itself is tainted with death—rather than to the Creator Himself—who is the essence of life—is such folly. You cannot wash the taste of death out of your mouth by gargling with water also tainted by the same death.

A *Taste of Death*
It should be clear that people experiencing despair are tasting the re-sults of living on a fallen planet without the life-giving satisfaction of the Thirst-Quencher Himself. When man fell, he distanced himself

---

[28]A. W. Tozer, *The Pursuit of God* (Camp Hill, Pa.: Christian Publications, 1982), 81.

from his Source of satisfaction and delight, and he was immediately shrouded in the darkness of a soul cut off from its Light. The tendency now that man's communion with God had been severed was to find his enjoyment in the creation—not in the Creator.[29]

Since man now had within him a treasonous bent against his Creator, which would result in his ultimate destruction, Adam's daily labor and Eve's childbearing were injected with "sorrow"—a taste of death—that tainted every part of their existence. The sorrow could be neutralized and overcome only by the creature's willful and continual submission again to his Creator.

The solution is to recognize what God is saying through the experiences of sorrow. They are a call to turn to Him in dependence. The result for the God-dependent child of God is a heart that deeply feels sorrow and at the same time experiences an abiding joy and peace. This is the testimony of Peter when he affirms that heaviness and rejoicing can exist in the same heart. After he speaks of the living hope of eternal fellowship with God, he says,

> Wherein [speaking of the living hope of verse 3] ye greatly *rejoice*, though now for a season, if need be, ye are in *heaviness* through manifold [trials] (I Peter 1:6).

Paul testifies of the same experience when he says,

> For our light affliction, which is but for a moment, worketh for us a far more exceeding and eternal weight of glory; *while we look not at the things which are seen, but at the things which are not seen:* for the things which are seen are temporal; but the things which are not seen are eternal (II Corinthians 4:17-18).

It is this view of "the things which are not seen" that is at the heart of our study. Paul in Ephesians compels us to scan the heavenlies with him and behold the glories that are ours from the God who made us. Here is a prison-bound saint whose spirit soars beyond the prison bars to show us the Milky Way of God's splendor. We want to join him in this study. We were created not to live in darkness to the boast of His enemy but to drink of His fullness and spread the word that He is sufficient.

---

[29]Romans 1:25.

PART ONE

Rejoicing in the Grand Reality of God

CHAPTER TWO

THE REALITY OF GOD'S SUPREMACY

PAGAN MYTHOLOGY

When I was in high school, I took two semesters of Latin. During that year we studied not only the language but also the mythology of ancient Rome. As I look back, I am struck with several lessons from those studies.

The mortals—the humans here on earth—formed a view of the gods entirely from their experience. They reflected on the weather, their personal trials, and their national difficulties and then proposed what seemed to them a *logical, yet supernatural,* reason that things happened as they did in their daily lives. For example, a grieving Roman father might have reasoned, "Since the weather was bad on the ocean and my son's ship was lost, it must have been because Neptune[1] was angry." Romans sought supernatural explanations for physical phenomena based upon their experiences. Eventually a body of accumulated folklore—both written and oral—governed their understanding of the gods and life.

The ancient Romans were always fearful because they never knew where they stood with the gods. They did not know from one day to the next whether the gods were going to rain on their crops or burn them. The gods were very unpredictable; they did not act from any set of consistent principles but were driven by capricious whims and desires. They possessed great power—at least in their particular domain—but that power was useful to man only if he happened to be on the good side of the god. If he had antagonized the god, or if the god

---

[1]Neptune was the Roman god of the sea.

was in a bad mood, he might be in for great trouble. There was no such thing as permanent favor with a god, so a person was never quite sure if a certain god considered him friend or foe. The response of the mortals to the gods' temperamental behavior ranged from cowering fear of the gods on the one hand to bold disregard of the gods on the other hand.

This wanton variableness on the part of the gods prompted most mortals to hope that the gods would be too busy—doing whatever the gods did—to notice or interfere with their lives. The mortals were quite content for the gods to leave them alone. At least that way, their own personal destinies were somewhat within their own hands. Once the gods intervened, life could get very complicated and very miserable. Most mortals did not want the gods watching them too closely.

If the mortals really needed supernatural intervention from one of the gods to win a war, to survive a storm at sea, or to achieve some great and dangerous quest, they would attempt to find out what pleased that god and give it to him in exchange for the god's assistance. Most gods could be bribed and bought by the highest bidder.

As you can see, ancient Roman mythology certainly had its drawbacks. It did not provide a consistent view of the world, nor was it personally satisfying to its adherents.

Unfortunately, many parallels exist between the experiences of the ancient Romans and countless modern Christians. Many believers today form their views of the true God much as the pagan mythologists did. Their view of God is the product of their own experiences or the experiences they have heard recounted by others and is not formed by seeing God's inerrant revelation of Himself in the Scriptures. The resulting "Christian mythology" isn't any more satisfying to these modern Christians than the pagan mythology was to the Romans. When something goes wrong, these modern believers try to fit that situation into their limited view of God.

For example, they might reason, "I don't know why God let me have that flat tire and miss the sales presentation, but perhaps it was His way of delaying me so that I would not have the car accident that would have occurred if I had kept my original schedule." Others might surmise, "Maybe God took that baby to heaven at childbirth because He knew it would grow up to be a wicked sinner."

The fact that every calamity is a divinely appointed way for a believer to demonstrate God's unique excellence in some way—a way to manifest His glory—does not enter their minds. Their reasoning is limited to a shallow cause and effect that revolves around putting a good spin on bad situations so that they can make some sense of the calamity. *For the illuminated believer, however, the unifying and satisfying element in every circumstance is always the glory of God*, not some sentimental, rose-colored view of the situation that makes him feel better about it. Paul faced many excruciating hardships[2] while on earth. His concern for God's glory and his view of unseen things sustained him. He testified,

> For which cause [to demonstrate God's glory] we faint not; but though our outward man perish, yet the inward man is renewed day by day. For our light affliction, which is but for a moment, worketh for us a far more exceeding and eternal weight of glory; *while we look not at the things which are seen, but at the things which are not seen*: for the things which are seen are temporal; but the things which are not seen are eternal (II Corinthians 4:16-18).

We are not biblical Christians simply because we *affirm* the right doctrines. We are biblical Christians when we *practice* a supernatural worldview based upon right doctrine. Paul in these verses testified that "seeing" the right things in the supernatural realm resulted in a certain kind of endurance (i.e., "we faint not") in the physical realm. The natural realm of life is profoundly affected by the supernatural realm, and we must live in *both* realms. Both are real, and the Christian who lives in only the half he can see with his physical eyes will be just as confused and as easily corrupted as the ancient Romans, for his worldview is incomplete, and therefore, just as mythological. The supernatural isn't something merely to be believed; it is something to be lived, to be experienced, to be seen, to be enjoyed! Illuminated revelation shows us what we cannot see. We must, above all, see God, and we must see Him above all!

---

[2]See II Corinthians 4:7-11; 6:4-10; 11:23-30.

B. B. Warfield has captured this truth in his comments on the text of John 3:16, "God so loved the world":

> We shall not make the slightest step forward in understanding our text . . . so long as we permit ourselves to treat the great term "God" merely as the subject of a sentence. We must endeavor rather to rise as nearly as may be to its fullest significance. When we pronounce the word *we must see to it that our minds are flooded with some wondering sense of God's infinitude, of His majesty, of His ineffable [i.e., indescribable] exaltation of His holiness, of His righteousness, of His flaming purity and stainless perfection.* This is the Lord God Almighty whom the heaven of heavens cannot contain, to whom the earth is less than the small dust on the balance. He has no need of aught, nor can His unsullied [i.e., unstained] blessedness be in any way affected—whether by way of increase or decrease—by any act of the creatures of His hands. What we call infinite space is but a speck on the horizon of His contemplation: what we call infinite time is in His sight but as yesterday when it is past. Serene in His unapproachable glory, His will is the resistless law of existence to which their every motion conforms. Appareled in majesty and girded with strength, righteousness and judgment are the foundations of His throne. He sits in the heavens and does whatsoever He pleases. It is this God, a God of whom to say that He is the Lord of all the earth is to say so little that it is to say nothing at all, of whom our text speaks. And if we are ever to catch its meaning we must bear this fully in mind.[3]

Warfield is admonishing us to have a proper, exalted understanding of who God is. Without an accurate, Spirit-taught view of God, we are doomed to the deficiencies of a "Christian mythology." Let's look at how this played out in Paul's life through the Book of Ephesians.

NOT YOUR AVERAGE PRISONER

Paul wrote Ephesians from a prison cell, yet he is not your average prisoner. He is not grousing and complaining. He is not despairing and moaning. He is not angry and attacking. In fact, when we study his prison epistles—Ephesians, Philippians, Colossians, and Philemon—we find a joyful, contented man concerned about how he could demonstrate the greatness of His God through his responses. He also

---

[3]B. B. Warfield, *Biblical and Theological Studies* (Grand Rapids: Baker Book House, 1968), 513.

showed a selfless concern for the spiritual condition of others around him—both those in the jail and those in the churches. Obviously, he could "see" some things that made all the difference. He was physically bound but not spiritually blind. His body was in chains but his spirit was not shackled by a deficient view of reality. He opens his Ephesian letter with the words

> Blessed be the God and Father of our Lord Jesus Christ, who hath blessed us with all spiritual blessings in heavenly places in Christ (1:3).

I have asked myself while studying these opening words in Ephesians, "If I were in jail because of religious persecution and had the opportunity to write a letter home, I wonder if I would have thought of saying the same kinds of things to the people at home?" Perhaps I would just bitterly complain about the injustice of my imprisonment and beg for someone to send me help. An amazing testimony of Paul's vibrant Christianity is what comes out of his pen when he sits down to write this letter. After the opening doxology[4] we just saw in verse 3, he launches into a three-stanza hymn praising the Father, Son, and Holy Spirit. "Blessed be the God . . . who hath blessed us" echoes the sentiment of the well-known musical doxology:

> Praise God, from whom all blessings flow;
> Praise Him all creatures here below;
> Praise Him above, ye heavenly host;
> Praise Father, Son, and Holy Ghost!

We must ask ourselves, "If these are not the most dominant thoughts when we are under pressure, what does Paul know that we do not know? What—or rather whom—is he seeing that we are blind to?" The answer, of course, has everything to do with our view of God. So the questions before us are "Who is God?" and "What is He like?" Paul gives us a wonderful overview of God and His work in the first three chapters of Ephesians. We will look at some of them in this chapter and in the three to follow in our study. The lessons for us can be life changing.

---

[4]"Doxology" means literally "a word of praise."

NOT YOUR AVERAGE GOD!

The *grand reality* is God.[5] His eternal existence and absolute supremacy are the central fact of all the universe. He is *first* of all!

If this truth is ever compromised or forgotten, everything is off-center. The reality of this exclusive fact that He is the greatest and the first—His supremacy—is taught throughout the entire Bible. Here is a sampling of its teaching.

> In the beginning God created the heaven and the earth (Genesis 1:1).

> I am the Lord thy God. . . . Thou shalt have *no other gods before me* (Exodus 20:2-3).

> Know therefore this day, and consider it in thine heart, that *the Lord he is God* in heaven above, and upon the earth beneath: *there is none else* (Deuteronomy 4:39).

> For *of him*, and *through him*, and *to him*, are all things: *to whom* be glory for ever. Amen (Romans 11:36).

> I am Alpha and Omega, *the beginning and the ending*, saith the Lord, which is, and which was, and which is to come, *the Almighty* (Revelation 1:8).

Unless we spend much time considering that God is the first and the greatest, all kinds of other things will loom large in our eyes—our problems, our temptations, our goals, our achievements, and so forth, and we are sentenced to plod through life with our eyes pinched shut—for truly we see no better than that. And tragically, if we are a leader of some sort, we can be only "blind leaders of the blind. And if the blind lead the blind, both shall fall into the ditch."[6] The satisfied and stable believer sees God as *first* of all—supreme—and delights to have it so!

---

[5]"Grand" here is used in the dictionary sense of "the most important; principal; main" (*The American Heritage Dictionary of the English Language*, s.v. "grand").
[6]Matthew 15:14.

THE GLORY OF GOD IS HIS SUPREMACY

We cannot speak of God's supremacy without a discussion of His glory. Many believers use the phrase "the glory of God" with little or no understanding of what it means. Noted theologian Charles Ryrie defines the glory of God as "the awesomeness, splendor, and importance of God seen in some way."[7] The glory of anything is the excellence that makes it first, and therefore, unique.

Consider Mt. Everest in the Himalayas on the border of Nepal and Tibet. It is the highest mountain in the world. It rises 29,028 feet above sea level and is the only mountaintop to puncture the jet stream. The glory of Mt. Everest is that there is no peak anywhere on the earth that towers over it. Its unique excellence—its glory—is its peerless height. It does not share this glory with any other mountain. It is supreme among mountains. It is first!

The glory of God is that unique excellence that makes Him supreme—towering over everything else. He is uniquely the Source and Sustainer of everything else; He alone is the Creator-God. He is unique in His eternal existence; He alone has neither beginning nor end. He always has been and forever will be. He is unique in His infinitude; He alone cannot be measured or contained. His unblemished purity is unique; He alone has no moral deficit. His infinite knowledge and wisdom are unique; He alone knows everything intuitively and perfectly. His infinite power is unique; no one else can stay His hand or stop His works. What He purposes to do comes to pass without fail. He alone accomplishes everything He purposes to do.

Every one of His glories—these unsurpassed attributes—towers infinitely above the landscape of the rest of His creation, both celestial and terrestrial. He is not like Mt. Everest, which while it is the highest of all mountains, still has its conquerors—Edmund Hillary being the first. God has no peer and no conqueror. He is *alone* in this position as Lord of all. It is this uniqueness in His infinite attributes that is the glory of God; it is His unique boast. This uniqueness of God as *first* is the most important consideration of all existence.

---

[7]Charles Ryrie, *Transformed by His Glory* (Wheaton: Victor Books, 1990), 18.

In fact, it is this uniqueness of God that is at the essence of His holiness. We tend to think that His holiness is merely God's *separateness from evil*—speaking of His perfect *goodness*, which establishes His *morality*. All of that is certainly true, but that is merely a subset of what His holiness really is. The fact that God is holy, as Isaiah saw Him in Isaiah 6, is that He is *separate from His whole creation*. This speaks of His Godness and establishes His ultimate *authority*. This is the meaning of the following verses and many others like them:

> To whom then will ye liken me, or shall I be equal? saith the Holy One [i.e., the Entirely-Separate-from-All-Creation-One] (Isaiah 40:25).

> Who is like unto thee, O Lord, among the gods? who is like thee, glorious in holiness [i.e., separateness], [awesome] in praises, doing wonders? (Exodus 15:11).

If we do not spend time meditating upon these unique excellencies, we cannot understand how it is that we are to "glorify God," nor will we know what it means that "all have sinned, and come short of the glory of God."[8] The Bible writers everywhere admonish us to "glorify God"—to show His supremacy. Read over these passages and then we shall consider how we are to put them into practice.

> Let your light so shine before men, that they may see your good works, and *glorify* your Father which is in heaven (Matthew 5:16).

> Herein is my Father *glorified*, that ye bear much fruit; so shall ye be my disciples (John 15:8).

> That ye may with one mind and one mouth *glorify* God, even the Father of our Lord Jesus Christ (Romans 15:6).

> For ye are bought with a price: therefore *glorify* God in your body, and in your spirit, which are God's (I Corinthians 6:20).

> Whether therefore ye eat, or drink, or whatsoever ye do, do all to the *glory* of God (I Corinthians 10:31).

---

[8]Romans 3:23.

You cannot understand God or His ways unless you understand what His glory is and why it is important. One Bible teacher has put it this way.

> God does everything for His glory. That is a basic axiom of sound hermeneutics.[9] That is an important key to understanding His ways and interpreting His Word. God's grace, God's government, and God's greatness may be other keys to understanding the Scriptures and God's ways with men and nations. But these keys only unlock certain doors. God's glory is the master key that unlocks all doors.[10]

Several times in Ephesians Paul enunciates that God's overarching purpose for His redemptive acts is so that His glory would be displayed. He said the reason the Father chose us was "to the praise of the glory of his grace."[11] The reason Christ redeemed us was "that we should be to the praise of his glory."[12] And the reason the Spirit sealed us was "unto the praise of his glory."[13] Paul even winds up his three-chapter discussion of God's great works on our behalf with the statement, "Unto him be glory in the church by Christ Jesus throughout all ages, world without end. Amen."[14]

So you see, the glory of God is not something we can ignore. Glorifying God must become the heartbeat of every believer. Ask yourself, "What part does a concern for the glory of God play in my daily choices?" It is the most fundamental question of your Christian life, and your answer will be the difference between spiritual mediocrity and fullness of joy and peace.

FALLING SHORT OF THE GLORY OF GOD

Before the Fall, every part of God's creation pointed to His unique excellence. The celestial bodies were created to testify of His unique "firstness" by showing the Creator's skill and power unmatched by any

---

[9]Hermeneutics is the science of interpreting the Bible. Phillips is stating that it is impossible to rightly interpret the Bible without understanding the issue of God's glory.

[10]John Phillips, *Exploring Ephesians* (Neptune, N.J.: Loizeaux Brothers, 1993), 102.

[11]Ephesians 1:4-6.

[12]Ephesians 1:7-12.

[13]Ephesians 1:13-14.

[14]Ephesians 3:21.

other being. David exclaimed, "The *heavens* declare the glory of God."[15]

In the same way, *man* was created to bear witness of God's unique excellence. Man was created with qualities that put him in an order above all the celestial bodies and above the flora and fauna of the earth. He was given personal qualities—the image of God—that equipped him to fellowship directly with God.

Prefallen man and unfallen angels willingly and joyfully acknowledged the fact that God was first and above all. It was Adam's highest delight to turn his face to God in entire dependence and unrestrained praise, acknowledging God as the first and the greatest. Adam instinctively knew that God was the Source and Sustainer of his existence. He rejoiced "that the Lord he is God in heaven above, and upon the earth beneath: *there is none else.*"[16] God was his highest delight.

Then Adam fell, and man's nature was corrupted. His darkened nature put *himself* first. He saw *himself* as the most significant part of reality. He turned to *himself* for direction, strength, and survival. He gloried in *himself*—saw *himself* as the supreme one in his universe. His focus became instinctively "*me*-first" instead of instinctively "*God*-first." He fell short of his purpose of reflecting and enjoying God's unique excellence—His glory.[17]

Are you getting the picture? You may think this is too heavy, but these are important issues. Stay with me now. It is precisely *because* God's people in recent years have not thought upon these things that we are left with such a malnourished Christianity in our day. It may be that you will have to read and reread sections of this book in order to grasp the importance of what we are studying together.

Do not be discouraged by that. Edmund Hillary had to stop at nine camps to rest and refresh himself as he made his way up Mt. Everest. His fatiguing journey started on March 10, 1953, with a 188-mile hike from Kathmandu to the base camp at 17,900 feet. He and his fellow

---

[15]Psalm 19:1.

[16]Deuteronomy 4:39.

[17]Romans 3:23.

climber, Tenzing Norgay, were rewarded on May 29—two months later—with a view from the "top of the world!"[18]

You will be richly rewarded for your efforts as well. Only, you will be compensated with a view of the heavenlies—a view that thrilled and sustained Paul while he wrote Ephesians and a view that has thrilled and sustained centuries of saints. I hope you have understood all we have discussed so far because we are about to apply this matter of God's glory to daily experience.

CREATED FOR HIS GLORY

We have learned that God is glorified when He is seen as supreme—first. What does it mean that *we* were created for His glory? And further, how does that translate into practice in our daily lives? One of my favorite Bible texts is the statement of the redeemed representatives of the Church who cry out in heaven,

> Thou art worthy, O Lord, to receive glory and honour and power: for thou hast created all things, and *for thy pleasure* they are and were created (Revelation 4:11).

The First One created all things—including me—for *His* pleasure. Many questions come into my mind as I ponder that statement. How can *I* bring God pleasure? What can *I* do that He cannot do better? What can *I* make that He cannot create better? I feel my own sinfulness and finiteness so acutely. How can such a limited being like me bring any delight to the Creator-God? A simple illustration helped me understand something of the gist of this mind-boggling truth.

Just One of God's Pets—Many people have pet dogs. I had one as a young boy on the farm. Though there is a vast difference between an animal and a human being, nonetheless, there can be a special relationship that brings pleasure to both.

A dog may sleep peacefully curled up at the foot of his owner's chair before a crackling fire. As soon as the master rises out of his chair and heads for the door, the dog is immediately on his feet and may even beat his master to the door. The master may say, "Get the paper, boy,"

---

[18]Ron Tagliapietra, *Great Adventurers of the Twentieth Century* (Greenville, S.C.: Bob Jones University Press, 1998), 73-80.

and the dog prances down the driveway to retrieve the daily news. He wags his tail as he returns to the house and deposits the paper into his owner's hand. A pat on the head and a "Good boy!" tells the dog that he has pleased his master. Both man and dog are pleased.

When I think of my position as a servant of God, I think of how my service is so primitive when compared to His own capabilities. I can "fetch His paper," but I get saliva on the rolled-up newsprint and may even tear a portion of a page with my fangs in the process. When I come into the house, I track mud on His carpet before I know what I'm doing. Yet He still says, "well done, thou good and faithful servant." That amazes me! Somehow my eagerness to obey Him and my attempt to do His bidding to the best of my "canine" ability is pleasing to Him, though my efforts are so flawed. When I think of these things, I can only look up at His face and say to Him, "What a wonderful Master You are! No one compares to You. I'm so delighted to be Your pet."[19] When He hears that eager praise from me, He is particularly delighted because I see Him as He really is—first above all! In this small way, I glorify Him by finding my greatest delight in Him.

The difference between God and me and a pet owner and his dog is that because God has created me in His image, I have the capability to understand to some degree what is happening in this relationship. A dog is not aware of these things. I, however, can actually see the great distance between us in terms of the kind of beings we are, yet I can sense the nearness that I can have to Him as my Father. I can stand in awe at His patience at my flawed service and at His forgiveness for my dirty feet. I know I'm limited and beyond that, defiled. Yet He loves me and desires to let me "dwell in the house of the Lord for ever."[20] I want everyone to see what it is like to be a dog in the house of this wonderful Master! I want the world to know that He is the best! He is *first*—supreme—among masters!

---

[19]Some may object to being called one of God's "dogs." If that analogy bothers them, they can rethink the whole picture, thinking of themselves then as "sheep," for that is God's own analogy—dumb, helpless sheep.

[20]Psalm 23:6.

It is in this way that we were created for His glory. We can glorify Him as one of His "pets"—beings created for His pleasure—*as we acknowledge and enjoy His "firstness."* We can do so in several ways.

Demonstrating His Firstness in Our Decisions

First, if we are to glorify God, we must make decisions that reflect His "firstness." The treasonous depravity of our sinful natures naturally pulls us to consider ourselves first. This was exactly the sin of Lucifer. Notice God's own description of the original angelic rebellion against God.

> How art thou fallen from heaven, O Lucifer, son of the morning! how art thou cut down to the ground, which didst weaken the nations! For thou hast said in thine heart, *I* will ascend into heaven, *I* will exalt *my* throne above the stars of God: *I* will sit also upon the mount of the congregation, in the sides of the north: *I* will ascend above the heights of the clouds; *I* will be like the most High (Isaiah 14:12-14).

Notice that Satan insisted upon being *first*. He was a created being himself—certainly not worthy of being first above his Creator. But in his pride he demanded what rightly belonged to God. A third of the angelic creation followed him in his rebellion.

God created another race of creatures—mankind—who were created with the capacity to personally fellowship with the Creator and to join with the unfallen heavenly hosts in acknowledging and enjoying the unique excellence—the firstness—of their God. Adam fulfilled that primary function of being *created for His glory* until he and Eve listened to the serpent and joined the rebellion of Lucifer. Think with me about that initial temptation in Eden. Adam could have glorified God in that temptation if his response had been something like this.

> Eve, I hear what the serpent has said, but it is contradictory to what the First One has said. Our Creator is certainly *first in wisdom.* No creature—neither I nor the serpent—can match His understanding of what is best. The First One said, "Of every tree of the garden thou mayest freely eat: but of the tree of the knowledge of good and evil, thou shalt not eat of it: for in the day that thou eatest thereof thou shalt surely die."[21] The First One certainly has good reasons for His

---

[21]Genesis 2:16-17.

command. I can't pretend that I know better than He, no matter what the serpent says.

The serpent also implied that God is withholding something from us that we should have. How can the First One not be also *first in goodness*? The serpent said we would not die. How could the First One not be also *first in truth*? If I were to listen to the serpent, I would have to deny that the First One is indeed *first in all these things*. I certainly don't understand what is going on, but I will not betray the First One, our Creator.

If Adam had responded this way, he would have "glorified God." He would have by his decision shown that God is indeed *first*—supreme. As we have already seen, sin is when we "come short of the glory of God"[22]—when we do not respond in such a way that shows Him to be first with a unique excellence that is worthy of our trust and obedience.

It is this kind of acknowledgment that is at the heart of the greatest commandments the Creator-God ever gave to His rational creatures:

Thou shalt have no other gods before me (Exodus 20:3).

Jesus said unto him, Thou shalt love[23] the Lord thy God with all thy heart, and with all thy soul, and with all thy mind. This is the first and great commandment (Matthew 22:37-38).

David got it right when he prayed,

Thine, O Lord, is the greatness, and the power, and the glory, and the victory, and the majesty: for all that is in the heaven and in the earth is thine; thine is the kingdom, O Lord, and *thou art exalted as head above all* (I Chronicles 29:11).

The health and happiness of the creature and the delight of the Creator both rest upon the creature's worship of God as *supreme*—first of all! It is totally unrighteous that it should be any other way in view of

---

[22]Romans 3:23.

[23]Don't be confused by the word "love" in this passage. Godlike love is a self-sacrificing choice that seeks to benefit another. It certainly can contain the element of affection, but that is not always the case—especially when the love is first exercised while still underdeveloped. Its primary meaning is still to put someone else *first*!

the nature of the parties involved. Notice Paul's response to who God is and what He has done in his words from II Corinthians 5:14-15.

> For the love of Christ constraineth us; because we thus judge, that if one died for all, then were all dead: and that he died for all, that they which live *should not henceforth live unto themselves*, but unto him which died for them, and rose again.

The *only* acceptable response a man can make to God's supremacy is repentance for living for *himself* followed by a life that aligns itself obediently *under* God. The world speaks much today about various psychological "disorders." The greatest "disorder," however, is that any man should place *himself* first before God. This is the ultimate "disorder"!

It is this personal mutiny of the creature that brings upon him the just penalty of eternal death.[24] He has willfully banished God to the hold of the ship of his life while the creature stands self-confidently at the helm usurping God's rightful place as *first* in command.

Reflecting on His Firstness in Our Meditations
We have seen how our decisions reveal who is supreme in our lives—God or ourselves. There is no way, however, that our decisions will acknowledge God's unique excellence unless our minds are constantly dwelling upon His preeminence as seen in the Word. We must take time to behold His glory—His unique firstness. Adam cannot "argue himself back to reality" about what indeed is right and first if he has not made the invisible things of God a constant focus of his meditation. That is exactly what we want to do in the opening chapters of this book just as Paul did in the opening chapters of Ephesians. We must be continually "seeing the invisible." Our hearts drift back to "*me*-firstness" without daily and sometimes hourly reflections on the Grand Reality as revealed in the Scriptures.

Declaring His Firstness in Our Evangelism
I shall not fully develop this theme here, but lastly, I want you to notice in Psalm 96:3-10 how David explained the basic motive behind world evangelization. He said in effect, "None should withhold the

---

[24]Romans 6:23.

glory due to God! He should be praised by all men! Therefore, go tell the entire world that 'Our God reigns!' He is *first!*"

> Declare his glory among the heathen, his wonders among all people. *For the Lord is great, and greatly to be praised:* he is to be feared *above all gods.* For all the gods of the nations are idols: but the Lord made the heavens. Honour and majesty are before him: strength and beauty are in his sanctuary. Give unto the Lord, O ye kindreds of the people, give unto the Lord glory and strength. *Give unto the Lord the glory due unto his name:* bring an offering, and come into his courts. O worship the Lord in the beauty of holiness: fear before him, all the earth. Say among the heathen that *the Lord* reigneth.

Believers who have not seen His supremacy in this way will not gladly proclaim to the lost the wonderful news of what they have seen. This is the heartbeat of the missionary heart! Evangelism is the natural response of a heart that sees God as supreme.

CONCLUDING THOUGHT

In his classic work *The Pursuit of God,* Tozer sums up what we have been looking at. Reverently reflect on his words as we close this portion of our study.

> "Be *thou* exalted" (Psalm 21:13) is the language of victorious spiritual experience. It is a little key to unlock the door to great treasures of grace. *It is central in the life of God in the soul.* Let the seeking man reach a place where life and lips join to say continually "Be *thou* exalted," and a thousand minor problems will be solved at once. *His Christian life ceases to be the complicated thing it had been before and becomes the very essence of simplicity.* . . . Made as we are in the image of God, we scarcely find it strange to take again our God as our All. God was our original habitat and our hearts cannot but feel at home when they enter again that ancient and beautiful abode. I hope it is clear that there is a logic behind God's claim to preeminence. That place is His by every right in earth or heaven. While we take to ourselves the place that is His, the whole course of our lives is out of joint. Nothing will or can restore order till our hearts make the great decision: God shall be exalted above.[25]

---

[25]Tozer, *Pursuit of God,* 95-96.

A man who is not rejoicing in the reality that God is supreme—the first and the greatest—and who is not ordering his own thoughts and decisions accordingly is living a life with a severely flawed worldview. He lives out his own "Christian mythology" and will find life unsatisfying. More fundamentally, he will find God resisting him because he puts *himself* first rather than God.

The questions below are ones that every thoughtful and growing Christian will have already faced in life. He will have encountered them often and will have humbly responded in ways that show that he regards God as *first* in his life. If the questions seem strange to you or you resist answering them truthfully, you have much work to do before you get to first base in your Christian experience. Seeing God as *first* and living in the light of that reality is the initial step toward vibrant, joyful Christianity.

TAKE TIME TO REFLECT

1. Have you come to a time in your life when you recognized you were living for *yourself* and you were broken by the realization that you were robbing God of *His* glory? Describe the time when God showed you the rebellion of your self-focus. What did you do about it? If you did come to that point at some time in the past, are you still living in the light of that realization?

2. Think of the areas of your greatest temptations. If you were rejoicing in the reality of God's supremacy—His firstness—what aspects of God's nature would you be calling to mind during those temptations that would help you make the right decision? Write out the conversation you *should* be having with yourself about God's "firstness" if you are to overcome that temptation. Review the conversation Adam *should* have had with himself on pages 35-36 for ideas of how you should be handling your temptations.

3. Since you are one of God's "pets"—beings created for *His* pleasure—how can you bring pleasure to God today?

4. What place does the reading and studying of God's Word have in your life? What have you "seen" of the invisible God recently that altered the way you looked at and handled life?

5. In the past how has your view of God been wrong; how have you
   had a Christian "mythology" rather than a biblical understanding
   of some aspect of God?

A WORD TO DISCIPLE-MAKERS

A Transcendent Worldview[26]

When we say that it is important that a man be able to "see the invisible" as we have been talking about in these first two chapters, we are saying that he must live with a *transcendent worldview*—a view of life and the world around him that rises above that which he can see and experience in the material realm. "Transcendence" is a theological and philosophical term that means that something exists above and apart from the material world. Most notably, *God* is transcendent. He exists separately from His creation. He exists above and over His creation. *Spiritual truth*, since its author is God, is also transcendent. It rises above everything in the material universe and is not affected by it.

God has placed within every man a sense of that transcendence. Ecclesiastes 3:11 says, "[God] hath made every thing [appropriate] in his time: also he hath set [eternity] in their heart." That "eternity" is a sense that there is something more to life than what he can see. A

---

[26]Jerry Solomon, general editor of *Arts, Entertainment, and Christian Values* (Grand Rapids: Kregel Publications, 2000), provides a helpful description of a worldview. He says, "Worldviews act somewhat like eyeglasses or contact lenses. That is, a worldview should provide the correct 'prescription' for making sense of the world just as wearing the correct prescription for your eyes brings things into focus. In either example, an incorrect prescription can be dangerous, even life-threatening" (44).

"A worldview should pass certain tests. First, it should be rational. It should not ask us to believe contradictory things. Second, it should be supported by evidence. It should be consistent with what we observe. Third, it should give a satisfying, comprehensive explanation of reality. It should be able to explain why things are the way they are. Fourth, it should provide a satisfactory basis for living. It should not leave us feeling compelled to borrow elements of another worldview to live in this world" (45).

Solomon further states that worldviews answer the following six questions. "1. Why is there something rather than nothing? . . . 2. How do you know that you know? . . . 3. How do you explain human nature? . . . 4. How do you determine right from wrong? . . . 5. What is the meaning of history? . . . 6. What happens to a person at death?" He further asserts that modern believers should be somewhat acquainted with the "most influential worldviews of the past and present: deism, nihilism, atheistic existentialism, Christian theism, postmodernism, New Age, and Eastern pantheism" (47-49).

thoughtful man has a yearning to see the things beyond what he is experiencing. This is important for us to understand if we are to comprehend the philosophies that affect the world around us and if we are to prepare those we disciple to live biblically in this world.

Transcendence Without God

It is this longing for the transcendent that produced romanticism toward the end of the eighteenth century. Rationalism, the theory that reason—not spiritual revelation—provided the only basis for understanding and handling life, had removed the supernatural from man's view. The result was that man found the material world by itself unsatisfying. Romanticism attempted to restore a sense of transcendence, but it was a transcendence without God. Romanticism brought about a return to transcendent themes of beauty, order, and nobility. Without God to inject humility into the worldview, however, it produced a snobbishness of high culture in some and degenerated into the primitivism of a low culture in others—both unattractive options.[27] What romanticism verified was the soul's quest for something beyond what the material world offered. Rationalism was not satisfying. The thinking man wanted something he could feel—something that rose above the material world. Thus, Lord Byron, called "the model romantic," wrote,

> The great object of life is Sensation—to feel that we exist—even though in pain—it is this "craving void" which drives us to Gaming—to Battle—to Travel—to intemperate but keenly felt pursuits of every description.[28]

It is this same "craving void"—for a transcendent reason for existence—that drives the interest in the "spiritual" pursuits of today's New Age Movement, neo-paganism, the "signs and wonders" movement, "spiritual" box-office hits, and goddess religions. Byron admits it is also the same void behind the "intemperate . . . pursuits" of

---

[27]Primitivism extolled the virtues of man without the corrupting influence of civilization and promoted the "noble savage." It taught the myth that evil in life comes from structure and tradition and championed a "back to nature," even pantheistic, approach to life. Because of its unrestrained individualism, however, primitivism could lead only to the vulgar.

[28]Quoted in Kenneth Myers, *All God's Children and Blue Suede Shoes: Christians and Popular Culture* (Wheaton: Crossway, 1989), 139.

"Gaming," "Battle" [i.e., conquest], and "Travel." The parallels with today's restless pursuits of these exact passions are noteworthy.

A Culture of Transcendence

Kenneth Myers closes his insightful book on popular culture with a well-deserved indictment of the Church. He calls it "A Lost Opportunity."

> In the two decades since the cultural collapse provoked by The Sixties, there have been numerous laments from a cultural remnant about the loss of a sense of transcendence, absolutes, and human dignity. Many intellectuals are chafing under the yoke of oppression from ideologies that see all cultural expressions as political, expressive only of interests of class, race, and gender. What a shame that these individuals (many of them agnostic or atheistic) could not look at the church and see *in its cultural expressions as well as in its teaching a living testimony to a culture of transcendence*, a dynamic cultural life rooted in permanent things [emphasis his].[29]

He is right. We who have the truth have lived as if it didn't matter. Even in many Christian homes, parents have bathed their families with a worldview that is essentially worldly. They have tried merely to edit out some of its profanity, some of its rock music, and some of its nudity. The remaining fare is assumed to be worthwhile. *What a shame that a Christian worldview is defined by worldliness minus its excesses!*

A biblical, transcendent worldview must dictate our view of death, recreation, ministry, work, education, worship, music, art, history, science, entertainment, study, business, love, sex, and a thousand other issues. The reality of God's supremacy means that He has the first and last word on every issue. Everything is evaluated, not on the basis of "is this or that blatantly evil" but on the basis of "does my view of and participation in this or that truly show to the world and testify to our God that in my view of things He is supreme above everything He has created? Am I doing it 'all to the glory of God?'[30] Does it show that I realize I was *created for* His *glory?*"

---

[29] Myers, 183.
[30] I Corinthians 10:31.

CHAPTER THREE
THE REALITY OF THE FATHER'S SOVEREIGNTY

THREE STANZAS AND A CHORUS

In the last chapter we looked at Paul's opening doxology of the first chapter of Ephesians. He says, "Blessed be God who blessed us!" declaring that God was *first* above all—supreme! Paul follows this statement of praise with the lengthiest sentence in the Bible. In the Greek New Testament it goes from verse 3 to verse 14!

Though it is a long sentence, Paul isn't rambling. This extended sentence is really a hymn of praise to God. It is divided into three stanzas, each with a recurring chorus about God's glory. Take a moment to read the description of each stanza below and then read the verses themselves from Ephesians 1. These stanzas will direct our study together through chapter 5 of this book.

Stanza 1: *The Reality of the Father's Sovereignty*—the thrust of this chapter

"God the Father *chose* us . . . to the praise of the glory of his grace" (vv. 4-6a).

Stanza 2: *The Reality of Christ's Sufficiency*—chapter 4 of this book

"The Father sent the Son to *redeem* us . . . that we should be to the praise of his glory" (vv. 6b-12).

Stanza 3: *The Reality of the Spirit's Security*—chapter 5 of this book

"The Father sent the Spirit to *seal* us . . . unto the praise of his glory" (vv. 12-14).

Before we look at these topics in more detail, however, we need to step back to get a picture in our mind of where Paul is headed in this book. One of his overarching purposes is to show to the Church for the first time ever one of the great "mysteries" of God. Let's look at it.

THE SECRET IS OUT

Most people love a good mystery story. There is something captivating about an unresolved plot, and there is something in all of us that likes to see the story come to a just conclusion. Every believer needs to have an understanding of what a divine mystery is and why that mystery is so important. Deuteronomy 29:29 is a verse of great importance to us. Consider it carefully.

> The secret things belong unto the Lord our God: but those things which are revealed belong unto us and to our children for ever, that we may do all the words of this law.

This verse teaches us that there will always be a certain mystery in the things that God is doing. Part of that is because He is infinite and there is no possible way for us to understand all that God is or what He is doing. Our eternal existence will be always filled with wonder as we learn more of our fathomless God. Though much of life is filled with mystery, there are certain things God *has* revealed to us that should govern the way we live before Him in this life.

God used Paul as the instrument to publish many of His "secrets"—His mysteries. We must understand, however, that a "mystery" in the Bible is somewhat different from a mystery like those confronting Sherlock Holmes. We must see that *mysteries in the Bible are divine secrets previously unknown at this level of detail.*[1] For example, God had previously promised to bless the whole world through Abraham. It was not clear, however, how that was to be done until the unfolding of God's plan in the New Testament. The specific details of the Church were not uncovered until Paul wrote Ephesians. Paul was used of God to add much detail to a previously sketchy plan. That extra "detail" is the unfolding of a biblical "mystery."

---

[1]See Ephesians 3:3, 5 and Romans 16:25-27.

THE GREAT "MYSTERY" OF EPHESIANS

The New Testament reveals several "mysteries." Ephesians contains at least three, which are all really dimensions of one great "mystery of his will" (1:9).[2] *That mystery is the previously unrevealed ultimate purpose of God to reunite everything in Christ to the praise of His glory.*[3]

The human race has dreamed about this in every civilization. All the utopias, the towers of Babel, the Star Trek dreams of a unified universe at peace with itself, and the ideas of a global village are testimony that man knows something is drastically wrong with this world and that something drastic must be done to unify it in peace again.

We have congressional studies, philosophical think tanks, and world conventions on an endless series of topics—children, women, nuclear disarmament, global warming, world economics, disease, and famine— to study how to reverse the effects of the disunity we experience. Evangelists for economic renewal, social reform, racial unity, and ecological responsibility each have their own version of what drastic measure must be done to bring about the utopia they dream of.

We believers sense the incompleteness too. This is what Paul testified of in the following passages.

> For we know that the whole creation groaneth and travaileth in pain together until now. And not only [does the creation groan], but ourselves also, which have the firstfruits of the Spirit, even we ourselves groan within ourselves, waiting for the [final] adoption, [that is], the redemption of our body (Romans 8:22-23).

> For we that are in this tabernacle do groan, being burdened: not for that we would be unclothed, but clothed upon, that mortality might be swallowed up of life (II Corinthians 5:4).

"Groaning" is unavoidable. We are not home yet. We were made to live in another world. Paul announces in Ephesians that *the world we*

---

[2]The "mystery of his will" is also called the "mystery of Christ" (Ephesians 3:4; Colossians 1:25-27) and the "mystery of the gospel" (Ephesians 6:19).

[3]This phrase does not imply universalism. Universalists believe that everyone will be finally restored to salvation—even the damned in hell and the fallen angels. This is a direct contradiction to the Bible's teaching regarding judgment and hell.

long for is coming, and God has made His Church a major player in His coming agenda: to restore all the glory to Himself!

Read carefully through the following portions of Ephesians—you may have to read them slowly several times—and try to catch something of the flavor of what is now being revealed to us about this ultimate mission of God, which has previously been hidden.

> *The mystery of his will,* according to his good pleasure which he hath purposed in himself *[is] that* in the dispensation of the fulness of times [i.e., in the management of the divine plan when the time is right] *he might gather together [again] in one all things in Christ,* both which are in heaven, and which are on earth . . . that in the ages to come he might [display] the exceeding riches of his grace in his kindness toward us through Christ Jesus . . . according to the eternal purpose which he purposed in Christ Jesus our Lord . . . to the intent that now unto the principalities and powers in heavenly places might be known by the church the manifold wisdom of God . . . [so that] *unto him [will] be glory* in the church by Christ Jesus throughout all ages, world without end. Amen (Ephesians 1:9-10; 2:7; 3:11-10, 21).

Now this may seem like quite a mouthful, but don't miss the teaching here: *our salvation is not only about God's forgiveness of our sins so that we can stay out of hell.* That is merely a part of a much greater goal He has in mind. Read the words in *italics* in the passage above to get a summary of the truth Paul is revealing. Our salvation means that *God has chosen us to be redeemed by His Son so that we can be one of the witnesses He will display before His holy angels, before fallen men, and before redeemed men to vindicate His maligned character.* At that time every knee will once again bow, and He will receive the praise of all His creation, for all will once again see His infinite worth! Everyone will see His firstness and worship Him as supreme.

A DOG SHOW PARABLE

No story can perfectly illustrate these truths, but perhaps an analogy will shed some light upon the powerful truth that God is going to reunite everything together again in Christ to restore all the glory to Himself.

46

Let us suppose that there were a world-class dog trainer who through his skill and effort produced a team of trained animals unmatched anywhere else in the world. So widely acclaimed was his skill that he was given the title Master-Trainer. One night under cover of darkness his archenemy, who wanted to be the recognized top trainer, sneaked into the Master-Trainer's kennels and infected the dogs with rabies. The virus not only disfigured the bodies of the animals but confused their minds as well. They were not only disqualified from being world-class show dogs but were also, according to the laws of the land, required to be exterminated because of the deadliness of their disease. While waiting the coming extermination, some dogs snapped at and fought each other, and others tried to attack the Master-Trainer when he came near. None of them functioned according to their former capabilities, and all were poor advertisements of the true skill and wisdom of the Master-Trainer's former training and grooming.

The picture for the animals was bleak. As the day of extermination drew near so did the day of the world-class show of the century. The Master-Trainer's enemy appeared to be gaining a world-class reputation of his own now that the Master-Trainer's dogs were not on the show circuit. The reputation of the Master-Trainer was severely damaged. It looked like his show days were over.

The enemy however had not taken into account the extent of the Master-Trainer's skill *or the extent of his determination to rescue the reputation of his character and skill in the eyes of the world.* He engineered a genetic transplant for each dog that would reverse the effects of the virus and then put his dogs through training rigors like they had never before experienced. The improvement was marginal in some dogs and absolutely unbelievable in others.

On the day of the world-class show, before the enemy himself, before all of the Master-Trainer's helpers, and before the entire watching world, the prize dogs of the Master-Trainer were shown. When the dogs were displayed, the results left everyone in stunned silence! The genetic transplant had been timed to accomplish a *full restoration* on the day of the show. Every dog was perfected beyond his former glory, and the whole story of the enemy's activities was unveiled.

Everyone saw not only the Master-Trainer's original skill and wisdom but also aspects of his skill and wisdom that could not have been displayed had the dogs not been infected. No one present would ever question again who reigned as the Master-Trainer. *His character and skill were vindicated by the restored dogs he displayed at that grand demonstration.*

From the dogs' perspective, their "salvation" was about the healing of their bodies and minds. From the Master-Trainer's viewpoint, however, the "salvation" of his animals was also about a greater issue: the worldwide vindication of his own character and wisdom.

The central "mystery" of Ephesians is the unveiling of God's ultimate purpose for everything He has done for man. He is getting His Church—His pet show dogs—ready for the grand demonstration of His own character. At that day He will bring all of His creation together again in such a way that will restore all the glory to Himself! This comprehensive plan is revealed in Ephesians so that we can know "what God is doing in the Church through His Son for His own glory forever"[4] (Ephesians 3:20-21).

I like to call this glorious display the "end-time demonstration" of His glory through the Church.[5] All rational created beings—earthly and heavenly—will behold the amazing glory of the Creator-God when they see how He wraps up His wonderful redemptive plan for mankind.

Though His glory will be seen in its most sublime revelation at that time, there are many "real-time demonstrations" of His glory through His people during their earthly pilgrimage. The Bible is full of examples of people who glorified God by their willingness to carry out His plan for their lives even though Satan opposed them on every side. They never abandoned their commitment to God and His ways. Though "infected" by the Fall, they willingly submitted to the "Master-Trainer's" cure and never betrayed their loyalty to Him.

These "real-time demonstrations" occur today when a child takes a stand against his friends when they want him to do wrong with them.

---

[4]Mark Minnick, "Glory to God Through the Church," taped sermon preached January 25, 1998.
[5]See I Corinthians 15:20-28, 51-58.

Or when a teen avoids bitterness because she is trying to respond rightly though her parents are making life hard for her by their fights with each other and their threats of divorce. Or when a believer enduring continual physical pain or a terminal cancerous condition continues to look to God for daily grace to sustain him and looks around for others to minister to with what strength he has. They also include the times when a wife remains confident in the Lord's plans and provisions for her though she sees her husband making choices that will be financially and morally devastating.

These are "real-time demonstrations" by God's people. God is glorified when these believers testify, by the way they choose to handle life's difficulties, that God is first and worthy of their undivided confidence though life in His will right now is extremely difficult. These contests are played out on earth, but the score is kept in heaven. God's glory is at stake. Is He who He says He is? Can He sustain His people in hardship so that they do not deny Him even to their dying breath? Can He perfect them and bring them to share in His glory? These demonstrations show "God is First!"

God is shown to be powerful and trustworthy during these "real-time *individual* demonstrations," and the believers involved rejoice that they are counted worthy to suffer for Christ.[6] But the best demonstration is yet to come! The "end-time *universal* demonstration" will show the excellencies of God before all of creation and every knee will bow and testify to His firstness! That will be a glorious day!

THE CAST IS CHOSEN

Paul is rejoicing in Ephesians 1 because he, along with every other believer, has been sovereignly chosen by God to be a cast member—one of His pets—for that end-time demonstration. Paul speaks in Ephesians of God's choices in the following ways:

According as *he hath chosen us* in him before the foundation of the world, that we should be holy and without blame before him (1:4).

---

[6]Acts 5:41. Note the entire context of Acts 4-5.

[In love]⁷ having predestinated us unto the adoption of children by Jesus Christ to himself, *according to the good pleasure of his will* (1:5).

[In all wisdom and prudence]⁸ having made known unto us the mystery of his will, *according to his good pleasure which he hath purposed in himself* (1:9).

Who worketh all things after the counsel of his own will (1:11).

According to the eternal purpose which he purposed in Christ Jesus our Lord (3:11).

It is clear from these passages that Paul understood God to be in total control of everything. The theological term for that total control is "sovereignty." It means that God is King—the Sovereign—and is ruling His world as He wishes. God's sovereignty is perhaps the most misunderstood, yet one of the most comforting, truths about God taught in the Bible.

This is a scary doctrine to some. It frightens them to think that someone else is in total control of their lives. That is frightening to them only because they do not know well the loving nature and the surpassing wisdom of the one who has everything under His control. Some even protest, "I'm not sure that I like it that God is running everything!" My question to them is "Well, whom *do* you want to be running it?" I don't know of anyone else besides God I would want to be running it. But their fear isn't uncommon. Even Jonathan Edwards himself had an early struggle with God's sovereignty. He says,

> From my childhood up, my mind had been full of objections against the doctrine of God's sovereignty. . . . It used to appear like a horrible doctrine to me. But I remember the time very well when I seemed to be convinced, and fully satisfied, as to this sovereignty of God. . . . And there has been a wonderful alteration in my mind, with respect to the doctrine of God's sovereignty, from that day to this; so that I scarce ever have found so much as the rising of an ob-

---

⁷This phrase "in love" fits better at the start of verse 5 than as a conclusion to verse 4.

⁸Again, the phrase in brackets more likely goes at the beginning of verse 9 than at the end of verse 8.

jection against it, in the most absolute sense. . . . I have often since had not only a conviction, but a *delightful* conviction. The doctrine has very often appeared exceedingly pleasant, bright, and sweet. Absolute sovereignty is what I love to ascribe to God. But my first conviction was not so [emphasis his].[9]

Though Jonathan Edwards believed in God's sovereignty, he did not learn it from others; he learned it from his Bible. It is a well-ingrained teaching of the Scriptures:

> But our God is in the heavens: *he hath done whatsoever he hath pleased* (Psalm 115:3).

> A man's heart deviseth his way: but *the Lord directeth his steps* (Proverbs 16:9).

> There are many devices [i.e., plans] in a man's heart; nevertheless *the counsel of the Lord, that shall stand* (Proverbs 19:21).

> Remember the former things of old: for I am God, and there is none else; I am God, and there is none like me [i.e., God declares His supremacy]. Declaring the end from the beginning, and from ancient times the things that are not yet done, saying, My *counsel shall stand, and I will do all my pleasure* [i.e., God declares His sovereignty] (Isaiah 46:9-10).

> *All [authority] is given unto me* in heaven and in earth (Matthew 28:18).

> Go to now, ye that say, To day or to morrow we will go into such a city, and continue there a year, and buy and sell, and get gain: Whereas ye know not what shall be on the morrow. For what is your life? It is even a vapour, that appeareth for a little time, and then vanisheth away. For that ye ought to say, *If the Lord will, we shall live, and do this, or that* (James 4:13-15).

These passages should comfort us, not frighten us. Let's look briefly at what they tell us to be true about God. These passages—and countless others—teach us first of all that . . .

---

[9]"Memoirs of Jonathan Edwards," Jonathan Edwards, *The Works of Jonathan Edwards*, vol. 1 (1834; reprint, Peabody, Mass.: Hendrickson Publishers, 2000), liv-lv.

GOD *DECIDES* WHAT HE WILL DO

Nothing that He has decided to do will ever fail to come to pass.

His sovereignty applies to His creative acts.

The Bible begins with the bold statement "In the beginning *God* created the heaven and the earth."[10] *He* decided what He would create, when He would create it, and how He would create all things. He acted sovereignly in creation.

His sovereignty applies to His providential acts.

God not only created all things but also continues to superintend all things. Psalm 103:19 says, "The Lord hath prepared his throne in the heavens; and his kingdom ruleth over all." We call this continued management of all things His "providence." Isaiah 40 is perhaps one of the most soaring descriptions of God's sovereign rule over His entire creation. Verse 26 reads,

> Lift up your eyes on high, and behold who hath created these [stars], that bringeth out their host by number: he calleth them all by names by the greatness of his might, for that he is strong in power; not one faileth.

Tozer has a wonderful comment on this verse. He says,

> Now this passage is probably the most daring flight of imagination ever made by the human mind. We have here in Isaiah that which is vaster and more awesome than anything that ever came out of the mind of Shakespeare. It is the thought of the great God, the Shepherd of the universe, moving through His universe, with its billions and trillions of light years, with its worlds so big that our whole solar system would look like a grain of sand by comparison. And God stands out yonder and calls all of these millions of worlds as His sheep; He calls them all by name and leads them out across the vast sky.

> I'd say this is the highest thought I know of, in the Bible or out. And God does this "by the greatness of his might, for that he is strong in power; not one faileth" (40:26). Just as a shepherd keeps all of his sheep and not one is lost, so God keeps all of His universe. Men point their tiny little glasses [i.e., their telescopes] at the stars and

---

[10]Genesis 1:1.

talk learnedly, but they've just been counting God's sheep, nothing more. God is running His universe.[11]

Isaiah refers to His providential control over the nations in chapter 40, verses 15-17. He says,

> Behold, the nations are as a drop of a bucket, and are counted as the small dust of the balance: behold, he [lifts] up the isles as [fine dust]. And Lebanon is not sufficient to burn, nor the beasts thereof sufficient for a burnt offering. All nations before him are as nothing; and they are counted to him less than nothing, and vanity.

He controls not only the nations but also the weather, including the famines, the floods, the hurricanes, the volcanic eruptions, and every earthquake. He does this all simply with His words. Truly, He possesses amazing power and wisdom!

His sovereignty applies to His redemptive acts.

I will not spend any time on this aspect of His wonderful works on behalf of our salvation because I will discuss His sovereignty in redemption later in this chapter.

This brief discussion of His decisions hardly does justice to God's sovereignty. My purpose is not to teach the details of this wonderful doctrine but merely to acquaint you with the extent of God's comforting control over all things.[12] He alone decides what He will do.

GOD *DELIGHTS* IN WHAT HE DOES

God not only *decides* ahead of time what He will do, but we must understand that He also is pleased with His decisions. He *delights* in Himself and in His works. Think about these passages:

---

[11]A. W. Tozer, *The Attributes of God* (Camp Hill, Pa.: Christian Publications, 1977), 25.

[12]For more study on God's sovereignty and providence, see Layton Talbert, *Not by Chance: Learning to Trust a Sovereign God* (Greenville, S.C.: BJU Press, 2001). This book is a wonderful presentation of God's rulership over all things. It should be read by layman and pastor alike. It is one of those delightful books that bears repeated readings. See also Jerry Bridges, *Trusting God* (Colorado Springs: NavPress, 1988).

I will do all my pleasure (Isaiah 46:10).

He hath done whatsoever he hath pleased (Psalm 115:3).

According to the good pleasure of his will (Ephesians 1:5).

According to his good pleasure (Ephesians 1:9).

We must remember that *everything God does is consistent with His perfection in every one of His attributes*: wisdom, love, justice, holiness, and so forth. So His decisions have behind them infinite wisdom, infinite love, infinite justice, and infinite holiness. He doesn't make decisions based upon flawed or imperfect information or on the basis that He "woke up grumpy today." All of His perfections are reflected in all of His decisions. The perfection of His decisions makes them delightful to Himself and a joy to His illuminated creatures. Note these brief considerations about those perfections—those attributes—that control His decisions.

First, consider that His attributes don't fight each other. God's mercy doesn't have to "balance" His justice. His love doesn't "mellow" His wrath. His compassion doesn't "temper" His power. Everything He does, He does with everything He is. God never has internal conflicts with Himself. He is always at perfect peace with Himself.

Secondly, God is immutable, or unchangeable. He isn't capricious. Therefore, He is *always* wise, He is *always* loving, He is *always* powerful—*always* sovereign. Everything that God is, He will always be. It is this unchangeable consistency that produces in us a great confidence in Him.

Lastly, we must consider that His attributes are not limited in any way. They are all infinite, giving Him unlimited perfection in every part of Himself. He never runs out of power, wisdom, love, patience, and so forth. This makes all of His actions perfect in every way and makes Him delightful to behold when viewed by His creatures. It is precisely because He is absolutely perfect in every way that God delights most in Himself. If He were to find His greatest delight in something outside of Himself, He would be guilty of idolatry, for His greatest delight would be in an unworthy object.

He not only delights in Himself but also delights in His works of creation and redemption. All of these works are designed to draw out of His rational creatures the praise that belongs to Him as a worthy object of their adoration. He has made them to be the most joyful and satisfied themselves when they are beholding and praising the glories He manifests to them through His works. This is exactly what happens with Paul as he marvels that God should sovereignly choose him for salvation! Paul is rejoicing in God's decisions, just as God Himself rejoices in His decisions.

It is this kind of sovereignty that prompted the hymn writers to say,

> *Every joy or trial*
> *Falleth from above,*
> *Traced upon our dial*
> *By the Sun of Love.*
> *We may trust Him fully*
> *All for us to do;*
> *They who trust Him wholly*
> *Find Him wholly true.*[13]

> *This is my Father's world,*
> *O let me ne'er forget*
> *That though the wrong seems oft so strong,*
> *God is the Ruler yet.*
> *This is my Father's world:*
> *The battle is not done;*
> *Jesus who died shall be satisfied,*
> *And earth and heaven be one.*[14]

> *"Fear not, I am with thee, O be not dismayed,*
> *For I am thy God, I will still give thee aid;*
> *I'll strengthen thee, help thee, and cause thee to stand,*
> *Upheld by My gracious, omnipotent hand."*[15]

---

[13]Frances R. Havergal, "Like a River Glorious," in *Worship and Service Hymnal* (Carol Stream, Ill.: Hope Publishing Co., 1957).

[14]Maltbie D. Babcock, "This Is My Father's World," in *Worship and Service Hymnal* (Carol Stream, Ill.: Hope Publishing Co., 1957).

[15]"How Firm a Foundation," in *Worship and Service Hymnal* (Carol Stream, Ill.: 1957).

These hymn writers, like Paul, delighted in the fact that God rules sovereignly and absolutely over His entire creation. As I said earlier, that
rulership applies to His creation, His providence, and His redemption.
Let's look more fully at His sovereignty as it applies to our salvation.

THE BLESSING OF ELECTION:
"GOD THE FATHER CHOSE US!"

We should not draw back in fear when we see the word "election." To
be sure there are many aspects of this doctrine we cannot grasp, but
Paul clearly states in Ephesians 1:4 that the Father chose us. The Bible
plainly teaches us that we who are His children are members of His
family because He elected it to be so. Believers in the Body of Christ
are even called "the elect" by the apostles.[16]

Some Cautions

Some believers are concerned—and rightly so—that this matter of
election will cause Christians to feel that they do not have to evangelize the lost. If wrongly understood, it certainly can create that problem, but God foresaw this and provided an answer in Romans 10:14:

> How then shall they call on him in whom they have not be-
> lieved? and how shall they believe in him of whom they have not
> heard? and how shall they hear without a preacher?

God has chosen to call His elect to salvation through the evangelizing
work of someone who will tell them the gospel! God Himself says if
there is no one to tell them, they cannot call on Him and, therefore,
cannot be saved. The issue seems pretty clear. We have a responsibility to evangelize while God has assumed the responsibility to be at
work in the hearts of the lost.

Notice that God told Paul to continue preaching in Corinth because
"I have much people in this city."[17] What an encouragement that is!
God calls us to evangelize because He has people whom He has chosen that He still wants to save! Paul says the same thing in II Timothy
2:10, when he says, "Therefore I endure all things for the elect's sakes
[remember, these people he calls 'elect' are not yet saved] that they

---

[16]See Romans 8:33; Colossians 3:12; Titus 1:1; and I Peter 1:2.
[17]Acts 18:10.

may also obtain the salvation which is in Christ Jesus with eternal glory."

H. A. Ironside used to explain God's election and man's responsibility with this illustration. He said that it is as if there were a large sign over the gate of heaven. As you approach the gate, you see the words "Whosoever will may come." Once you pass through the gate, if you turn and look at the sign from the inside, it reads, "Elect from the foundation of the earth." The resolution of those two truths will remain a mystery until we ourselves are in heaven.

Rather than dissuading us from evangelism, the knowledge that God's elect will come to Christ when they hear the gospel should inspire us to be ready witnesses for Him! The message to the lost is simply "*whosoever* will may come."[18] The message to the redeemed is "chosen . . . in him before the foundation of the world."[19] What comforting and motivating words these are for the believer!

Election, being chosen by God, is not a doctrine that can be ignored; it is to be embraced. Over fifty-one times the word "elect" is used in one form or another to show that *God* chooses men both for salvation and for service.

Neither is it a doctrine to be argued; it is to be celebrated. It is clearly taught in the Bible for the comfort of the saints. This is precisely what Paul is doing in Ephesians 1. He is rejoicing in His election!

Does that mean that every question about our election is answered for us in the Bible? Certainly it doesn't. Many other questions about our salvation are not answered for us either.

Do we think we know how God could send Jesus Christ to earth in a human body? Do we think we know how it was possible for Him to be raised from the dead? Of course not. These aspects of our great redemption will be withheld from us until we see Him face to face in glory.

---

[18]See Revelation 22:17.
[19]Ephesians 1:4.

Some might say, "If God chooses some and doesn't choose others, doesn't that make God unfair?" Paul anticipated that question too and addressed it clearly in Romans 9:14, 19-20. He said,

> What shall we say then? Is there unrighteousness with God? God forbid. . . . Thou wilt say then unto me, Why doth he yet find fault? For who hath resisted his will? Nay but, O man, who art thou that repliest against God? Shall the thing formed say to him that formed it, Why hast thou made me thus?"

Paul replies, "Can God's righteousness fail? Can God ever be unjust?" We could also ask, "Can God ever be unloving? Can God ever be unmerciful or unkind?" The answer, of course, is no! Does that mean we can understand all His ways? Again, the answer is no. We can take great comfort, however, in the fact that whatever God is doing in this matter of election is not contradictory to His love for the whole world nor contrary to the desire that none should perish.

Think with me for a moment about how the redeemed, perfected, glorified saints in heaven rejoice at God's decisions. They sing in Revelation 15:3-4,

> Great and marvellous are thy works, Lord God Almighty; *just* [i.e., righteous] and true are thy ways, thou King of saints. Who shall not fear thee, O Lord, and glorify thy name? for thou only art holy: for all nations shall come and worship before thee; for thy *judgments* [i.e., decisions] are made manifest.

The psalmist said, "The Lord is *righteous* in *all* his ways, and holy in *all* his works."[20] Paul, after discussing God's decisions for three chapters in Romans 9-11, finishes his discussion with this amazing declaration:

> O the depth of the riches both of the wisdom and knowledge of God! *how unsearchable are his judgments* [i.e., His decisions], and his ways past finding out! For who hath known the mind of the Lord? or who hath been his counsellor? (11:33-34).

---

[20]Psalm 145:17.

We, too, should come away with humbled hearts that bow before God's *unsearchable* wisdom and bow in grateful submission to His *judgments*—His decisions.

There is no room for a self-exalting pride that flaunts itself before others, saying, "I [and my group] understand it all and have it right." Nor is there room for a self-protective pride that says, "I don't bother with such things." Paul "bothered" with them, and in fact, the first statement out of his mouth in Ephesians was "Bless the Father, who chose us!" This was not a small issue with him. It was first in his mind, and he wanted it to be first in ours as well!

Remember, too, that these truths were written originally to first-century converts fresh out of paganism. They didn't have libraries of commentaries or the benefit of centuries of theological fine-tuning. They didn't even have the rest of the New Testament! These Ephesian Christians had probably never seen the epistle Paul sent to the Romans. They had only this letter and perhaps a copy of the one written to the Colossian church. Apparently, Paul—and God, who inspired Ephesians—felt that what was said in this epistle would be enough to rejoice and quiet their hearts. *It should have the same effect upon us!* If it does not, either our pride or our unbelief has kept us from the peace and joy these truths are intended to bring.

Some Distinctions

We have already seen that great "mysteries" still remain for us. If we are to understand what parts *are* understandable about our salvation, however, we must be sure to use certain terms properly. Unfortunately, the terms "election," "predestination," and "foreknowledge" are used almost interchangeably, which is a serious mistake. Two key passages will help us see their relationship.

> And we know that all things work together for good to them that love God, to them who are the called according to his purpose. For whom he did *foreknow*, he also did *predestinate* to be conformed to the image of his Son, that he might be the firstborn among many brethren. Moreover whom he did *predestinate*, them he also *called*: and whom he *called*, them he also justified: and whom he justified, them he also glorified (Romans 8:28-30).

Elect according to the *foreknowledge* of God the Father . . . (I Peter 1:2).

My friend and colleague Dr. Mark Minnick has likened the terms "election," "predestination," and "foreknowledge" to three bases on a baseball diamond. You cannot hit a home run if the bases are stacked up on top of each other. They have to be spread out and put in order. Let's look at the "bases." We will start with third base and work our way back to first base.

Election is *what* God did before the foundation of the world—He chose us! We know this is third base because Ephesians 1:4-5 and I Peter 1:2 put election after foreknowledge and predestination.

Predestination is second base because Romans 8:29 puts it after foreknowledge. It speaks of *why* God chose us. It describes His purpose in election. Let me illustrate the difference between election and predestination this way. When I purchase an automobile, I am making a choice. My *choice* of that particular car is my *election* of it. My *predestination* of the car is my predetermined *purpose* for the *choice*.

Recently, I acquired a 1974 Volkswagen bug. It was in pretty good shape but had a seized engine. I chose that car for the *purpose* of making it a dependable "daily driver."[21] Others might choose that same vehicle for the *purpose* of restoring it for show at any number of annual VW bug festivals around the country. Still another might choose that car for the *purpose* of hot-rodding the engine for drag racing or the thrill of leaving more reputable sports cars in the dust at a traffic light. My "election"—my choice—of that car was to *predestinate* it to daily use. I had a specific *purpose* for my choice.

God clearly tells us that He *chose* us, having *predestinated* us to "the adoption of children."[22] His *purpose* is to bring us to the enjoyment of our full inheritance that He has planned for His own. Romans tells us further that the predestination was to bring us to the full restoration of the image of Christ in us that was lost in the fall.[23] The next question

---

[21]I'm sure that the fact that I grew up in a mechanic's family that drove Volkswagen bugs and buses had something to do with the decision.

[22]Ephesians 1:5.

[23]Romans 8:29.

is, on what basis did He elect and predestinate us? That brings us to first base: foreknowledge.

Foreknowledge is the *basis* for our predestination and election. But what does foreknowledge mean? Does it mean that God *knew* ahead of time what He would do with every man because He had *decided* ahead of time what He would do? Does it mean that God chose the ones He knew in His omniscience would respond to Him? God has not clearly spelled out the answer to that question.

This should not trouble us. We must remember that most of this is still unrevealed, and these "secret things belong to God."

We can rejoice in what we know but must bow in humility at what we cannot know and say with the prophet, "O Lord God, *thou* knowest."[24] And there our wondering minds must rest. Any attempt to uncover the secret things will be an exercise in philosophic conjecture. They cannot be known. They are divine secrets and no one can pry the information out of God until we are in His presence and He is ready for us to know. Until then we rejoice in His decisions, though we "see through a glass, darkly."[25]

H. C. G. Moule describes this mystery factor in election with these words:

> Who does not know the awfulness of the shadows that lie close to this glory—the dread questionings of the mind over the election of God? But these shadows are cast, as shadows always are, by light. And the purpose of the light is, not to cast shadows but to guide our steps. Do we indeed believe on the Son of God? Have we indeed been 'sealed with the Spirit of the Promise'? Then let us leave absolutely to the Lord *the unknown* of the matter; we shall not be disappointed when He lets us know more about it, another day. But let us boldly grasp for our strength and joy *the known* of the matter; the sovereign grace that lies behind the sinner's repentance, faith, hope, and love" [emphasis his].[26]

---

[24]Ezekiel 37:3.

[25]I Corinthians 13:12.

[26]H. C. G. Moule, *Ephesian Studies* (Fort Washington, Pa.: Christian Literature Crusade, 1937), 37.

Conclusion

God is getting His Church ready for a grand demonstration that will vindicate His character and restore all the glory to Himself. We who are His children can rejoice with Paul in our salvation. He has chosen us to be a part of His cast for that final day. We do, however, have a commission from Him that is to occupy us until He comes for us. We must take the good news of His salvation to every creature. Our message is "Whosoever will may come." For all who have not come, the invitation is still open. For all of us who have come, we can rejoice with Paul that He chose us as a part of His sovereign plan. For your continued reflection I have included in Appendix B an extended discussion of this mystery aspect of God's work. It is called "Salvation: Divine Determination or Human Responsibility" by Layton Talbert. The discussion itself is an appendix article in Dr. Talbert's excellent book, *Not by Chance: Learning to Trust a Sovereign God.*

TAKE TIME TO REFLECT

1. Put into your own words the great "mystery" revealed in Ephesians.

2. If you are a believer, you are one of God's "show dogs" He will display in the end-time universal demonstration, which will vindicate His maligned character. He is now using you as one of the real-time individual demonstrations of His glory. How well are you doing at showing others that God is *first* above all things?

3. In what specific areas are you failing to do so?

4. If you are *not* showing God to be first in these areas, who are you proclaiming to be more important than God?

5. If you are falling "short of the glory of God"—failing to show Him as worthy of being first—what is your failure called, according to Romans 3:23? What do you need to do about it, according to I John 1:9? Have you done that?

A WORD TO DISCIPLE-MAKERS

Do You Listen to Yourself or Talk to Yourself?

One of the greatest indicators of our understanding of and acknowledgment of these great truths about God is what we say to ourselves when *we* are in a "prison" experience—a constraining hardship that seems to have no end. An unrenewed, unilluminated mind evaluates problems and pressures from a purely human perspective. It makes comments to itself and others like the following:

- That's one more crummy thing I have to do this week. I'll never make it!

- I think this requirement is stupid, but if that's the only way I can get what I want, I'll put up with it.

- This kind of stuff always happens to me! Doesn't anybody care?

- I've got enough to worry about already. I don't need this!

- He can't get away with that. I don't have to take it!

Can you imagine Paul—or Christ—handling pressures this way? Remember that the great declarations about God that we have been looking at from Ephesians come from Paul's lips while in prison. D. Martyn Lloyd-Jones, a doctor who left his medical practice to preach, addresses this issue when speaking about depression. He says, "the ultimate cause of all spiritual depression is unbelief." He goes on to say,

> I suggest that the main trouble in this whole matter of spiritual depression in a sense is this, that we allow our self to talk to us instead of talking to our self. Am I just trying to be deliberately paradoxical? Far from it. This is the very essence of wisdom in this matter. *Have you realized that most of your unhappiness in life is due to the fact that you are listening to yourself instead of talking to yourself?* Take those thoughts which come to you the moment you wake up in the morning. . . . They start talking to you, they bring back the problems of yesterday, etc. Somebody is talking. Who is talking to you? Your self is talking to you. Now this man's treatment [speaking of the psalmist in Psalm 42] was this; instead of allowing his self to talk to him, he starts talking to himself. "Why art thou cast down, O my soul?" he asks. His soul has been depressing him, crushing him. So he stands up and says: "Self, listen for a moment, I will speak to you." Do you know what I mean? If you do not, you have had but little experience.

> The main art in the matter of spiritual living is to know how to handle yourself. You have to take yourself in hand, you have to address yourself, preach to yourself, question yourself. You must say to your soul: "Why art thou cast down"—what business have you to be disquieted? You must turn on yourself, upbraid yourself, condemn yourself, exhort yourself, and say to yourself: "Hope thou in God"—instead of muttering in this depressed, unhappy way. *And*

then you must go on to remind yourself of God, Who God is, and what God is and what God has done, and what God has pledged Himself to do. Then having done that, end on this great note: defy yourself, and defy other people [who discourage you], and defy the devil and the whole world, and say with this man: "I shall yet praise Him for the help of His countenance, who is [also] the health of my countenance, and my God."

This is the essence of the treatment in a nutshell.[27]

Now we can administer that kind of treatment to our problems only if we have something to preach to ourselves—something true about God. How much do we really know about God? Do we have some sermons ready to preach to ourselves? Paul is smiling and rejoicing in prison because he knows some things about God, and he reminds himself about those things continually—every time he is tempted to get discouraged. And God wanted us to know these same things too, so He directed this apostle in his prison to write out for us under inspiration the things Paul rehearses in his own mind about God so that we can do the same thing.

---

[27]D. Martyn Lloyd-Jones, *Spiritual Depression: Its Causes and Cure* (Grand Rapids: W. B. Eerdmans Publishing Company, 1965), 20-21.

CHAPTER FOUR
THE REALITY OF CHRIST'S SUFFICIENCY

HAVE YOU MERELY "DONE" THE MUSEUM AND GALLERY?[1]

The BJU Museum and Gallery, housed on the campus of Bob Jones University, is one of the world's largest collections of religious art. Its holdings include over four hundred great works of art by scores of lauded artists, including Reni, Botticelli, Van Dyck, Rubens, Ribera, Titian, Tintoretto, Rembrandt, Le Brun, and Cranach—to name a few.

Visitors to the Museum and Gallery can purchase a self-guided tour brochure as they enter the collection and walk through the almost thirty galleries to examine the paintings, furniture, and sculptures. As they progress through the collection, they may pause to look at a famous painting highlighted in the brochure. They notice it is by Peter Paul Rubens and comment to the friends touring with them, "Here's a famous painting!" They quickly move to the next gallery to pick out a painting by Rembrandt. There they stop momentarily but move on to the next gallery quite gratified that they have seen a work by such a famous artist. So on it goes through their self-guided tour as they visit gallery after gallery until they have finished the tour. In all, they have spent probably no more than ninety minutes for the entire tour.

They know that the War Memorial Chapel on the campus houses a collection of seven massive masterpieces by the American artist Benjamin West, originally commissioned for the chapel of Windsor

---

[1] Art gallery illustration adapted from D. Martyn Lloyd-Jones, *God's Ultimate Purpose: An Exposition of Ephesians 1* (Grand Rapids: Baker Books, 1978), 171.

Castle in England. One of the visitors may comment to his friends, "Well, we have 'done' the Museum and Gallery. Let's go see the chapel paintings."

In reality, they haven't 'done' the Museum and Gallery at all. Art critics from around the world will spend entire days studying a particular artist or works from a certain school of artists. They will leave reluctantly at the end of their visit, thrilled with what they have experienced during the visit but very much aware that they have not begun to explore all there is to gain from their target paintings, let alone gleaned all they could from the rest of the collection. They could spend a lifetime in the building and would never feel they have 'done' the Museum and Gallery.

When you are not yet skilled at discerning art, it is normal to go through the Museum and Gallery quickly. You have a sense that you are looking at unusually magnificent art although you do not yet know exactly why it is so splendid. You readily admit you have no knowledge of the artist, the painting's background, the medium used, the artist's techniques or style of representation. You don't yet know enough to be exhilarated by the painting, but you see enough excellence, though your eyes are untrained, to desire to visit it again and perhaps to do some study before you come again so that you can see some things you didn't see before. That is the sense we ought to have when we visit the "Gallery of the Heavenlies" in Ephesians. I have prepared for you a "brochure" of the two "paintings" we have been looking at in the last two chapters and have added a description of the third one we are to see in this chapter.

"PAINTINGS" IN THE EPHESIANS 1 "GALLERY OF THE HEAVENLIES"

Item 1: "The Supreme One"
Here is pictured the First One, who **created** the heaven and earth. He alone towers **high above** His creation and is worthy of the constant adoration and entire submission of every creature He has made.

Rather than just read the catalog descriptions in this "Gallery of the Heavenlies," we have stopped to ponder the beauty on the canvases before us. In chapter two, we have gloried in the all-encompassing supremacy of God. No doubt is left in our minds as to who has "created all things" and for whose "pleasure they are and were created." We marveled at God's plans to reunite all things together in Christ.

Remember, His purpose in the ages to come is to display His Church before all of creation as material witnesses to vindicate His character. He intends to show that He can be "just, and the justifier of him which believeth in Jesus,"[2] and He wishes to display "the exceeding riches of his grace in his kindness toward us through Christ Jesus."[3] The result will be that Lucifer and his minions will be justly condemned and damned along with all who rejected His claims, and the redeemed and the unfallen spirits will rejoice at the wisdom, love, and power of the one who could bring this all to pass! That was Item 1—"The Supreme One." After viewing Item 1, we paused in chapter three at Item 2.

> Item 2: "The Sovereign One"
> This painting shows that God **reigns** absolutely over every part of His creation. He **chooses** to bring to pass the things that will bring Him the greatest pleasure.

As we gazed upon this treasure, we bowed before the humbling sovereignty of God. We saw that what is even more amazing to us *personally* is that He chose *us* to be a part of those who will be reunited with Him in the new creation! He didn't choose us reluctantly; He did so because it made Him happy to do so. And we sing with Wesley, "And can it be that *I* should gain an interest in the Savior's blood?" and later, "'Tis mercy all, immense and free! For, O my God, it found out *me*."

That brings us to Item 3 in the "Gallery of the Heavenlies"—our topic in this chapter.

> Item 3: "The Sufficient One"
> Notice in this portrait the astonishing **provisions** He has made through His Son for His sovereign plan to be executed for His supreme glory and for the salvation of men.

---

[2]Romans 3:26.
[3]Ephesians 2:7.

We do not want to merely read the brochure description of this portrait. We want to stop to meditate upon the beauties of our salvation and rejoice at the wise and loving sufficiency of God for His skill and provision for redeeming a lost race through His Son. It is not possible for us to stop to look at every phrase of Ephesians 1, but we must not miss the overall impact of Paul's lengthy sentence in verses 3-14.

FIREWORKS IN THE HEAVENLIES

Within this sentence Paul rehearses the major truths of the Christian faith that lit up for him the darkness of his prison. I like to think of these statements of truth as individual skyrockets in a great fireworks display. As his lengthy sentence runs on and on, Paul doesn't even seem to take a breath between the individual skyrockets of truth; he is so excited about their beauty![4]

Any believer who has ever meditated upon these phrases himself stands back as well and says "oooh" and "aaah" in his heart as Paul mentions each one. The illuminated believer has seen them before, and as each skyrocket of truth is launched into his consciousness, it bursts with a colorful, majestic explosion upon his memory as he recalls the sparkle and brilliance of each truth. He can't wait for the next one because he knows what is coming! He nudges his neighbor and says, "Wait till you see the next one! It's beautiful!" We might imagine a conversation like this as each skyrocket bursts in the sky:

Did you see that?! He chose us before the foundation of the world!

O look, we're adopted as children according to the good pleasure of His will!

There's my favorite! We're redeemed by His blood!

And there's another! We're accepted in the Beloved!

And what about that one?! Forgiven according to the riches of His grace!

Look over there! It's our inheritance!

See that one?! We're sealed with the Holy Spirit of promise!

---

[4]Of course, the analogy breaks down because fireworks are momentary, soon-forgotten displays, but the truths Paul was seeing are eternal.

Now, we need to ask ourselves a penetrating question: "Did those statements draw from us the same kind of excitement and brilliance that Paul experienced?" If not, we need to ask ourselves why not because through the ages they have exhilarated the saints who knew God well. They certainly cause the angels and the saints in glory now to respond in wondering praise. In heaven, the voices of innumerable angels, heavenly creatures, and the blood-bought Church triumphant,[5] who behold these things, sing with loud voices. Their praises echo through the ages of eternity because of these things. They are seeing the excellence of Christianity, the beauty of a Lamb, slain from the foundation of the earth, the wisdom of the Father, who planned it all, and the skillful work of the Spirit, who executed the plan.

Why then do these truths mean so little to us? How often have we read Ephesians 1, and the phrases seemed to run together meaninglessly? These truths aren't to be packed in boxes to be forgotten in some remote warehouse. They are to be written "upon the table of [our] heart"[6] and deployed regularly in the milieu of life. Paul is laying a solid foundation for a vibrant Christian walk. We must see these truths for ourselves if we are to be stable and joyful in our "prison" experiences. We certainly cannot explore them all in this chapter, but we can appreciate more of their beauty as we take a look at what Jesus Christ accomplished by His cross according to Ephesians 2. Consider them with me.

DEAD AND DIVIDED

To make our salvation possible, God faced some major obstacles.[7] How could He righteously forgive His own treasonous creatures, who had sided with Lucifer to disobey Him and who set themselves up as the rulers of their own lives, robbing Him of His glory? The first major

---

[5]The "Church triumphant" is the multitude of believers who have died and are with the Lord now in heaven. They are no longer the "Church militant" as we who yet live on the earth are called. Their battles with the world, the flesh, and the Devil are over. They have "triumphed" over these enemies and are now at rest from the fight.

[6]Proverbs 7:1-3.

[7]Please understand the limitation of human language here. Nothing is an "obstacle" when viewed from God's perspective. Viewed from our perspective, however, these are staggering problems.

complication then was that we were justly condemned to eternal death; *we were dead and needed to be redeemed unto God.*[8]

Secondly, how could He make a Bride for His Son out of "every kindred, and tongue, and people, and nation"[9] when Jews and Gentiles were so hostile to each other? How could He unite two such antagonistic groups of people so that together they could be the centerpiece of His restored creation—the Church? *The Jews and Gentiles were divided and needed to be reconciled to each other.*[10] We will see how He united these two factions in chapter seven and will turn our attention to what He had to do to rescue us from being "dead in trespasses and sins."[11]

CHILDREN OF DISOBEDIENCE

Philosophers and psychologists have tried for years to describe the human condition. They have produced countless theories and categorized innumerable disorders in an attempt to understand the various dilemmas man has produced for himself. There never has been any better presentation of human psychology, however, than the God-inspired portraits of man painted by the apostle Paul. And of all of Paul's portraits, none present a more succinct picture than the ones outlined in Ephesians.

> And you . . . were dead in trespasses and sins; wherein in time past ye walked according to the course of this world, according to the prince of the power of the air, the [mindset] that now [energizes] the children of disobedience: among whom also we all [lived] in times past in the lusts of our flesh, [indulging] the desires of the flesh and of the mind; and were by nature the children of wrath, even as others (2:1-3).

> Having the understanding darkened, being alienated from the life of God through the ignorance that is in them, because of the [hardness] of their heart: who being past feeling have given them-

---

[8]Ephesians 2:1-10.
[9]Revelation 5:9.
[10]Ephesians 2:11–3:13.
[11]Ephesians 2:1.

selves over unto [sensuality], to work all uncleanness with greedi-ness (4:18-19).

It is precisely because we do not see the heinousness of the above para-graphs and because we do not see ourselves described in them that we place little value upon what Jesus Christ did for us at Calvary. These passages clearly tell us that before salvation our *mind* is darkened; it cannot see anything as it should. Our *will* is hardened; it obstinately chooses self over God every time and has no inclination to bow to any-one unless it serves self to do so. Our *soul* is dead; it no longer has the capacity to fellowship with God. It is not only dead in its receptive ability—like a dead radio that cannot tune in the stations—it is also dead because it is under condemnation—like a convicted killer is as good as dead while he awaits execution on death row.

The words of Moule in his commentary on Ephesians capture the treachery of the scene.[12]

> "Other [i.e., false] Gospels" . . . present [man] as . . . an unfortunate traveller upon some bye-road of the universe, fallen among thieves, "more sinned against than sinning," cruelly robbed and maimed, with nothing to blame but his enemies and his circumstances; so that the supreme King stands in some sense obligated to redress him, and to recover him, and to comfort him after his long calamities. . . . But it is not the true Gospel of the Lord and His Apostles. . . .
>
> [Man] lies not only wounded but guilty on the wayside. Man is not merely a sufferer; he is a runaway, a criminal, a rebel, a conspirator. Eternal Love regards him. But eternal Law, lodged in the same Will with eternal Love lays its arrest upon him, and shews the death-war-rant. And meanwhile, as part of the phenomenon of man's mysteri-ous self-ruin, he lies there not only guilty and arrested, but alienated and resisting still. His destruction of himself expresses itself above all in this—that in the Fall, he does not love God, he does not choose God. He "forsakes his own mercy." He lays the blame anywhere but on his own head. He loves himself best. Of himself, he is not con-trite, penitent, submissive, believing. He is dead to his true life, which is to know God in His redeeming Son. . . .
>
> I linger upon this side of truth [i.e., of the sinfulness of man], not as if I could forget the glorious other side [i.e., of what he is in Christ];

---

[12]Moule, 66-70.

what would life be without it? But I am sure that *this* [emphasis his] side is what the Christian world is forgetting far and wide, while salvation is either taken all too indolently, (a very different thing from taking it simply,) or is practically put aside as what "humanity" can do without. . . .

Let the Church come to be strange to the experience of conviction of sin; it will come to be equally strange to that of "joy in God through our Lord Jesus Christ."

"Never was there a heresy, but it had something to do with an insufficient estimate of sin." And an insufficient estimate of the "thing which God hateth" is not only the parent of speculative error; it is the secret death of true spiritual joy.

So here we have a messy picture. Paul heaps picture upon picture and says, furthermore, that before salvation all of us followed the "course of this world,"[13] a course that was blazed by the Devil himself. Just like the water in the Colorado River follows the course of the riverbed at the bottom of the Grand Canyon, so the soul estranged from God can do nothing but take the same twists and turns that the Devil has dictated for the world to follow. Since that course is diametrically opposed to the intention of God, to follow it is to be disobedient.

A Boy and a Judge

The thought of our disobedience to God ought to cause us to shudder, but tragically it does not because we do not know well the nature and stature of the one whom we disobey. We see this in a small way in various levels of disobedience to men. Certainly a brother disobeying his older brother's insistence to play a game fairly is not seen to be nearly as serious as that same brother disobeying his father, who has told him he cannot ride his bike until he empties the trash. The boy's statement "You can't make me!" takes on a different seriousness when it represents his defiance to his father than when it is said to his brother.

Suppose, however, that that same young man several years later says, "You can't make me!" to a district judge who has just ruled that he must not leave the state pending a felony trial. He would be in contempt of court. No judge would stand for that kind of defiance against

---

[13]Ephesians 2:2.

72

his authority. Neither would the judge be out of line if he imposed a stiff fine or jail sentence for the young man's defiance. If we can understand the gravity of the man's disobedience to a district judge, why do we not understand the infinitely more heinous nature of our defiance against the Judge of the earth? The infinite nature and unsurpassed stature of this Law-Giver as the Creator of us all make any disobedience to any of His commands a grievous offense.

The Real Offense of Our Sin

Think through these previous situations of disobedience with me and place yourself in the position of the disobedient boy. The gravity of the offense is determined by how much authority you had the audacity to ignore to get what you wanted. To defy an older brother is to ignore his seniority, though it be only a few years, and to place yourself on an imaginary[14] level that is higher than his natural seniority.

To defy a father's command, you must ignore not only his seniority by age but also his seniority as your progenitor and his God-ordained authority as your ruler. You then have to imagine yourself on a self-exalted level that is higher than his authority. You have to believe that your authority to do what you want supersedes his authority to command you otherwise.

To defy a district judge's order, you must ignore his constitutionally granted and God-ordained powers to bring law and order to the citizenry under his jurisdiction. To defy him, you have to exalt yourself to an imaginary level of authority that can overrule his rule.

I hope you see the growing arrogance of the defiance as you see the growing levels of self-exaltation that must be imagined and claimed in order to disobey increasingly higher levels of authority. In reality, to defy their orders is to usurp their rightful place over you while imposing *your* will on them.

Now lastly, think about your disobedience to God. To defy the Creator's commands, you must ignore His exclusive right to rule His own

---

[14]I say "imaginary" because there is no legitimate claim to power in these cases except that which we grant to ourselves in our willful self-deception. Though the supposed right to rule our lives may "feel" right, that is a reflection of the extent of our self-deception, not a reflection of things as they are in reality.

creation as He wishes. You have to exalt yourself to a level of imaginary importance that would make Him at least second in command—if you are that generous—and place yourself first in command over the part of His creation you want to control—in this case, yourself. The arrogance of such a feat is astounding, and the act can be considered nothing less than treason against the Most High God—the First One! No wonder God created a hell! It is the just end for Satan and any who would follow him in his rebellion. No punishment existed that was strong enough to address the severity of dishonoring God in this way—robbing Him of the glory of His *firstness* to which He alone is worthy. And that brings us to the second title Paul gave to the unbelieving heart: children of wrath. We shall discuss it shortly. Before we do, let's examine one more aspect of our disobedience.

The Reason for Our Insensibility to Sin

Have you ever asked yourself why we who are believers are still so insensitive to our disobedience to God? The Puritan preacher John Owen explains it this way when commenting on Ephesians 4:18ff:

> Custom [i.e., the frequency] of sinning takes away the *sense* of it; the course of the world takes away the *shame* of it; and love to it makes men greedy in the pursuit of it.[15]

When our frequent disobedience makes it commonplace to us, and when the world assures us that disobedience is entirely acceptable, and when our self-deceived hearts have such an affection for it that it seems to be beneficial to us, our sinfulness does not seem bad to us at all. Indeed, unless the Spirit of God opens our eyes to see our condition of defiance against God—and to see the just penalty of eternal death that it deserves—we cannot be saved.

Furthermore, unless after our salvation we continually ask the Spirit of God to be searching us and to be bringing our actions to trial before God's righteous standards,[16] we will be lulled back into a complacency that will breed all manner of carelessness, blindness, and wickedness in our lives. Unless our view of our sinfulness is kept right through frequent meditation and regular preaching on the subject,

---

[15]Sinclair B. Ferguson, *John Owen on the Christian Life* (Carlisle, Pa.: The Banner of Truth Trust, 1987), 40.

[16]Psalm 139:23-24.

we cannot get the Christian life right. We shall look at this in some depth in chapter six.

Paul called unredeemed fallen man "[sons] of disobedience." We are truly the offspring of an evil idea—the devilish idea that God does not have to be obeyed in all things whatsoever He commands. Instead we have obeyed the lusts of our flesh. Paul gives us an even closer look at the psychology of fallen man in Ephesians 2:3 when he discusses those lusts and labels them "desires of the [body] and of the mind." Again, it is noteworthy that every part of every man has been affected as he continues to perpetuate the disobedience of Satan himself against God.[17] Every man since Adam has this self-serving bent in him. That bent cannot be eradicated in this life. It cannot be coddled or ignored. And what is even more frightening is that it cannot be atoned for by anything a man can do to make the wrongs against the Most High God right. We are not only "children of disobedience" but also "children of wrath."[18] Let us consider that awful statement.

CHILDREN OF WRATH

Imagine that you are in the courtroom as the young man defies the judge with his words "You can't make me!" What would go through your mind? You probably would be thinking, "Oh, son, you are about to learn that the judge *can* make you! And you are also about to learn the limitation of your own imaginary authority and the reality of the judge's authority!"

That young man will soon experience some indication of the judge's displeasure at being challenged and will receive a penalty with enough severity to show the seriousness of the offense. The judge's stern rebuke and reasonable penalty would be the only righteous response he could make if he takes seriously his responsibilities to uphold the law in his jurisdiction. For the judge to overlook the infraction because he felt sentimentally "warm and fuzzy" toward offenders today would be a travesty of justice. The judge himself would be unrighteous.

---

[17]This truth that every part of man has been defiled is called "total depravity." It does not mean that a man is as wicked as he possibly can be but that his wickedness has permeated his "total" being.

[18]Ephesians 2:2-3.

The wrath of God is His righteous response to the high crime of mutiny against His rule. His wrath is the manifestation of His hatred of evil. It is the revulsion of His moral excellence against wickedness in the creature. God would be unrighteous if He were morally indifferent to evil. He would not be assigning to evil its true weight. He would cease to be perfect if He did not rejoice in obedience and hate defiance. His wrath is not like the anger of most men, however. It is not cruel or capricious. In His righteousness every men gets exactly what he deserves.

What Is Your Tolerance of Vomit?

The fact that we do not share with God this same revulsion of wickedness is testimony to the numbing effect of sin upon our own sensibilities. To our shame we are more repulsed by the sight of vomit than by the presence of sin.

When someone gets airsick on a flight or a family member vomits because of an illness, most everyone turns away in revulsion. We do not want to view the sight—much less clean it up. In fact, we are still uncomfortable when the mess is cleaned up because the smell is still in the air. We simply have no tolerance for vomit—nor should we. God uses a rather graphic picture in II Peter 2:22 to make this very point. He says,

> But it is happened unto them according to the true proverb, The dog is turned to his own vomit again.

The dog returns to his vomit because he does not think it is so bad. We return to our sin for the same reason. The picture—though unpleasant—should make us pause to think of how distasteful the sight of our sin is to God. Perhaps now you can understand more fully the definition we just looked at for the wrath of God: *It is the revulsion of His moral excellence against wickedness in the creature that causes a righteous and severe response to it.*

If we did not have strong reactions against vomit—if we had the same acceptance of it as the dog has that we saw in II Peter—there would be something dreadfully wrong with our sensibilities. If God were to have anything but strong hatred for wickedness, something would be dreadfully wrong as well. The Scriptures, however, show God's strong reaction against sin. Consider these inspired accounts of God's righteous wrath.

> The Lord Jesus shall be revealed from heaven with his mighty angels, in flaming fire taking vengeance on them that know not God, and that obey not the gospel of our Lord Jesus Christ: who shall be punished with everlasting destruction from the presence of the Lord, and from the glory of his power (II Thessalonians 1:7-9).

> For [in the gospel] the wrath of God is revealed from heaven against all ungodliness and unrighteousness of men, who [suppress] the truth in unrighteousness . . . so that they are without excuse (Romans 1:18, 20).

> For the wages of sin is [eternal] death (Romans 6:23).

> He that believeth on the Son hath everlasting life: and he that believeth not the Son shall not see life; but the wrath of God abideth on him (John 3:36).

> And the kings of the earth, and the great men, and the rich men, and the chief captains, and the mighty men, and every bondman, and every free man, hid themselves in the dens and in the rocks of the mountains; and said to the mountains and rocks, Fall on us, and hide us from the face of him that sitteth on the throne, and from the wrath of the Lamb: for the great day of his wrath is come; and who shall be able to stand? (Revelation 6:15-17).

These passages are not isolated texts; they are mere samplings of the plethora of times that this theme appears in the Word of God. Jesus, in fact, had more to say about hell than He did about heaven. The way to hell is broad with many traveling on its path, and our Lord was concerned that men know the outcome of their life if their sinfulness was not pardoned by the one they had offended. And it is into this heavy plight that Paul interjects the hope of the gospel for fallen man:

> But God, who is rich in mercy, for his great love wherewith he loved us, even when we were dead in sins, hath [made us alive] together with Christ, (by grace are ye saved;) and hath raised us up together, and made us sit together in heavenly places in Christ Jesus: that in the ages to come he might shew the exceeding

riches of his grace in his kindness toward us through Christ Jesus (Ephesians 2:4-7).

CHILDREN OF GOD

Though God must pour out His wrath as the righteous statement of His aversion to evil, nonetheless, for reasons known only within the divine counsels of the Trinity, God loved the world. And here my mind wonders at the seeming incongruity of the statement that God loves sinners—more specifically that He loved *me*!

I am amazed as I contemplate *"Why* should He do this?" but I am just as stunned when I consider *"How* could He do this?" His plan was not one that made good men merely better for there is none good;[19] it made sons out of His enemies! John tells us, "But as many as received him, to them gave he [authority] to become the sons of God, even to them that believe on his name."[20] How can it be that I, a "child of disobedience," and thus, a "child of wrath," can become a "child of God"? That brings us to a beautiful story—the true account of God's plan to rescue us from our miserable plight.

An Old, Old Story

The story began in the Garden of Eden after the fall of man, when God promised that through Eve's offspring one would come who would crush the Serpent's rule on the earth. We have already seen why the Serpent's defiance—and ours—was worthy of eternal separation from God in hell. Thus, God's declaration, "the soul that sinneth, it shall die."[21]

God also revealed to Moses, however, that in the place of the sinner's death, He would accept the death of a blemish-free lamb whose blood would be poured out as an atonement—a means to satisfy God's righteous wrath against sin. That substitutionary, ceremonial lamb, however, was only a token sacrifice. It was limited in scope and had to be repeated daily by each individual sinner. The elaborate Mosaic sacrificial system was merely foreshadowing a Sacrifice of staggering proportions, which was yet to come. But "when the fulness of the time was come, God sent forth his Son, made of a woman, made under the law,

---

[19]Romans 3:10-18.
[20]John 1:12.
[21]Ezekiel 18:4.

to redeem them that were under the law, that we might receive the adoption of sons."[22]

Within the counsels of the Trinity, God Himself decided He would provide His own substitutionary sacrifice to appease His own wrath so that all who would accept His atonement could become guilt-free sons purchased for Himself by the blood of His own Son, Jesus Christ. Precisely on schedule, Jesus Christ, the Creator and God Himself, stepped out of heaven's splendor, still fully God, added to all the qualities of His godhood the body and qualities of a man,[23] and physically and historically lived on planet earth for thirty-three years. The evangelist John states it succinctly: "The Word was made flesh, and dwelt among us."[24]

He did not come to this earth merely to teach us principles of living—how to forgive, how to love, and how to care for the less fortunate. The babe lying in a manger in a Bethlehem stable was to become a sacrifice to atone for sin. He would qualify as a perfect Lamb by thirty-three years of life on this planet subject to every evil influence and every divine law experienced by created men. Since He perfectly kept the law, His death would not have to be for His own sin. The whole idea was to satisfy the wrath of God, impart resurrection life to dead souls, and thereby give to redeemed men the capacity to once again fellowship with the Creator.

It is of vast importance that we understand that the death of Jesus Christ was not just another Roman execution. It was the ultimate blood sacrifice for sin. Because Jesus Christ was God—an infinite being Himself—His death could have infinite proportions. One Man could die for the sins of the whole world! It was a perfect plan—a credit to the wisdom, love, and power of our perfect Creator.

On that cross, Jesus Christ became a "lightning rod" that attracted all the fury of the righteous anger of God against the sin of men. For three hours of excruciating physical torture and an even more torturous spiritual defilement, our sinfulness and its guilt were placed upon Him by the Father, and He endured the rod of the Father's displeasure *for us*!

---

[22]Galatians 4:4-5.
[23]Philippians 2:5-11.
[24]John 1:14.

How my soul shrinks in shame as I think that such unsullied purity should take upon Himself such defilement for me! While my eyes fill with tears at the horrible spectacle, my heart convulses with "joy unspeakable and full of glory"[25] that I, a child of hell, should become a son of God! I never want to recover from the sight, and I want to—yea must—return to the scene often.

When the wrath was spent, the sacrificial Lamb cried out in agonizing triumph, "It is finished!" and surrendered His human life to the Father. The atonement was made! This is why Paul in Ephesians exclaims, "in whom we have redemption through his blood, the forgiveness of sins, according to the riches of his grace; wherein he hath abounded toward us!"[26] Don't rush over this verse. It is rich with meaning for anyone who has spent time at the foot of the cross gazing upon the sight.

After His death on the cross, His body was placed into a borrowed tomb to await His own resurrection three days and three nights later. And rise He did! He "was delivered [up to death] for our offences, and was raised again for our justification."[27] His resurrection was the proof that God's holiness was satisfied. He could now be both "just [in the full punishment of sin] and the justifier of him which believeth in Jesus."[28] It was furthermore a statement that He was indeed God's heaven-sent Messiah: He was "declared to be the Son of God . . . by the resurrection from the dead."[29] And most happily for us, His resurrection guaranteed our own resurrection to new life here on this earth and to eternal life in the world to come![30]

No single chapter of any book could even begin to show the beauty of the wisdom and love and power of this great God, who would do such a thing for us! I can only urge you to meditate upon these great themes of our redemption so that you will come to love Jesus Christ more fully. As you spend time contemplating these things, you will learn why no

---

[25]I Peter 1:8.
[26]Ephesians 1:7-8.
[27]Romans 4:25.
[28]Romans 3:26.
[29]Romans 1:4.
[30]I Corinthians 15:17-28.

title of our blessed Lord is more precious to the believer than that of Redeemer.[31]

As we return to Ephesians, we note that the various blessings of the Christian life come because we are "in Christ," or "in Him." Indeed, Paul wraps up the whole of the Christian life with his statement in a passage in Colossians that is parallel to his discussions in Ephesians. He declares that we are "complete in Him."[32] In my own Bible, I have underlined the passages in Ephesians that point this out. Notice how Jesus Christ is central to every part of our Christian experience.

1:1 "to the faithful *in Christ Jesus*"

1:3 "who hath blessed us with all spiritual blessings in heavenly places *in Christ*"

1:4 "According as he hath chosen us *in him*"

1:6 "wherein he hath made us accepted *in the beloved*"

1:7 "*In whom* we have redemption through his blood"

1:10 "That . . . he might gather together in one all things *in Christ*, both which are in heaven, and which are on earth; even *in him*"

1:11 "*In whom* also we [believing Jews] have obtained an inheritance"

1:13 "*In whom* ye [Gentiles] also [obtained an inheritance], after that ye heard the word of truth"

2:5 [God] "hath [made us alive] together *with Christ*"

2:6 "and made us sit together in heavenly places *in Christ Jesus*"

---

[31] An afternoon or evening of meditation on old hymn texts such as "Redeemed, How I Love to Proclaim It," "O, for a Thousand Tongues to Sing," "I Will Sing of My Redeemer," "Since I Have Been Redeemed," "Crown Him with Many Crowns," "Praise Him, Praise Him," and "There Is a Fountain" will provide a great feast for your soul.

[32] Colossians 2:10.

2:10 "For we are his workmanship, created *in Christ Jesus*"

2:21 "*In whom* all the building fitly framed together groweth unto an holy temple"

2:22 "*In whom* ye also are builded together for an habitation of God"

3:6 "That the Gentiles should be . . . partakers of his promise *in Christ*"

3:11 "According to the eternal purpose which he purposed *in Christ Jesus our Lord*"

Paul is trying to teach us something very vital to vibrant Christianity, and that is that *you cannot understand or live Christianity well unless you understand how central Jesus Christ is to this whole arrangement.* This is the mystery of Christ—the heretofore divine secret previously unknown at this level of detail—that Jesus Christ is the central factor in God's reuniting of all things. God does nothing for any of us without our right relationship to Jesus Christ. Let me illustrate it this way.

What Is He Doing Here?

Suppose a wealthy businessman, while driving downtown looking over some properties, notices a young girl—obviously a prostitute—standing on a street corner. Her "benefactor"—there are other, more profane, terms for the man she works for—is just walking away from her in anger. Perhaps she has just missed an important client or has failed her contract in some other way. The businessman notices the despair and hopelessness written on the young girl's face. He suspects she probably ran away from home only to find herself in a worse situation than she had ever experienced with her parents. The businessman drives on by, but the pathetic image of her bondage and emptiness is forever emblazoned on his mind.

He returns home determined to do something about it. To care for her in his own home would look inappropriate, to say the least. It would not be proper for him to do something for the girl if she were not part of the family.

The businessman confers with his son, and they decide to rescue her. She is probably infected with innumerable diseases she has contracted in her profession but is also in trouble with the law. The son is to find her, convince her to marry him, and, while wedding arrangements are being made, get her the medical attention she needs, pay off her debt to her "benefactor," and square her record with the law. As the son seeks her in the brothels, he exposes himself to the worst ignominy of his life. Upon seeing him in "that part of town," those who know him ask each other, "What is *he* doing down *there?*" Nonetheless, he pursues her until he finds her, convinces her of his love, proposes to her, and seeks to right all the wrongs she has committed.

A short while later he marries her, and now she is "in the family." *Now the father can righteously bless her by blessing the son.* Whatever the father does for the son benefits his son's wife.

What Is Done for the Groom Is Done for the Bride!

O Christian, that is what it means to be "in Christ"! If you are a believer, the Father chose you, the Spirit sought you out, the Son redeemed you, and now you are "in the family." Now, because the Father raised up the Son, you benefit from His resurrection. When the Son reigns in heaven over all, you will reign with Him. As the Father loves the Son, so He loves the Bride. And the Father can do it all righteously and for the purpose of showing "the exceeding riches of his grace in his kindness toward us *through Jesus Christ. . . .* that we should be to the praise of his glory."[33]

The heavenly Father said to the Son, "Go pay her debts; it will cost You Your own blood. You will have to take the form of a mortal, live in rejection, face an excruciating death, and pay the penalty for her sin. You will have to become her Redeemer. You Yourself must become the atoning sacrifice to appease My just wrath against her. I will charge You with her sin and will turn My back on You, but I have chosen to love her. She will be My Church and Your Bride. And with that, the Father "spared not his own Son, but delivered him up for us all."[34] The

---

[33]Ephesians 2:7; 1:12.
[34]Romans 8:32.

Son rejoiced at the plan and became "obedient unto death, even the death of the cross."[35] He paid the price and *redeemed* us!

I suppose that as the angels watched the incarnation take place, they must have wondered why the Son would leave the glories of heaven to live in the filth of the fallen world. They may have asked each other the same question asked about the businessman's son, "What is *He* doing down *there*!" That is why Charles Wesley penned the following stanza in his hymn "And Can It Be That I Should Gain?"

> *'Tis mystery all! Th' Immortal dies!*
> *Who can explore His strange design?*
> *In vain, the first-born seraph tries*
> *To sound the depths of love Divine!*
> *'Tis mercy all! let earth adore,*
> *Let angel minds inquire no more.*[36]

And in wonder we who know Him as our Redeemer exclaim with William Newell, author of "At Calvary,"

> *Oh, the love that drew salvation's plan!*
> *Oh, the grace that brought it down to man!*
> *Oh, the mighty gulf that God did span*
> *At Calvary!*
> *Mercy there was great, and grace was free;*
> *Pardon there was multiplied to me;*
> *There my burdened soul found liberty,*
> *At Calvary.*[37]

Dear reader, do you see the beauty of this plan? Does this old, old story strike any chord of wonder in you? Does it humble you to think that the God you have offended would Himself pay your just debt? Does your heart still pull back in rebellion when this one who died for you says, "Come follow Me"? Do you have any inward compulsion to be like Him in His self-sacrificing love for others and His explicit obedience to the will of His Father?

---

[35]Philippians 2:8.

[36]Charles Wesley, "And Can It Be That I Should Gain?" in *Worship and Service Hymnal* (Carol Stream, Ill.: Hope Publishing Co., 1957).

[37]William R. Newell, "At Calvary," in *Worship and Service Hymnal* (Carol Stream, Ill.: Hope Publishing Co., 1957).

If you draw back from these questions in self-protective resistance, either you have never experienced this redemption for yourself, or you like the prodigal son have so distanced yourself from Him by your continual self-will that you hardly recognize His voice, nor remember your place in your Father's house.[38] The words of Jesus Christ Himself to the Ephesian church several years later are appropriate for you.

> I have somewhat against thee, because thou hast left thy first love. Remember therefore from whence thou art fallen, and repent, and do the first works; or else I will come unto thee quickly, and will remove thy candlestick out of his place, except thou repent (Revelation 2:4-5).

I close this chapter with some admonitions from John Owen on how to remedy the condition described above. He says,

> Make every effort to prepare your minds for such heavenly thoughts. If your thoughts are filled with earthly things, then a sense of Christ's love and its glory will not abide in them. Few minds are prepared for this duty. The outward behaviour of most reveals the attitude of their souls. Their thoughts wander up and down to the corners of the earth. It is useless to call such persons to the duty of contemplating the glory of Christ's love. . . . *A holy calmness of mind ruled by spiritual principles, a heavenly mindedness, and a realization of how excellent this divine glory is, are required for this duty of meditation.*

> We must not allow ourselves to be satisfied with vague ideas of the love of Christ which present nothing of his glory to our minds, for it is by such thoughts that many deceive themselves. All who believe that Christ is God value his love and so are never happy with vague ideas of his love. . . . To have clear, distinct ideas of Christ's love, ask yourself the following questions:

>   (i)   Whose love is it? . . . (*1 John 3:16*).

>   (ii) How did this love of the Son of God show itself? . . . (*Ephesians 3:19, Hebrews 2:14-15, Revelation 1:5*).

>   (iii) Did we deserve Christ's love?

>   (iv) What did the love of God procure for us?[39]

---

[38]Luke 15:11-32.
[39]Owen, 54-55.

I have tried to answer those questions in this chapter. Read it over and over until something of the glory of Christ's work begins to glow in your soul. Sit down with an old hymnal and pause long over the texts of saints who have seen the glory of Christ's person and work. Sing them, memorize them, and make their messages your own praise to your Redeemer. Fill your mind with the wonder of Isaiah 53 and the spiritual logic of I Corinthians 15. All the while, beg God to show you the excellency of these things. Ask Him to show you the beauty of His plan and the wonder of His love. Keep coming back to this cross until your stubborn and insensitive heart bows in broken submission and loving devotion to "the Lamb of God, which taketh away the sin of the world."[40]

TAKE TIME TO REFLECT

1. Has God, indeed, made you alive in Christ Jesus, or are you still dead to God, governed by the world's atmosphere, living only to please your desires, and therefore, under the just wrath of God?

2. Rate your own "disobedience index." Do you think of your disobedience to God on the same level as disobeying an older brother, your father, or a district judge, or do you sense the gravity of it and shudder at the thought that you are disobeying the Most High God?

3. If you are redeemed, do you "love to proclaim it," or are you "hesitant to admit it"?

4. Since God is preparing you to be a material witness of the greatness of His power and of His grace, how is His "project" in you coming? Are you cooperating with Him as He prepares you for the grand display in the ages to come and for the smaller displays in which you represent Him now? Are you resisting His efforts to make you "holy and without blame" (Ephesians 1:4), or are you daily asking Him to show you how you can be a better display for Him?

5. Is your heart filled with wonder that He should love *you*, and is your tongue filled with praise to God Himself for letting *you* be a part of His marvelous plan?

---

[40]John 1:29.

A WORD TO DISCIPLE-MAKERS

The Importance of Jesus Christ

Remember, in this chapter we are standing before Item 3 in the Gallery of the Heavenlies and beholding "The Sufficient One." We are gazing upon our Savior, Jesus Christ. *There is no better way to find out what God is like than to become intimately acquainted with Jesus Christ.*

Think about these passages.

> God, who . . . spake in time past unto the fathers by the prophets, hath in these last days spoken unto us by his Son . . . *who being the brightness of his glory, and the [exact] image of his person,* and upholding all things by the word of his power, when he had by himself purged our sins, sat down on the right hand of the Majesty on high (Hebrews 1:1-3).

> But if our gospel be hid, it is hid to them that are lost: in whom the god of this world hath blinded the minds of them which believe not, lest the light of the glorious gospel of Christ, *who is the image of God,* should shine unto them. For we preach not ourselves, but Christ Jesus the Lord; and ourselves your servants for Jesus' sake. For God, who commanded the light to shine out of darkness, hath shined in our hearts, *to give the light of the knowledge of the glory of God in the face of Jesus Christ* (II Corinthians 4:3-6).

> [Jesus Christ] is *the image of the invisible God,* the firstborn of every creature[41] (Colossians 1:15).

> And the Word was made flesh, and dwelt among us, *(and we beheld his glory, the glory as of the only begotten of the Father,)* full of grace and truth (John 1:14).

> Jesus saith unto him, Have I been so long time with you, and yet hast thou not known me, Philip? *he that hath seen me hath seen the Father* (John 14:9).

---

[41]"Firstborn" here does not mean that Jesus Christ is the ranking "creature." He is not created. The use of "firstborn" calls attention to the fact that He is the one who has the right of inheritance over all the creation. It is all His by right and will all be returned to Him at the restoration of all things (Psalm 89:27; Hebrews 2:6-8).

Many people today have distorted views of God. The most vivid picture of who God is and what He is like is revealed in "the face of Jesus Christ," particularly in His death, burial, and resurrection. All of the attributes of God that can be comprehended by finite man are revealed in their most brilliant splendor at Calvary. Here in one event is the most complete revelation of the wrath of God, the righteousness of God, the holiness of God, the love of God, the mercy of God, the grace of God, the power of God, the wisdom of God, the faithfulness of God—and everything else there is to be known about God! And it is precisely because most believers spend so little time contemplating the work of Jesus Christ at Calvary that they know so little about God Himself.

No one who has seen the cross with illuminated eyes would ever say that God is not loving or that God does not care for him. Nor would he ever doubt God's power or His wisdom. He would instinctively cry out to God in times of need, for he would know that "he that spared not his own Son, but delivered him up for us all, how shall he not with him also freely give us all things?"[42] His heart would be full of praise for His faithfulness, His mercy, and His grace. He would never tire of telling the "old, old story of Jesus and His love." His lips would be ready to give the gospel to any who would listen. His heart would be ready to hear more of this wonderful Savior, "who his own self bare our sins in his own body on the tree, that we, being dead to sins, should live unto righteousness."[43] His life would know a power for overcoming sin that would free him from the bondage of his lusts, and he would yearn for the day when He could look on his Beloved One face to face "lost in wonder, love, and grace." These are the effects on the life of one who has been beholding the cross.

This is why Paul never got tired of speaking of Jesus Christ. The apostle can hardly pen a phrase without mentioning how some blessing or benefit was because we are "in Christ Jesus" or "in Him" or "in the Beloved." *Paul loved Jesus Christ!*

That fact alone is the difference between Paul's Christianity and ours. Most believers today do not have a deep sense of devotion to and ad-

---

[42]Romans 8:32.
[43]I Peter 2:24.

miration of the person of Jesus Christ. They may be straight in their theology. They may be careful in their Christian standards, but all of that can be done out of love for a certain theological position or love for a certain image they want to have before others. The message that rang loud and clear from Paul's heart was that nothing thrilled his heart more than to think of His beloved Lord. Listen to his testimony.

> For I determined not to know any thing among you, save Jesus Christ, and him crucified (I Corinthians 2:2).

> For to me to live is Christ, and to die is gain. . . . I am [hardpressed from both directions], having a desire to depart, and to be with Christ (Philippians 1:21-23).

> I count all things but loss for the excellency of the knowledge of Christ Jesus my Lord: for whom I have suffered the loss of all things, and do count them but dung, that I may win Christ (Philippians 3:8).

We must ask ourselves, "Is this our heartbeat today? Do we speak of Jesus Christ in these exalted terms? Is He truly lovely to us? Do we desire above all things to sacrifice whatever is necessary to learn more of the excellency of Jesus Christ? These aren't merely poetic phrases from some silver-tongued orator. They are the heartthrobs of a man who adored Jesus Christ. It is that devotion that drove and rejoiced the first-century church. It motivated this Ephesian church through its infancy.

Tragically, however, Jesus Christ Himself had to tell this assembly less than fifty years later that they had "left [their] first love" for Him and that they must repent of their fallen condition or He would remove the impact of their testimony.[44] *Indeed, there is no power in a testimony that is not passionate about Jesus Christ.* That kind of devotion and admiration, however, does not come by sitting around thinking dreamy thoughts of a compassionate Teacher who walked in Galilee two thousand years ago healing the sick and confronting religious hypocrisy.

It is built only by an increased, illuminated understanding of what is revealed about Jesus Christ in His work at Calvary. The death, burial,

---

[44]Revelation 2:1-7.

and resurrection of Jesus Christ was Paul's focal point. Notice his words.

> But God forbid that I should glory, save in the cross of our Lord Jesus Christ, by whom the world is crucified unto me, and I unto the world (Galatians 6:14).

This same emphasis upon the person and the work of our Lord Jesus Christ must dominate our ministry to others as well. Be very cautious about movements and ministries that primarily emphasize another member of the Trinity.

For example, some movements highlight the ministry of the Holy Spirit through His gifts and supposed modern-day "signs and wonders." This is a misplaced emphasis.

In addition, much music and many books today focus on the greatness and the power of God as the Creator. Though the creation displays God's existence and His power, Ephesians 1:19-21 tells us that the greatest manifestation of God's power was His raising Jesus Christ from the dead and exalting Him to His position of honor in the heavenlies. The apostles taught that the touchstone of true belief was a person's view of Jesus Christ.[45]

Whole genres of contemporary music seldom place Jesus Christ in the spotlight. In fact, a Unitarian or a Mormon could subscribe to many of the currently produced songs since both of these false religions respect God as the majestic Creator over all. Truly, songs that exalt the majesty of God should bring a great sense of awe to the believer and compel him to bow in worship, but the true test of the believer's understanding of the works of God is whether He possesses an even greater sense of awe and compulsion to worship when he contemplates the *redemptive* themes of Scripture.

The work of Jesus Christ as the Redeemer was the most common theme of the hymnody of the past two centuries. A movement away from that emphasis tells us much about the lack of Bible understanding of today's lyricists. The use of the rock idiom to communicate the

---

[45]II John 9-11.

lyrics is also a telling sign of the low level of spiritual understanding in today's church.

It is the *Lamb's* redemptive work that evokes the "new song" of praise in the heavenlies because He has "redeemed us to God by [His] blood!"[46] The redeeming work of Jesus Christ should be the center of our thoughts and praises now as well.

---

[46]Revelation 5:9.

CHAPTER FIVE

THE REALITY OF THE SPIRIT'S SECURITY

We have one more painting to consider before we move out of the "Gallery of the Heavenlies." I hope you have spent considerable time meditating before each one we have studied so far. If so, you should have a new sense of their beauty and a new admiration for the Artist behind them. We will start our study of this fourth portrait by reading the brief description of it found in the tour brochure.

> Item 4: "The Securing One"
> Here is portrayed the work of the Holy Spirit, who **seals** us, certifying that everything God has promised will indeed come to pass for us. The **presence** of the Holy Spirit Himself within believers is the down payment guaranteeing the full redemption of our body and soul. He alone can **illuminate** our hearts, showing us the certainty of these things.

NO FEARS OR ANXIETIES HERE

We have learned in the previous portraits that God is the Supreme One above us, that the Father chose us, and that the Son redeemed us. Now the subject changes to the work of the Spirit of God. In fact, the greater portion of Ephesians 1 (verses 13-23) is taken up with the wonderful work of the Holy Spirit on our behalf.

We learn in this passage that it is the work of the Spirit to assure us—to teach us the security we have both eternally and temporally since we are in Christ. One of the most precious names given to the Holy Spirit by Christ Himself is that of the "Comforter," whom Jesus said He would send after His own departure.[1] He certainly knew how much we would need a Comforter while we live on this fallen planet!

It is this lack of comfort, security, and assurance that characterizes modern civilization. People today are filled with anxiety and fear. Even among Christians, worry seems to be an acceptable pastime. People have turned to drugs and therapies in unprecedented ways to deal with the mounting "disorders" of this fearful, anxious, and discouraged generation. Yoga is enjoying a resurgence of interest in the name of stress reduction, and people flock to any seminar or workshop that promises to bring a measure of peace and fulfillment to their harried lives. In general, our civilization is filled with anxious, fretful, unsettled, restless, and agitated people. Even many believers experience very little comfort directly from the Spirit of God.

STANZA THREE—THE SPIRIT THAT SECURES US

Paul completes his three-stanza hymn of praise in verses 13-14 of Ephesians 1. He says,

> In whom [speaking of Christ] also after that ye believed, ye were sealed with that holy Spirit of promise, which is the earnest of our inheritance until the redemption of the purchased possession, [and then Paul closes the stanza with the familiar chorus] unto the praise of his glory.

The Holy Spirit takes up residence in us immediately upon our salvation.[2] So clearly did the apostle Paul want us to know this that he dogmatically stated in Romans 8:9, "Now if any man have not the Spirit of Christ, he is none of [Christ's]." These two verses in Ephesians show us further that the Holy Spirit's presence in us provides two wonderful blessings for us. His presence is our "seal" and our "earnest." I want to take some time to discuss these two powerful truths that guarantee our security. I will do that, however, as a part of the discussion of the verses that follow in this passage—verses 15-23. Read them thoughtfully since they provide the foundation for the rest of this chapter's discussion.

---

[1] John 16:7.
[2] This fact is often called the "indwelling of the Spirit."

Wherefore I also, after I heard of your faith in the Lord Jesus, and love unto all the saints,

Cease not to give thanks for you, making mention of you in my prayers,

That the God of our Lord Jesus Christ, the Father of glory, may give unto you the spirit of wisdom and revelation in the knowledge of him:

The eyes of your understanding being enlightened; that ye may know what is the hope of his calling, and what [are] the riches of the glory of his inheritance in the saints,

And what is the exceeding greatness of his power to us-ward who believe, [these are] according to the working of his mighty power,

Which he wrought in Christ, when he raised him from the dead, and set him at his own right hand in the heavenly places,

Far above all principality, and power, and might, and dominion, and every name that is named, not only in this world, but also in that which is to come:

And hath put all things under his feet, and gave him to be the head over all things to the church,

Which is his body, the fulness of him that filleth all in all.

Paul begins this prayer after he has just presented, in the form of this three-stanza hymn, the most foundational and heart-stirring truths of the Christian faith. But he was afraid that many believers would not understand the significance of them to their Christian lives. Because these are spiritual truths, they could be understood only with eyes that were opened to see spiritual things. So now he prays for them. The content of his prayer is

That the God of our Lord Jesus Christ, the Father of glory, may give unto you the Spirit of wisdom [i.e., insight] and revelation [i.e., unveiling] in the knowledge of [God]: the eyes of your [heart] being enlightened; that ye may know . . . [certain things].[3]

---

[3]By the way, it is this specific kind of knowledge of God Himself through the Word that differentiates illumination from mysticism. Mysticism is the belief that

It is the particular function of the Holy Spirit to teach the believer the truths that will help him see Jesus Christ more clearly. Paul discusses this in I Corinthians 2:9-10.

> But as it is written, Eye hath not seen, nor ear heard, neither have entered into the heart of man, the things which God hath prepared for them that love him. But God hath revealed them unto us *by his Spirit*.

Jesus Himself spoke of this particular responsibility of the Holy Spirit in John 16:13-14.

> Howbeit when he, the Spirit of truth, is come, he will guide you into all truth: for *he shall not speak of himself*; but whatsoever he shall hear, that shall he speak: and he will shew you things to come. *He shall glorify me:* for he shall receive of mine, and shall shew it unto you.

Paul is praying that this special work of the Holy Spirit would be experienced by these believers. Our Bible text calls it "being enlightened." The word we would use today is "illumination." It is important to understand why Paul had to pray for the illumination of his fellow believers. He did so because illumination is not automatic. Unfortunately, neither is it common. Listen to how Lewis Sperry Chafer describes this work of the Spirit in the heart of a believer. Note the italicized phrases he uses to show the effects of illumination upon the heart.

> By this particular manifestation of the Spirit, unseen things become *blessedly real*. There is such a thing as "ever learning and never coming to the knowledge of the truth." Truth must become real to us. We may know by faith that we are forgiven and justified forever: it is quite another thing to have *a heart experience wherein all is as real*

---

spiritual knowledge is gained from some "inner light" or religious experience either apart from or at least superior to what is revealed in the Scriptures. It is an appeal to personal, intuitive experience for knowledge of spiritual things.

Paul warns of false teachers—and they are still prevalent today—who pride themselves in their visions and statements about their "word from the Lord." The apostle says in Colossians 2:18, "Let no man beguile [i.e., defraud] you of your reward in a voluntary [i.e., false] humility and worshipping of angels, intruding into those things which he hath not seen [i.e., investigating his visions], vainly puffed up [i.e., inflated] by his fleshly mind."

as it is true. We may believe in our security and coming glory: it is different to *feel its power in the heart.* We may believe in "things to come" through the exact teaching of the Word: it is a precious experience to have it *made actual to us by the Spirit* that "the Lord is at hand," and that our eternal glory with Him may be but a moment removed. Such *heart experience* is provided in the boundless grace of God for each of His children: but only those who abide in Him can know the *ecstasy of life.*[4]

The necessity of illumination is such a neglected teaching in Bible-believing circles today! There was a time when this truth was known by most evangelical believers, though even then only a minority ever sought the Lord seriously enough to experience much illumination of the Word by the Spirit. Perhaps its effect can be better understood by an illustration.

ILLUMINATION: THE DIFFERENCE BETWEEN KNOWING AND SEEING

Recently my wife and I were speaking at a convention in another state and were staying in a hotel. While we were relaxing in the room after a morning of speaking, we turned on the television to catch the latest news. One channel featured a news documentary about a blind man whose sight in one eye was restored surgically. He was married and had two children. Of course, he had never seen any of them before the operation.

One of his eyes was totally blind from birth, and there was no hope for sight to be restored in that eye. The other eye, however, could discern the contrast between very bright lights and darkness. New surgical techniques had been developed to counteract the particular condition of that eye. The surgery promised a 50/50 chance of success in restoring sight to that eye. If the operation failed, however, he would lose even the ability to see the contrast of light and darkness and be plunged into even greater darkness. Of course, he had some misgivings about the risks, but he was nonetheless optimistic that the surgeon who recommended the procedure knew what he was doing.

---

[4]Lewis Sperry Chafer, *He That Is Spiritual* (Grand Rapids: Zondervan, 1967), 59.

The operation was a success, and the television cameras captured his first moments of sight several weeks later when the surgeon removed his bandages. The first person he saw was his wife. She had been apprehensive that he might not like what he saw. He, of course, was delighted with the sight of her! He quickly and lovingly put his hands on the sides of her face and kissed the woman he loved—and now could see.

The doctor next asked him to walk over to the mirror to look at his own face. Though he was quite handsome, he modestly replied, "What an ugly mug!" Next came the ride home from the doctor's office. He marveled at the buildings, the sky, and the green grass and was duly frightened by the number of cars that passed so quickly and so closely to their automobile.

When he reached home, he saw his children for the first time. It took them only a few minutes to realize that their dad did not recognize by sight anything he saw. They quickly went to work teaching him his colors, helping him recognize the letters of the alphabet, and showing him pictures of animals in their picture books—he was quite surprised when he learned what a giraffe "looked" like. He walked everywhere with his family—to the beach, to the outdoor vegetable market, to the park—*"seeing" for the first time all the things he "knew" existed but had never fully comprehended.*

This documentary illustrates very powerfully the effects of illumination. Many believers "know" that God has chosen them. They "know" that Christ has redeemed them, and they "know" that the Spirit of God dwells in them, but they have never "seen" these things with illuminated eyes.

Let me say again, *Paul prayed for this illumination to take place because it is not automatic for the believer; neither is it common.* This lack of Spirit-taught assurance of spiritual things is the main culprit whenever there is little joy, little wonder, little humility, and little certainty in the lives of God's people. Without it, they are filled with the same anxieties about daily life and about the future as the unbelieving world.

Boredom: The Sign of Darkness in the Soul

The greatest sign that believers are not illuminated is that there is no delight and savor of spiritual things. They can logically defend their salvation—just like the blind man in the documentary could defend the existence of his wife and children—but they have never seen the beauty and the glory of their salvation. Jonathan Edwards called the effect of this Spirit-taught revelation a "relish" of spiritual things.[5] By contrast, most believers are easily bored with spiritual things. That is never the condition of a believer who has seen a particular truth with illuminated eyes.

An unilluminated believer cannot understand why other believers seem to delight in the preaching and teaching of God's Word. His own Bible reading—when he even attempts it—is dry and unappealing. *Boredom is the result of hearing the Word of God without "seeing" it.* The result is that the truth has no relish to him because only the Spirit of God can open his eyes.

No man can understand the things of God's own heart until God places His own Spirit within the man. Even then, unless the Spirit of God within him chooses to show the man the meaning and the importance of the words of God, the man still will not understand though he hears the words themselves. He will be consequently bored with the truth. He may sit in church pretending to show interest, but he is truly bored.

A DOG'S LIFE

Think with me about the similarity between this unilluminated man in a church service and a dog lying peacefully at his master's feet while the master carries on a conversation with another human. The dog rests his head on his paws in front of him and appears "bored" with the whole ordeal. He has no interest in the conversation because he has no "understanding" of it. Since he is a dog, he cannot understand the conversation of his master and his friend.

Like the dog on the floor, the unilluminated believer may hear spiritual conversations and preaching going on around him, but they have no appeal—no "relish"—to him. It is extremely difficult for him to show an interest in these discussions because he has no understanding.

---

[5]Jonathan Edwards. *Religious Affections*, ed. James M. Houston (Minneapolis: Bethany House Publishers, 1984), 84.

The bored believer will dismiss the regular church attendance and regular devotional life of others as legalism or religious tradition and ceremony. He will assume they are doing these things to win some kind of favor with God or others. He cannot perceive any other motive and cannot understand their regularity or attentiveness. He is spiritually blind! He needs to pray for his eyes to be opened.[6]

Fascination ≠ Illumination

I would add one more thought before leaving this discussion. Spiritual illumination with its resulting sense of wonder and delight is not the same as intellectual fascination with a truth. There are some whose temperaments are quite stirred with the discovery of some new idea—whether it be theological, mechanical, philosophical, or scientific. When the pieces to a puzzle they have been trying to solve finally fit together, they are filled with a great sense of accomplishment and delight that the whole matter is now resolved in their thinking.

I would not for a moment minimize the triumphant feeling of this kind of discovery. It is one of the blessings of the common grace of God to all men—saved and unsaved. It oils the machinery of the research world, whether theological research or otherwise. It spurs men on to further experimentation and discovery. But it is not to be confused with illumination.

Illumination certainly contains a strong element of fascination, but fascination itself is not to be taken for illumination. An unbeliever can be fascinated with something—even theology—but he cannot experi-

---

[6]A word of admonition is in order here. If you are sitting under the sound preaching and teaching of the Word of God and find yourself bored, that is the time to recognize that the speaker is dealing with a truth for which you have never received any illumination. Rather than dismiss the whole presentation as boring, you should be praying, "God, here is a truth for which I have not had illumination. 'Open thou mine eyes, that I may behold wondrous things out of thy law' " (Psalm 119:18). Your boredom is the sign of your spiritual blindness to that truth.

Those in the audience who have experienced God's enlightening work about that truth will find great delight to hear it again—even if the speaker is dreadfully uninteresting in his delivery and perhaps has never been illuminated about that truth himself. Enlightened truth retains its relish and delight. It is never boring no matter how many times a believer hears it. This is what caused the hymn writer to say, "I love to tell the story, for those who know it best seem hungering and thirsting to hear it like the rest." When God opens your eyes to a passage, the truth never loses its luster and brilliance to you. It is always a delightful experience.

ence the illumination of that truth until the Spirit of God dwells within him. This is why the "discovery" of some theological issues send some believers—most notably young theologs—into such a fanatical tailspin. They may mistake for illumination the joy of discovery and the fascination of seeing intricate puzzle parts beginning to fall into place.

The telltale sign that they have *not* experienced Spirit-taught illumination is the lack of humility they demonstrate in the aftermath. If they have indeed seen something from God, it will have a serious humbling effect upon them. They will know that the truth did not come to them through their own devices. They will know that it is also quite possible that they have not seen the whole picture even yet.

An illuminated, and therefore humbled, believer will not argue truth with others with red-faced irritation or with know-it-all arrogance. He knows *he* did not come to understand the truth through the airtight argumentation of men pressing him to come to their side but by the gentle but unmistakable persuasion of God's Spirit through the Word. Therefore, he will not resort to fleshly methods to force others to come to his position.

Pile on the Firewood and Pray for the Fire!

So how is it then that we come to have this Spirit-taught assurance of spiritual things? As I wrote earlier in *Changed into His Image,*

> Believers must take the time and effort to hike into the forest of God's Word and harvest the logs of truth from that massive timberland. They must by reflection split the logs and stack them in the fireplace of their own heart while they pray for the illumination from God to set the logs ablaze. The resulting fire will provide the light that directs their paths and the heat that fuels their passion for God.
>
> Unfortunately, most people accumulate only a few sticks of kindling from their pastor's Sunday sermons—not because he doesn't present great truths from God's Word but because they think little upon those truths, even during the message. Even when God *does* ignite those splinters of truth, their fire blazes only momentarily because there is so little truth for the Holy Spirit to burn.
>
> Solomon's burden in Proverbs 2 is that men would embark on this earnest and diligent search for truth. He says that the man who will

do so will "find the knowledge of God" (2:5). He is the one who God says will "*receive* my words, and *hide* my commandments" (2:1). He will "*incline* [his] ear" and "*apply* [his] heart" (2:2). He is the one who "*criest* after knowledge" and "*liftest* up [his] voice for understanding" (2:3). He "*seekest* [wisdom] as silver" and "*searchest* for her as for hid treasures" (2:4). This is no casual "I'll-pursue-God-if-I-have-the-time-and-if-I-remember-to-do-it" attitude. It is the wholehearted pursuit of God within His revelation that is rewarded with a view of God Himself![7]

This is exactly what Paul is doing in chapter one of Ephesians. He is stacking logs of truth before these believers in verses 1-14 and then is praying in verses 17-18 for God to ignite them with the "Spirit of wisdom and revelation in the knowledge of Him." This is why I say "pile on the firewood and pray for the fire!" Many believers are doing neither. Admittedly, this takes much time. We must set aside enough unhurried time that we do not have to think about time. It is just not possible to "meditate upon these things" and to "give yourself wholly to them" on five to ten minutes per day.[8]

With these cautions and instructions about illumination in mind, let us probe further into Paul's prayers and notice what truths he wants these first-century believers—and us—to see.

PAUL WANTS THEM TO KNOW THE CERTAINTY OF THEIR OUTCOME

The apostle prays that "the eyes of your understanding being enlightened; that ye may know what is *the hope of his calling . . .* " (1:18).

The word "hope" in the Bible is never used in the way it is generally used today. Hundreds of high school graduates matriculate each fall to the university where I minister *hoping* to graduate from college in four years. In God's good providence most of them do. When a freshman says, "I hope to finish four years from now," he is expressing a strong desire to attain a certain goal. He does not know with absolute certainty

---

[7]*Changed*, 153. Note that chapter seven of *Changed into His Image* provides an extended look at this matter of illumination.

[8]I Timothy 4:15-16. See "Spending a Day with God" in *Changed into His Image* (pp. 156-59) for ideas about how to set aside and utilize extended periods of time for meditation and prayer.

that he will do so, however. He may be forced to sit out a semester because of financial needs or family setbacks. He may be delayed in his plans because of an illness or an accident that lays him up for several weeks or months. In a very few cases, the obstacles are so great that he never returns to finish at all. Most of the students who experience these reversals, however, at one time *hoped* to finish college within a certain time frame. Certainly there is nothing wrong with their use of the word "hope" in this way. We all know they are expressing a strong desire that seems to have a likelihood of being fulfilled. This, however, is not the way the word "hope" is used in the Bible.

Hope in the Bible is a "confident expectation." It is an "assured outcome." When Paul speaks of "looking for that blessed hope, and glorious appearing of the great God and our Saviour Jesus Christ,"[9] he is speaking about an event that is *definitely* going to take place. Nothing can stop it since God has promised it. Our hope in it is not a strong desire with a measure of uncertainty mixed with it. Our hope is a confident expectation that this event *will* indeed take place.

So Paul is saying here, "I am praying that God will open your eyes so that you will see the absolute certainty of the outcome of the salvation that originated with His call to you. It was a call that drew *you* to Himself because He wanted *you* to be a part of the Bride for His Son. Until that great day of the Wedding Supper of the Lamb, the Son is at work perfecting and purifying His Bride—*you!*" He does that by sanctifying and cleansing His Bride "with the washing of water by the word, that he might present [His Bride] to himself a glorious church, not having spot, or wrinkle, or any such thing; but that it should be holy and without blemish."[10]

There is no doubt about the certainty of this outcome. All of the trials of life are part of that purifying process getting us ready to step into the splendors of life with our heavenly Bridegroom. Certainly, it is painful letting Him get us ready for that day, but as the songwriter said, "It will be worth it all when we see Jesus." And the hope we have is that we *will* see Jesus. This assurance of the outcome is so important that I am going to spend the next entire chapter discussing it further. For now,

---

[9]Titus 2:13.
[10]Ephesians 5:26-27.

understand that an illuminated view of this wonderful hope provides the endurance necessary for the trials of the present life. Illuminated "seeing" is the basis for the endurance of the faithful witnesses of Hebrews 11. For example, it speaks of Moses, who "endured, as seeing him who is invisible."[11]

When a believer, discouraged by the setbacks of life, says, "I don't know if it is worth it to go on," or "Will I ever get through this problem?" he is demonstrating that his eyes have not been opened to the certainty of what God has begun in him. The believer who is illuminated about the "hope of his calling" is "confident of this very thing, that he which hath begun a good work in [him] will perform it until the day of Jesus Christ."[12] He knows with assurance that "it is God which worketh in [him] both to will and to do of his good pleasure."[13] His soul immediately comes to rest again when he recalls that "whom He called, them He also justified: and whom he justified, them he also glorified." His heart cries out in response, "If God be for [me], who can be against [me]? He that spared not his own Son, but delivered him up for [me], how shall he not with him also freely give [me] all things?"[14]

These statements of truth are not merely logical building blocks in his reasoning that he must put in place to shore up his sagging confidence—although he may have to start with just that sort of argumentation with himself. His hope—his confidence—is revived when his mind is again reminded of truths like these that at one time have been taught to him personally by the Spirit of God. He has "seen" them before, and the sight of them again fills his heart with an assurance that indeed all is well. His God is for him. He knows the "blessed assurance"—the hope, the absolute certainty that God's calling will have its intended end. He is certain of it!

The Seal of the Spirit

One truth that shores up this hope is the "sealing of the Spirit." Notice Paul's teaching about the Holy Spirit back in verses 13 and 14 just before he begins his prayer for illumination.

---

[11]Hebrews 11:27.
[12]Philippians 1:6.
[13]Philippians 2:13.
[14]Romans 8:30-32.

. . . after that ye believed, ye were sealed with that holy Spirit of promise, [who] is the earnest of our inheritance until the redemption of the purchased possession, unto the praise of his glory.

This statement, the last stanza of Paul's three-stanza hymn of praise, announces that the Holy Spirit seals the believer. A seal in New Testament times had many of the same functions as it has today. Important documents back then were "sealed" with the imprint of the dignitary's ring upon hot sealing wax. Today the important paper might be embossed with the seal of a notary public. The stamp indicated the certainty that the signatures of those on the document were indeed their own. The phrase "signed, sealed, and delivered" meant that a transaction was fully carried out.

The seal of the Spirit is His presence within the believer. His presence is the authorized signature of God that He will complete all that He has promised. His presence is evident to us as He convicts us of sin,[15] produces His fruit of Christlikeness in us when we yield to Him,[16] and teaches us the Word of God.[17] Any believer can and should put great confidence in the fact of God's calling on his life to salvation when this evidence is seen in his daily experience.

He will have an even more unshakeable hope when the Holy Spirit has opened His eyes regarding the beauty and the wonder that Jesus Christ Himself should take up residence in such a sinful dwelling as his heart. Every believer should be praying, "God, show me the certainty of these things. Show me the hope of Your calling!"

PAUL WANTS THEM TO KNOW THE SPLENDOR OF THEIR OUTCOME

The apostle goes on to pray that "the eyes of your understanding being enlightened; that ye may know . . . what [are] the riches of the glory of his inheritance in the saints."[18] Here he prays that they might catch a

---

[15]Romans 8:14. The "leading of the Spirit" spoken of here in this verse is His leading us away from sin. It is a synonym for sanctification.

[16]Galatians 5:22-23.

[17]I Corinthians 2:9-14.

[18]Ephesians 1:18.

glimpse of the glorious fullness that is ours when God brings His salvation to completion.

This is not a prayer that the believer might understand the dimensions of his "mansion" or be awed by the fact that he will walk on streets made of crystal-clear gold. The believer's inheritance is Christ Himself, and Christ's inheritance is His Bride, the Church. In that day of completion, we will see our Bridegroom and be entirely perfected before Him when we see Him as He is.[19] A believer who has seen these things is overwhelmed with the splendor of what awaits him in the new heaven and the new earth. His heart yearns to see every kindred, tongue, and nation bow before his Beloved and give Him the glory that is due to Him. His heart aches when he grieves his beloved Bridegroom, and he longs to stand complete in His presence, possessing a heart totally free to worship Him unhindered from the taint of sin and the limitations of finite understanding. His heart confesses, "now I know in part; but then shall I know even as also I am known."[20] His soul longs to see Christ and to possess Christ for his own just as a bride longs to see her husband on her wedding day and possess him for herself.

The effect upon one who has begun to see the glorious riches of this inheritance—the full possession of Christ—is that he is not easily tempted with temporal and material matters. If you said to him, "I can't wait to see _____ (the season's latest television mini-series)! How about you?" he would answer in his heart—if not to you—"I can't wait to see Jesus Christ face to face. I wish it were today! There isn't any adventure, any romance, or any feature that can compare with the thrill of seeing my Beloved!"

If you pointed to the latest and trendiest car as it drove by and asked him, "Don't you wish you had that car?" the answer in his heart would be "I guess it is all right for now, but I really wish I had a glorified body and a new heart! I'm far more tired of my sin-cursed body and mind than I am of my ten-year-old car."

If you asked him, "Don't you wish you could go touring in Europe?" he would reply, "I would rather be in heaven. If I got an opportunity to go

---

[19] I John 3:2.
[20] I Corinthians 13:12.

to Europe, I'd be grateful, but I want to see the 'new Jerusalem, coming down out from God out of heaven, prepared as a bride adorned for her husband.' "

An unilluminated believer might read these statements and reply, "Get real! No one thinks like that!" But he is wrong. The illuminated believer knows what it is like when "heaven came down and glory filled [his] soul." He has tasted something of heaven via the Spirit of God, and he wants more! He knows "this world is not [his] home, [he is] just a-passing through." These thoughts aren't the wide-eyed imagination of someone who is "so heavenly minded, he is no earthly good." They are the deep longings of a soul who has experienced the "riches of the glory of his inheritance in the saints." He is seeking "those things which are above, where Christ [his beloved Bridegroom] sitteth on the right hand of God." He is setting his "affection on things above, not on things on the earth."[21] There is a definite "otherworldliness" about him that counters the magnetic pull of this world upon his soul and draws him to another pole.

The Earnest of the Spirit

Paul stated in Ephesians 1:14 that the Holy Spirit was also the "*earnest of our inheritance.*" His presence within the believer is not only the *seal* that assures the validity and the certainty of the transaction. His presence within us is also the *down payment*—the earnest—that guarantees that the rest will be redeemed at the proper time. He is not merely collateral in the sense of a pawn shop that accepts your deposit of a gold high school ring, which becomes the property of the pawn shop if you do not repay the loan you took out against the ring's value. In this case the "deposit," the Holy Spirit, is the same kind of "currency" as the final payment. He is the promise of more holiness and more fullness to come. He is the "earnest" guaranteeing that the full inheritance of Christlikeness will definitely come for us. By Spirit-taught illumination we can know *now* something of the splendor of the outcome of our salvation. The joy and peace we can experience now as He reveals Jesus Christ to us is just a small taste—the down payment—of what is to come. Every believer should be praying, "God, show me the splendor of these things. Show me the glorious riches of

---

[21]Colossians 3:1-2.

Your inheritance in the saints! Show me more of what it is to be like Christ and to be possessed entirely by Christ."

PAUL WANTS THEM TO KNOW THE
POWER THAT GUARANTEES THEIR OUTCOME

Paul prayed that "the eyes of your understanding being enlightened; that ye may know . . . what is the exceeding greatness of his power to us-ward who believe."[22]

His third petition for them is not that they would experience some *new* manifestation of God's power. He wanted them to begin to understand the kind of power that had *already* been at work on their behalf and that would continue to be at work until the job was done. To give them some idea of that power, he said that it is

> according to the working of his mighty power, which He wrought in Christ, when he raised him from the dead, and set him at his own right hand in the heavenly places, far above all principality, and power, and might, and dominion, and every name that is named, not only in this world, but also in that which is to come.[23]

He wanted believers to have a Spirit-taught glimpse of the magnitude of the power at work for them. It was the same power that actually raised Christ from the tomb after He had suffered eternal death for all men. It not only raised Him from the dead but it also elevated Him to a position of glory above every part of the physical and spiritual creation. Every believer should be praying, "God, show me the provision for these things. Help me to see in the resurrection of Christ the nature and the extent of the power that You are even now deploying on my behalf to bring these things to completion. Show me the exceeding greatness of Your power to us who have believed!"

MORE TO COME

I hope you see how the kind of illuminated assurance I have been talking about is the basis for an anxiety-free existence on this earth. When you have seen God at work, choosing you because He loves you, redeeming you by the blood of His Son, and securing your final outcome

---

[22]Ephesians 1:18-19.
[23]Ephesians 1:19-21.

with the presence of His Spirit in you, your heart can rest that all the details of getting you from here to heaven will be taken care of. *Believers lacking a Spirit-taught eternal security will have the most difficulty with their temporal security.* If that thought is foggy to you, I pray that it will become crystal clear as we finish this discussion in the next chapter.

Other than the illustration of "piling on the firewood and praying for the fire," I have not given you any instruction about how to seek Spirit-taught illumination. I shall cover that in the next chapter when we look in detail at the second of Paul's prayers in Ephesians. For now, think on the questions in the "Take Time to Reflect" section that follows.

TAKE TIME TO REFLECT

1. Rate the "boredom factor" of your Christian life. On a scale of 1 to 5 (1 being "bored out of your mind" and 5 being "thrilled with the truth"), what is your "boredom factor" when you read the Word or hear it preached?

2. Do you have this Spirit-taught understanding of the things Paul was praying for? If so, answer the following:

   a. What passage of Scripture did the Holy Spirit illuminate to show you the certainty of the outcome of your salvation—the hope of His calling?

   b. What passage of Scripture did the Holy Spirit illuminate to show you the splendor of what awaits you in heaven—the riches of the glory of His inheritance?

   c. What passage of Scripture did the Holy Spirit illuminate to show you the magnitude of the power that makes all of this happen—the exceeding greatness of His power to usward who believe?

3. What kind of time are you spending throughout a normal week piling firewood—logs of truth—into the fireplace of your heart so that the Holy Spirit has something to set ablaze?

4. How consistently do you actually pray that God will illumine your heart when you read for yourself or hear the Scriptures preached at your local church?

5. Is there any evidence of the Spirit's actual presence in your heart (i.e., do you experience His "leading" away from sin; do you see His fruit in your life; does He personally teach you the Word as you study it)? If so, explain.

A WORD TO DISCIPLE-MAKERS

I want to take one more opportunity to impress upon your mind the necessity for illumination and meditation in your Christian walk. Without it, there is no clear view of Christ and consequently, no consistent joy, peace, and power in the Christian life.

A. W. Tozer on the Need for Illumination

Spiritual truths differ from natural truths both in their constitution and *in the manner of their apprehension by us*.

Natural truths can be learned by us regardless of our moral or spiritual condition. The truths of the natural sciences, for instance, can be grasped by anyone of normal intelligence, regardless of whether he is a good man or a scoundrel. There is no relation between say, chastity and logic, or between kindness and oceanography. In like manner a sufficient degree of mental vigor is all that is required to grasp philosophical propositions. A man may study philosophy for a lifetime, teach it, write books about it, and be all the while proud, covetous and thoroughly dishonest in his private dealings.

The same may be said of theology. *A man need not be godly to learn theology*. . . . Surely God has that to say to the pure in heart which He cannot say to the man of sinful life. But what He has to say is not theological, it is spiritual; and right there lies the weight of my argument. Spiritual truths cannot be received in the ordinary way of nature. "The natural man receiveth not the things of the Spirit of God: for they are foolishness unto him: neither can he know them, because they are spiritually discerned" (1 Corinthians 2:14). So wrote the apostle Paul to the believers at Corinth.

Our Lord referred to this kind of Spirit-enlightened knowledge many times. To Him it was the fruit of divine illumination, not contrary to but altogether *beyond* mere intellectual light. The fourth Gospel is full of this idea; indeed the idea is so important to the understanding of John's Gospel that anyone who denies it might as well give up trying to grasp our Lord's teachings as given by the apostle John. And the same idea is found in John's first epistle, making that epistle extremely difficult to understand but also making it one of the most beautiful and rewarding of all the epistles of the New Testament when its teachings are spiritually discerned.

The necessity for spiritual illumination before we can grasp spiritual truths is taught throughout the entire New Testament and is altogether in accord with the teachings of the Psalms, the Proverbs and the Prophets. . . .

The sum of what I am saying is that *there is an illumination, divinely bestowed, without which theological truth is information and nothing more.* While this illumination is never given apart from theology, it is entirely possible to have theology without the illumination.[24]

John Owen on the Need for Meditation

Let us regard it as our duty to meditate frequently on [Christ's] glory. It is the neglect of meditation that keeps so many Christians in a feeble state, regardless of their [divine] privileges. They hear of these things and assent to the truth of them or at least they do not question them. But they never solemnly meditate on them. They think that meditation is above their capabilities, or they are totally ignorant of how to go about it, or they are not too concerned about it, or they treat it as fanaticism. Many cannot meditate because their minds are so cluttered up with earthly things. The mind must be spiritual and holy, freed from all earthly clutter. It must be raised above things here below if we wish to meditate on the glory of Christ. So many are strangers to this duty because they do not mortify their earthly desires and concerns.

There are some who profess to be strict, disciplined Christians, but who never put aside time to meditate on the glory of Christ. Yet they tell us that they desire nothing more than to behold his glory in heaven for ever. They are wholly inconsistent. It is impossible that someone who never meditates with delight on the glory of Christ here in this world, who does not make every effort to behold it by faith as it is revealed in the Scripture, should ever have any real gracious desire to behold it in heaven. It is sad, therefore, that many can find time to think much about earthly, foolish things, but have no heart, no desire to meditate on this object. What is this faith and love they claim to have?[25]

---

[24]A. W. Tozer, *That Incredible Christian* (Camp Hill, Pa.: Christian Publications, 1964), 61-64.

[25]Owen, 34.

Please do not dismiss these admonitions of Tozer and Owen as unattainable for the common man. Both of these men preached and wrote for the common man of their day and to great profit to those who heard and heeded their words. The world knew its spiritual giants in the generations past, and in every case, they were men and women who took God seriously, spent much time in His Word, and spoke often with their Lord Himself. Spiritual giants would once again walk the earth if we would do the same.

PART TWO

EXPERIENCING THE GRAND REALITY OF GOD

CHAPTER SIX

RELISHING THE ASSURANCE

Ephesians contains two prayers of the apostle Paul. Both of them are petitions that God would show His people some things that they needed to comprehend more fully. The prayer in chapter 1 was for them to have a Spirit-taught assurance of the outcome of God's plan for them.

SPIRITUAL STRENGTHENING

In chapter 3, Paul prays again for a better comprehension of spiritual things. This time his prayer is for their spiritual strengthening. Let's look at it together in Ephesians 3:14-21.

> For this cause I bow my knees unto the Father of our Lord Jesus Christ,
>
> Of whom the whole [spiritual] family in heaven and earth is named,
>
> That he would grant you, according to the riches of his glory, to be strengthened with might by his Spirit in the inner man;
>
> That Christ may dwell in your hearts by faith; [and] that ye, [having been] rooted and grounded in love,
>
> May be able to comprehend with all saints what is the breadth, and length, and depth, and height;
>
> And to know the love of Christ, which passeth knowledge, that ye might be filled with all the fulness of God.
>
> Now unto him that is able to do exceeding abundantly above all that we ask or think, according to the power that worketh in us,

Unto him be glory in the church by Christ Jesus throughout all ages, world without end. Amen.

Now again, we must ask ourselves, "Why is Paul praying that they would be spiritually 'strengthened with might by his Spirit in the inner man'?" And again, we must answer, "It is because this kind of experience—at least to a depth he wants to see in them—isn't an automatic reality."

As we have noted in the last chapter, the Christian world contains many believers who are fretful, distraught, and fearful. They have no doubt that they are saved, and they try to claim one promise after another to quiet their troubled souls, but they are still left with great uncertainty about how they will get along in this life. What is it they need? Paul tells us.

He says they need a powerful spiritual strengthening in the inner man. The inner man—the person they are down inside the heart, the part nobody sees—is too weak. Some powerful work must be done deep in the inner man. A mere resurfacing of the outer image won't do. Everything that follows in Paul's prayer is descriptive of that request. Spiritually weak believers lack the things he is praying for. What are these things?

FIRST THINGS FIRST

The first requirement is that "Christ may dwell in your hearts by faith" (3:17). Now that seems like an odd prayer request. Isn't he talking to believers? Doesn't Christ already dwell in their hearts? Those are certainly valid questions, but as we look at this statement more closely, I think we shall see Paul's concerns.

The key to understanding this passage is knowing the meaning of the word "dwell." It means literally to "house-down." It has the idea of coming into a house, not as a guest, but as a ruling master—claiming and using every part for his own purposes.

When my wife and I were first married, we led a student ministry team for our university for two summers. The team traveled from church to church throughout the summer, presented a musical package, and gave personal testimonies, and then I would preach. As we drove up to a new church each afternoon, we all wondered what kind of homes we would be staying in that evening. Most families were very hospitable. They would help us carry our luggage in, show us to our bedroom, show us the closet space they had cleared out, and give us a tour of the bathroom facilities, pointing out the towels that were ours, and so forth. We would take a few minutes to unpack our hanging clothes in the closets, freshen up in the bathroom, and then join the family in the family room, den, or living room.

Later, after dinner was over and while we helped clear the dishes from the table, some hostesses would open the refrigerator door and tell us to be sure to help ourselves to anything we wanted to make ourselves at home. Such was the welcome we received in most homes.

Now, even though we felt wonderfully at ease with our new host family, we still never felt quite "at home." Though they *said* we could have anything we wanted in the kitchen, we would have never felt the liberty later that night after the service to excuse ourselves from the conversation in the living room, go to the kitchen, fix ourselves a bowl of cereal, and return with it to our place on the couch. Somehow that would have looked very presumptuous to our hosts. We knew we were welcome, but we were quite sure we weren't *that* welcome. We were still guests. To "house-down" in this way would have been rude.

"Come, Lord Jesus, be our guest, and let this food to us be blest."

And so goes the simple table blessing many of us were taught as small children. Now there may be nothing wrong with this simple prayer as a child's table grace, but it sadly reflects the attitude that many believers take toward Jesus Christ. To them He is only a Guest. He is welcome to dwell with them as long as He understands that He is just that—a Guest. He can have one of the bedrooms with a small section of closet cleaned out for Him, but He shouldn't disturb anything in the dresser drawers; they are already full of the past season's sweaters. And He is welcome to the refrigerator as long as He doesn't take anything for Himself that was purchased for this week's menus.

This kind of "welcome" is not out of line for a guest, but it is unthinkable for the Owner and Master of the house of our heart. And here is the first reason many, many believers do not know the blessing of an intimate relationship with Jesus Christ. He is not allowed to "house-down" in their hearts. Why would that be the case? Some of them stubbornly reject the rule of anyone else over them. Others have fleeting moments of tenderness when they realize they should allow Christ to rule, but they do not trust Him. They are afraid that He might take over too much. He might remove something from the house that is too dear to them. This is why Paul says, "That Christ may dwell in your hearts *by faith.*" We must *trust* Him if He is to be given the reign of Master instead of treated like a Guest.

This is also why Paul prays that they would be strengthened with might—empowered—by the Spirit in the inner man. We need the aid of the Holy Spirit to expose the selfish protectiveness that so naturally rules in us and to fan the flames of our feeble desires to have Christ rule in us. Consider the words of Moule on this point as he answers the question "Why do we need a supreme empowering just in order to receive our Life, our Light?"

> The heart, though it immeasurably needs the blessed Indweller, has that in it which *dreads* His absolute Indwelling. *Can it trust Him with* complete internal authority? Will He not use it to purposes terrible to the human heart, asserting His position by some infliction, some exaction, awful and unpitying? So the hand, stretched out to "open the door" (Rev. iii. 20), the inner door—for the King is supposed to be already received into the porch, and hall, and more public chambers of the being—falls again, and shrinks from that turning of the key which is to set the last recess quite open to the MASTER. . . . Come, Holy Ghost, and shew to the hesitating heart "the glory of God in the face of Jesus Christ," that lovely glory, shewn in that fair Countenance; then it shall hesitate no more. Beholding His love in His look it shall not dread His power in His grasp. It shall be strong to welcome Him wholly in, for it shall see, in the light of the Spirit, that *"in His presence* is fulness of joy," that "to serve Him is to reign" [emphasis his].[1]

Glad Surrender
What we have before us then is the first requirement for spiritual strength. We need a Spirit-taught glad surrender to Jesus Christ as the Master of the house. Self cannot rule on the throne if Christ is to have permission to "house-down" in the inner man of our heart. I say "glad"

---

[1]Moule, 136-37.

surrender because if it is Spirit-taught we will see the divine necessity of it and want it though we do not yet know all that it will mean.

This is where the vast majority of believers drop out of the race. And this is precisely why so many lack the blessed assurance that comes with an intimate relationship with Jesus Christ. They cannot enjoy that kind of comfort because there is always tension in the house. They insist on treating the Master as a Guest. There must come a time when Jesus Christ is acknowledged as the Lord and Master of the house. We ask *His* permission to use what is in the house. We exist to do *His* bidding. And every breach of that divine right must be settled personally with the Master by confessing the mutiny and seeking His forgiveness so that the fellowship is restored and the tension is gone.

All of this we do *by faith*—taking God at His Word—that this is something we should pray for. We trust the Holy Spirit to empower us; therefore, we gladly surrender to Him as Master of the house. Notice Lloyd-Jones's comments.

> Faith enables you to say to yourself as you read it, or as you hear it, That is God's word, which says that it is possible to any Christian, to all Christians; well therefore, it is possible for me. It is possible for me to know the Lord Jesus Christ in this intimate manner. Faith lays hold upon the promise, personally and individually.

> So you begin to pray, and you go on praying thus in faith until some marvelous moment comes and suddenly you find yourself knowing Christ. He will have manifested Himself to you, He will have taken up His abode in you, and settled down in your heart. And you will say with amazement: How could I have spent so many years being satisfied with the mere beginnings of Christianity, the mere portals of the temple, when it was so wondrously and gloriously possible for me to enter into "the Holiest of all"?[2]

So Paul says first, "I am praying that you would become spiritually strong in the inner man. It will take the empowering of God's Spirit, but you must by faith let Christ become the Master of your house." The effect of that glad surrender will be that the believer will no longer be living for himself but fulfilling the Great Commandments of loving

---

[2]D. Martyn Lloyd-Jones, *The Unsearchable Riches of Christ: An Exposition of Ephesians 3* (Grand Rapids: Baker Books, 1979), 152.

God and others at his own expense. The actions of his life will be "rooted and grounded in love."

CLEANING THE CARPET

Romans 5:5 tells us that "the love of God is shed abroad in our hearts by the Holy Ghost which is given unto us." The words "shed abroad" mean to "pour out" as one would cover a floor with water. I like to think of it as laying down carpet. We don't say that we just "shed abroad" new carpet in our house, but that is the sense of this word. God demonstrated that love at Calvary.[3] It is the basis for His actions towards us and is to be the "root and ground" of our actions towards others.

When Christ is allowed to reign as Master of the house, He rips up the old, worn area rugs of self-interest, self-indulgence, self-protection, and self-preoccupation and cleans the underlying floor covering of Christian love, which He put there at salvation. He intends that every piece of furniture be enhanced by love and every step in the house be cushioned by love.

When Christ is reigning, and the believer is submitting to His reign, that believer's life bears the marks of his loving Savior. He lives for God and others, no longer for himself. The love of God for us taught in Romans 5:5 becomes the wellspring of the believer's love to God and others in return. In his commentary on Ephesians, Charles Hodge addresses what it means to be "rooted and grounded in love."

> The love in which we are to be rooted is not the love of God or of Christ toward us, but either brotherly love, or love as a Christian grace, without determining its object. It is that love which flows from faith, and of which both God and the brethren are the objects. It is for the increase and ascendency of this grace through the indwelling of Christ, till it sustains and strengthens the whole inner man, so that the believer may stand as a well-rooted tree or as a well-founded building, that the apostle here prays.[4]

Jesus very clearly told us, "A new commandment I give unto you, That ye love one another; as I have loved you, that ye also love one another.

---

[3]Romans 5:8.

[4]Charles Hodge, A *Commentary on Ephesians* (Carlisle, Pa.: The Banner of Truth Trust, 1964), 131.

By this shall all men know that ye are my disciples, if ye have love one to another."[5] It is that love for others that is the true sign that Christ has taken possession of the house as Master. He always cleans the carpet. It has a new brilliance. It shows Christ's love for us and displays a love in us that chooses the glory of God and the good of others before it seeks its own good.

Self-Centeredness at Home

The sad state of many Christian marriages reveals that the carpet has not been cleaned. As my wife and I travel and work with Christian families in trouble, we see husbands and wives who have been serving themselves for years. The result is gut-wrenching misery. To be sure, none of these believing couples walked to the marriage altar expecting their life together to be filled with heartache and disappointment. What they thought was going to be the experience of their dreams has turned into a nightmare from which they are hoping one day to awaken. Though their hopes of marital bliss gradually eroded during the first few years of marriage, the expected peace and satisfaction has almost completely vanished by the time their children are in their teens. Both spouses are in a survival mode, protecting what few personal resources have not been eaten up by the ravages of selfishness.

Children who seemed to them at the time of birth to be "bundles of joy," under the tutelage of self-centered parents, have become sources of great grief and pain because of their own self-centeredness. No child needs his parents' self-centeredness to *learn* how to be self-centered, but his parents' self-centeredness *authorizes* it in the home. It says, "Self-centeredness tolerated here. It won't be challenged unless it interferes with my particular brand of self-centeredness."

When the children finally move out, these couples realize they have gone entirely different directions for many years. There doesn't seem to be any point in continuing on together. If the marriage has not already been destroyed through pornography, affairs, materialism, ambition, and worldliness, it now ends simply out of despair. They see no purpose in continuing such a dead and meaningless relationship.

---

[5]John 13:34-35.

Other pleasures beckon—pleasures that cannot be easily pursued within the confines of the current marriage.

We see not only hurting marriages because the carpet has not been cleaned but also an alarming number of worldly children who have abandoned the God of their childhood professions. If they, indeed, have not forsaken God altogether, they are content with the mediocre level of Christianity they have seen in their parents. Tragically, the despair down the road for them will be the same that it is for their parents now.

We see many wives discouraged because often they alone are concerned about the spiritual condition of their families. We see their husbands, who are uninvolved—and often stubbornly so—in the spiritual leadership of their families. Often these men bear crushing burdens of personal failures. Some are spiritually lifeless because of pornography or affairs with other women—or men. We see church directories with more families on each page who are in need of serious help than families on that page who are able to help them.

We see singles passionately determined to stay single because of heart-rending sexual and physical abuses in their own homes. Others are passionately determined to be married at all costs, thinking that the marriage altar is the Holy Grail of satisfaction.

On the other hand, we are gratified to see numbers of teens and young adults who are dissatisfied with the low level of Christianity in the adults around them and who are seeking the Lord; they thirst for something more. We also see grieving parents, whose families have been shattered by teen rebellion, turn back to the Lord in genuine dependence. Some have seen as a cause their failure to live a Christianity vibrant enough to attract their children to God.[6] Now, as they help to raise the children of their own unwed offspring, they bow in humility

---

[6]As I mentioned in *Changed into His Image*, 12: "This is not to say that every failure of a child to follow God's way is entirely the fault of the parents. God Himself said, 'I have nourished and brought up children, and they have rebelled against me' (Isa. 1:2). He certainly didn't make any mistakes in His parenting goals or methods. Every child still has within him the inclination to 'turn every one to his own way' (Isa. 53:6). God does, however, place a heavy responsibility on parents to exemplify godliness and to saturate the child-rearing environment with the ways and the words of the living God lest they 'forget the Lord' (see Deut. 6:5-13)."

and repentance before the God of heaven, and a fresh breeze of God's own Spirit blows over their tired souls. Though life is still difficult, they have found a refreshing spring of life in relationship with Jesus Christ. They have let Him be Master, and He has cleaned the carpet of love that underlies everything they do.

This carpet-cleaning job isn't optional in the Christian life. It is absolutely essential. All of the miseries described in the paragraphs above were bred in homes where each lived for himself. Paul very clearly warned,

> Be not deceived; God is not mocked: for whatsoever a man soweth, that shall he also reap. For he that soweth to his flesh shall of the flesh reap corruption; but he that soweth to the Spirit shall of the Spirit reap life everlasting (Galatians 6:7-8).

Without "being rooted and grounded in love" (3:17), what I have described above is inevitable. So clearly is the carpet of love a sign that Christ reigns in the heart that the apostle John says,

> He that loveth his brother abideth in the light, and there is none occasion of stumbling in him. But he that hateth his brother is in darkness, and walketh in darkness, and knoweth not whither he goeth, because that darkness hath blinded his eyes (I John 2:10-11).

There just is no way of being a God-pleasing Christian without allowing Christ to "house-down" in our hearts so that He can clean the carpet of love He put down at salvation. *When that glad surrender is the norm of the life and the carpet of love stays fresh and inviting, we are demonstrating strength in the inner man.*

BLESSED ASSURANCE

The next inevitable result is a Spirit-taught sense of Christ's own love for us as His dear children. Paul says that then we will

> be able to comprehend with all saints what is the breadth, and length, and depth, and height; and to know the love of Christ, which passeth knowledge (3:18-19).

Here is the pinnacle of mature Christian assurance. And it is because few Christians really allow Christ to move in as Master—complete with clean carpet—that so few experience the kind of assurance we are about to look at. In fact, when summarizing the Puritan view of assurance, one writer said,

> "Full assurance" is a rare blessing, even among adults; it is a great and precious privilege, not indiscriminately bestowed. "Assurance is a mercy too good for most men's hearts. . . . God will only give it to his best and dearest friends." "Assurance is the beauty and top of a Christian's glory in this life. It is usually attended with the strongest joy, with the sweetest comforts, and with the greatest peace. It is a . . . crown that few wear. . . ." "Assurance is meat for strong men; few babes, if any, are able to bear it, and digest it."[7]

A spiritually strong believer knows the experience of letting Christ "house-down" in his heart. He also knows what it is to live a life that is carpeted with love toward God and others. Paul tells us in this prayer that the believer who has experienced those elements of the Christian life is a candidate to know personally the voice of the Master tenderly expressing to him His everlasting love for him personally.

Many people want to hear these comforting words of acceptance and assurance but are unwilling to give Christ His rightful rule in the house. And what is so sad is that Jesus Christ wants them to know deeply—in the inner man—that they are loved with everlasting love. How their fears would be dissolved, their despairing hearts uplifted, and their doubts removed. What they need to know above all is that God loves *them*! That would put them on an entirely different spiritual plane. Let me explain the difference this way.

Most people have the assurance of knowing *who* their earthly father is. There is not any doubt in their mind in whose family they belong. Many of those same people, however, have lived very fearful and unfulfilled childhoods because there never was a comforting sense that the man they knew to be their father really cared about them person-

---

[7]J. I. Packer, *A Quest for Godliness: The Puritan Vision of the Christian Life* (Wheaton: Crossway Books, 1990), 181. Great caution is in order when reading Packer. His theology in recent years has taken a sad nosedive as he has sought to advance worldwide ecumenicity. His book *A Quest for Godliness* however, is a valuable history of what the Puritans taught on various theological themes.

The quotes cited above in Packer's text are from Thomas Brooks as cited in Packer's endnotes.

ally. They may have shared the family name but never experienced the profound security of having a father who loved and delighted in them and took the time to express by tender words his love to them personally. To a person raised in this grievous condition, the difference I am explaining is excruciatingly real—and painful to think about. There is an assurance that God is my Father, but there is another kind of Spirit-taught assurance that the God who is my Father loves *me!* Let's examine these two different experiences.

Two Levels of Assurance

Paul spoke of these two levels of assurance in Romans 8:15-16.

> For ye have not received the spirit of bondage again to fear; but ye have received the Spirit of adoption, whereby ye cry, Abba, Father. *The Spirit [Himself] beareth witness with our spirit, that we are the children of God.*

Listen to R. A. Torrey's comment on this passage and then let's look at it in more detail.

> There are two witnesses to our sonship, first, our own spirit, taking God at His Word. . . . Our own spirit unhesitatingly affirms that what God says is true that we are sons of God because God says so. But there is another witness to our sonship, namely, the Holy Spirit. He bears witness *together with* our spirit. . . . When the Spirit of His Son bears witness together with our spirit to our sonship, then we are *filled and thrilled with the sense that we are sons.*[8]

The First Witness Is Our Own Spirit—This is the testimony within our own heart, where with the Spirit's aid we can discern that certain things have taken place. We see the divine logic of what has happened when we came to Christ, and we have seen the Spirit's fruit in one way or another in our lives. The first witness of our own spirit may go something like this.

> I know I am saved because I came under conviction that I was a sinner. After I understood the gospel, I asked Christ to save me. Since He promised to make me His Son if I would receive Him according

---

[8]R. A. Torrey, *The Person and Work of the Holy Spirit* (Grand Rapids: Zondervan, 1910), 136-37.

to John 1:12, I know I am saved because God cannot lie. Since then I have seen fruit in my life that shows me indeed I have been saved.

Now there is nothing wrong with that kind of reasoning. In fact, it is absolutely correct and necessary for us to think this way. We call this "taking it by faith," and this witness *must* be in place before a believer can come to have the assurance of the second witness. Consider the Puritan view of this first witness.

> The Puritans identified "our spirit" [in Romans 8:16] with the Christian's conscience, which, with the Spirit's aid, is able to discern in his heart the marks which Scripture specifies as tokens of the new birth and to conclude from them that he is a child of God. The Spirit "writes first of all graces in us, and then teaches our consciences to read his handwriting." Without the Spirit's aid, man can never recognize the Spirit's handiwork in himself; "if he do not give in his testimony with them, your graces will give no witness at all." Sometimes the Spirit's help here is given in full measure; sometimes, however, to chasten us for sin, or to try our faith for a time, this help is partly or wholly withdrawn; and because the Spirit is not always active to enable us to know ourselves to the same degree, the witness of our spirit inevitably fluctuates: "a man shall find the same signs sometimes witness to him, and sometimes not, as the Spirit irradiates them." We must recognize that God is sovereign here, to give more or less assurance in this way as he pleases. Thus far, all Puritans are agreed.[9]

The Witness of the Spirit Himself with Our Spirit—But Romans 8:16 and passages such as this one in Ephesians teach us that there is a second witness, a second kind of assurance, that is Spirit taught. It always begins with taking by faith the inferred deduction from truth we just saw, but it is enhanced by direct illumination from the Holy Spirit that allows the believer to see God's personal claim on his life as God's child. Again, let me quote a summary of the comments of several Puritans—Sibbes, Brooks, and Goodwin—who saw it this way.

> They take the text [Romans 8:16] as referring to two distinct modes of witness, the first being inferential as described [in the previous quote], and the second being that of the Spirit testifying, no longer indirectly, but immediately and intuitively; not merely by prompting

---

[9]Packer, 183-84. The quotes cited are from Thomas Goodwin and Thomas Brooks.

us to infer our adoption, but by what Goodwin calls an "overpowering light" whereby he bears direct witness to the Christian of God's everlasting love to him, of his election, and his sonship, and his - inheritance.[10]

Consider the testimony of Thomas Goodwin again and of John Owen.

When the direct testimony is experienced, it creates a degree of joy to which the [first witness] could never give rise. "It works that joy in the heart which the saints shall have in heaven. . . . It is not a bare conviction that a man shall go to heaven; but God telleth him in part what heaven is, and lets him feel it" [Goodwin].[11]

Of this joy there is no account to be given, but that the Spirit worketh it when and how he will; he secretly infuseth and distils it into the soul, prevailing against all fears and sorrows, filling it with gladness, exultations; and sometimes with unspeakable raptures of mind [Owen].[12]

I would remind you that these statements are not the statements of present-day Charismatics but the words of Puritan preachers of the 1600s! There is, indeed, in this heavenly assurance an added comfort that energizes and confirms on a personal level that everything the believer has known in his heart by faith is indeed wonderfully true. This is the kind of assurance for which Paul is praying on behalf of the Ephesian believers. It was the experience of Fanny Crosby, who wrote,

> Blessed assurance, Jesus is mine!
> Oh, what a foretaste of glory divine!
> Heir of salvation, purchase of God,
> Born of His Spirit, washed in His blood.
> This is my story, this is my song,
> Praising my Saviour all the day long.

Fanny Crosby's exuberance in these lines does not come from the lively, melodic tune with which we are so familiar. Her jubilation comes because she has "seen" these truths with illuminated eyes. Ask yourself, "Have I ever experienced from God Himself such assurance that if I were a poet I would describe it as . . . ?"

---

[10]Ibid., 184.
[11]Ibid., 185.
[12]Ibid., 189.

Perfect submission, perfect delight,
Visions of rapture now burst on my sight;
Angels descending, bring from above
Echoes of mercy, whispers of love.[13]

Is the reality of your salvation so vibrant in your soul that it brings a profound delight to you? When you think of those times when the Spirit taught you these truths, do they burst afresh on your mind like "visions of rapture"? Is it as if angels themselves have brought you a message from God, whispering to you that you personally are His own delight?

Fanny Crosby is not merely waxing poetic in these stanzas. She is testifying of what it means to have a Spirit-taught assurance whereby "I in my Saviour am happy and blessed" and have a wondering comfort that feels like being "lost in His love." Here is a physically blind believer who has "seen" something most believers will never see about assurance, though God wants every one of them to have the same kind of comforting security in their salvation.

Paul never knew the text or the music to the hymn "Blessed Assurance." But he knew the experience of this Spirit-taught assurance and wanted every believer who ever read his epistle to have it as well. Therefore, he prayed for the "eyes of your understanding"[14] to be "enlightened."[15] He knew that without this special work of the Spirit of God no believer can truly experience that "blessed assurance."

CAUTION—HOLY SPIRIT AT WORK

It would be folly, however, to say that the Holy Spirit has to work in every believer in exactly the same way, or that the main goal of asking Him to work is so that we can have some kind of emotional experience. The Holy Spirit's mission is to show us Jesus Christ.[16] This assurance is the fruit of His blessed rule in the house. It is the final redecoration and refurnishing after the carpet of love for God and others has been cleaned and renewed. These gracious works of the Holy

---

[13]Fanny J. Crosby, "Blessed Assurance," in *Worship and Service Hymnal* (Carol Stream, Ill.: Hope Publishing Co., 1957).

[14]Lit. "heart."

[15]Ephesians 1:18.

[16]John 16:13-14.

Spirit always point to the excellency of the resident Master, who has designed and ordered the refurbishing. Dr. F. B. Meyer's caution is in order here.

> We must carefully avoid making the Holy Spirit the figurehead in any movement, however sincere and well intentioned its promoters may be. It is surely a profound mistake to make any special experience of the Spirit the objective or aim of a religious movement. In the present dispensation, the one aim of the blessed Paraclete is to glorify our Savior. He must surely shrink from any attempt, however well intended, to divert one thought from Him, who must ever be the Alpha and the Omega of our faith.[17]

When the Holy Spirit opens our eyes to what we have in our salvation, we will see that what we have is in *Jesus Christ*, and because of *Christ*, and for the *Lord Jesus*. We will see that we are created for *His* glory. The Holy Spirit turns these theological truths into living realities in our heart.

Now it is true that when we experience "the love of Christ, which passeth knowledge"[18] we are prone to be excited about it. We certainly must not make an emotional experience the test of spirituality, but neither must we try to dampen the spirits of one who has experienced "joy unspeakable and full of glory."[19] There is always the danger of fleshly fanaticism in our midst when God begins to work. One time Dwight L. Moody, the noted evangelist of the past century, was asked why some people objected to praying for an awakening—a Spirit-sent revival in America. He replied,

> One argument that seems to carry great weight with so many people right now is that there is too much excitement in an awakening. I wish I could see as much excitement in the church of God, in the work of God, as I see in other areas. If you want to see excitement, go to some place of amusement! The moment there comes a breath of interest in spiritual things, some people cry, "Sensationalism, sensationalism!" But I tell you that I would rather have sensation than stagnation any time. Don't be afraid of a little excitement. It seems

---

[17]Leona Frances Choy, *Powerlines* (Camp Hill, Pa.: Christian Publications, 1990), 156.
[18]Ephesians 3:19.
[19]I Peter 1:8.

to me that almost anything is preferable to deadness. Where there is life, there will always be a commotion. What we need is *life!*[20]

Lloyd-Jones addresses this issue as well.

There is a real difference between emotion and emotionalism. Is it conceivable that anyone can be told directly by God that he is God's child, and yet feel nothing, feel no emotion? . . . *We must emphasize that for God to visit a soul is the most overwhelming experience one can ever know; and it is not surprising therefore that sometimes the physical frame cannot stand it.* . . . True emotion produced by the Holy Ghost always leads to humility, to reverence, to a holy love of God. . . . What proves genuineness is that *the man is filled with a sense of awe.* He has been near the Majesty of God and is of necessity humbled. This emerged clearly in the accounts of the experiences of several of the great men of God which I have quoted.[21] They very rarely spoke about it; there was no boastfulness. What had happened to them was almost too sacred to be mentioned. It leads to humility, and to a love of God, and a rejoicing in Christ with "a joy unspeakable and full of glory." It must do so because it is a revelation of something of "the breadth and length and depth and height; and to know the love of Christ which passeth knowledge" (Ephesians 3:18-19). It is impossible to have even a glimpse of such an experience without being moved to the very depth of one's being. Yet one is humbled and at the same time is filled with a sense of awe and of reverence and amazement. . . . The question for each of us is: Is the love of God shed abroad in my heart? Do I know, beyond argument, beyond having to convince myself, that I am a child of God, and a joint-heir with Jesus Christ?[22]

So while emotions are not the touchstone of authenticity, when the Spirit teaches a believer Christ's love for him personally, emotions probably will be affected in the transaction. We certainly do not seek some kind of experience, but when the light of God's Spirit dawns upon the soul, it is an experience!

The real test of whether God's Spirit is enlightening the eyes or whether our emotions have merely been manipulated is always the

---

[20]Ibid., 170-71.

[21]He has previously referred to Thomas Goodwin, John Wesley, John Flavel, Jonathan Edwards, D. L. Moody, Christmas Evans, George Whitefield, and Richard Sibbes.

[22]Lloyd-Jones, *God's Ultimate Purpose*, 286-88.

centrality of Jesus Christ in the life. The Bible clearly teaches that the Holy Spirit will work joy and peace in the life when He opens our eyes, but those are only *effects*—wonderful though they be. The Holy Spirit's *focus* is always upon Jesus Christ.

This is why so many of the good hymns of past years focus upon the love of Christ. These dear believers *saw* His love. They sang, "I love to tell the story / Of unseen things above, / Of Jesus and His glory, / Of Jesus and His love." "The love of God is greater far than tongue or pen can ever tell." "O, Love that wilt not let me go, / I rest my weary soul in Thee." "I stand amazed in the presence / Of Jesus the Nazarene, / And wonder how He could love me, / A sinner, condemned, unclean. . . . How marvelous! how wonderful! / Is my Saviour's love for me!"[23] These saints were not writing lyrics to keep a recording industry going; they were expressing what they had experienced of the love of God for them. There is no higher experience this side of heaven. It truly is a "foretaste of glory divine."

THE FULLNESS OF GOD

Paul says the result of this kind of work in the heart of the child of God is that the believer is "filled with all the fulness of God" (3:19). That means that he is becoming more and more conformed to the "perfect man, unto the measure of the stature of the fulness of Christ."[24] He is taking on by a divine work of the Spirit of God more and more of the characteristics of the Master of the house. He is being "changed into the same image from glory to glory, even as by the Spirit of the Lord."[25] In short, it is evident that he is being sanctified. He is relishing the assurance, and he sings now with understanding:

> *Loved with everlasting love,*
> *Led by grace that love to know;*
> *Spirit, breathing from above,*
> *Thou hast taught me it is so!*
> *Oh, this full and perfect peace!*
> *Oh, this transport all divine!*

---

[23]Charles H. Gabriel, "My Saviour's Love," in *Worship and Service Hymnal* (Carol Stream, Ill.: Hope Publishing Co., 1957).

[24]Ephesians 4:13.

[25]II Corinthians 3:18.

In a love which cannot cease,
I am His, and He is mine.

Heav'n above is softer blue,
Earth around is sweeter green!
Something lives in every hue
Christless eyes have never seen:
Birds with gladder songs o'erflow,
Flow'rs with deeper beauties shine,
Since I know, as now I know,
I am His, and He is mine.

Things that once were wild alarms
Cannot now disturb my rest;
Closed in everlasting arms,
Pillowed on the loving breast.
Oh, to lie forever here,
Doubt, and care, and self resign,
While He whispers in my ear,
I am His, and He is mine.

His forever, only His;
Who the Lord and me shall part?
Ah, with what a rest of bliss
Christ can fill the loving heart!
Heav'n and earth may fade and flee,
First-born light in gloom decline;
But while God and I shall be,
I am His, and He is mine.[26]

Ah, believer, are these your experiences? If not, Christ wants them to be so. Let Him strengthen you with might in the inner man. Let Him dwell in your heart, not as a tolerated Guest but as the resident Master. Let Him rip up your old, worn rugs of selfishness and let Him refurbish the underlying carpet of love in your heart. Then let Him totally refurnish and redecorate your heart with the hangings and furniture that speak of His own dear love for you, His dwelling place. This truly is the closest thing there is to "heaven on earth."

---

[26]George Wade Robinson, "I Am His, and He Is Mine," in *Worship and Service Hymnal* (Carol Stream, Ill.: Hope Publishing Co., 1957).

IS THIS POSSIBLE?

Paul must have known that all of this sounds too good to be true. Perhaps he could hear the whines of the doubters—those who would excuse themselves from this experience because life was too hard and the battle too strong. Thus, he finishes his prayer with a doxology that puts everything back into focus.

> Now unto him that is able to do exceeding abundantly above all that we ask or think, according to the power that worketh in us, unto him be glory in the church by Christ Jesus throughout all ages, world without end. Amen (3:20-21).

Is it really true that every believer's life could bring glory to God? Paul says a resounding "yes!" There is no limit to the "power that worketh in us." There is no generation that cannot see this accomplished, for it is for everyone "throughout all ages." No limitation here either. Therefore, let the remodeling begin!

TAKE TIME TO REFLECT

1. Do the inner life of your heart and the outer testimony of your actions in recent days demonstrate that you have been treating Jesus Christ as a Guest or as the Master of your heart?

2. What reasons do you give for your answer to the previous question?

3. Do the inner life of your heart and the outer testimony of your actions in recent days demonstrate that Jesus Christ has "cleaned the carpet" of love in your heart (i.e., is your life characterized by love for God and love for others), or does it show you to be self-centered?

4. What reasons do you give for your answer to the previous question?

5. Have you experienced the Holy Spirit's personal assurance that God loves *you*? If so, describe the time He first showed that to you. If it is not your experience, write out what may be hindering Him from "furnishing and decorating" the house of your heart with the personal knowledge of His love.

A WORD TO DISCIPLE-MAKERS

As you disciple others whose lukewarm Christianity has borne them only bitter fruit in life, you must continually remind them that mediocrity isn't supposed to work. Often a believer has gone along, like the man in "midlife crisis" of chapter one, thinking that because he was faithful at church and faithful in his Bible reading that somehow that was enough. James forcefully makes the point that a man who merely hears the Word but does not take the time to meditatively *reflect* upon it so that it actually becomes a controlling factor in his life is *deceiving* himself.

This kind of believer may hear a message or read a passage and agree with its thrust and truth but not take the time to reflect upon it! He does not sit with his heart open, begging God to show him what that means for him. He does not wait patiently for God to answer him through the conviction of His Holy Spirit. He does not wait for God to open his eyes. He gives mental assent to it but does not *think* about it. He does not reflect!

Lest you think I am too hard on this man, let's grant that he makes a decision to change in some way. But James says there is much more work to be done. He says, "But whoso looketh into the perfect law of liberty, and continueth therein, he being not a forgetful hearer, but a doer of the work, this man shall be blessed in his deed."[27] Without this focused reflection on the Word he will readily walk away from the experience like a man "beholding his natural face in a [mirror]. For he beholdeth himself, and goeth his way, and [immediately] forgetteth what manner of man he was."[28]

He may walk away momentarily "blessed" by what he saw today, but he will not be permanently changed by what he saw because he did not take time to reflect.[29]

This man is self-deceived because he thinks he is changed once he acknowledges his need and decides to change—when no lasting change

---

[27]James 1:25.

[28]James 1:23-24.

[29]For an extensive treatment on meditation and its part in biblical change, see "Part Two—Renewing Your Mind" in *Changed into His Image*.

has actually taken place at all. He is not yet a consistent "doer of the work." He is a "forgetful hearer." The sad end is that when the difficulties of life hit, he will think God has let him down, and as he reflects upon "all he has done for God," his bitterness will grow and the despair will set in.[30]

Revelation − Reflection = Self-Deception

Revelation (the hearing of truth) without reflection (meditating upon the truth while asking God for illumination) is dangerous. It leads to self-deception. The believers described above may walk away from their experiences of "hearing" the Word impressed with certain principles of Christian living. They may see that they should not lie,[31] they should not love the world,[32] they should regularly assemble themselves with other believers,[33] and so forth, but these will be only matters of Christian principle and ethics to them.

Of course, that is a noble beginning, but unless God has illuminated the truth to the believer, he will not see in these very principles of living the excellency and beauty of the Christian life. Neither will he see the ugliness of walking as he used to walk, in the vanity of his mind.

---

[30]Those of us especially who come from a revivalist background have seen this. Coming forward at an invitation for salvation is a one-time event. It is called the "new birth" (John 3) and is not to be repeated. That one visit to the altar, where the seeking soul confesses his sin and turns to Christ as the only substitute for his sin, need not ever be done again. The problem of his eternal destiny has been solved.

However, many pastors and evangelists give the impression that "if you as a Christian want a different kind of life than you are living now, you need to come to the altar, get right with God, and your troubles will be over." That is faulty advertising! Sin-ladened believers coming to the altar—as they did for salvation—expect on the basis of that appeal that a visit to the altar will again "fix their problem." Only their problem now is different. It isn't one of salvation—an event; it is one of sanctification—a process. Coming to the altar may be a "start"—an acknowledgment of surrender and humility, and an indication to the perceptive pastor that here is a sheep that needs additional shepherding, but it is *only* that—a start. Someone needs to begin discipling that believer from that point on until he is actually walking "in newness of life" in the area of struggle. When the trip to the altar doesn't "work" as the preacher promised, many a sin-burdened saint has begun to doubt his salvation—making him a candidate for another trip to the altar—when what he needed was help in sanctification.

[31]Ephesians 4:25.

[32]I John 2:15.

[33]Hebrews 10:25.

As he turns his eyes out to behold the disintegrating culture around him, he will not grieve over the despair and emptiness of the lost around him. Nor will he try to penetrate their lives with the gospel. He will castigate their waywardness and isolate himself from them. Even more tragically, when you try to show him his self-deception, he cannot see it. Such is the result of revelation without reflection. You must get him meditating on the Word if you are to see lasting change in his life.

Revelation + Reflection = Illumination

As you can discern by now, the kind of reflection I am talking about means that a believer seeks for God Himself to illuminate his heart with a spiritual understanding of the truths before him in the Word. Do you remember how many times in the Gospels our Lord would say something to the whole crowd, but then He would stop and personally explain it to His disciples?

Some modern believers unfairly judge the Lord for not telling *everyone* what He meant. For example, His words following the parable of the soil in Luke 8 seem harsh to them. He says to His disciples,

> Unto you it is given to know the mysteries of the kingdom of God: but to others in parables; that seeing they might not see, and hearing they might not understand (10).

What many readers of this passage miss is a simple question by the disciples that prompted our Lord's statement. They "asked him, saying, *What might this parable be?*"[34] Another time they "came unto him, saying, *Declare unto us the parable of the tares of the field.*"[35] When He finished His explanation, He asked them, "Have ye understood all these things? They say unto him, Yea, Lord."[36]

What is happening here? The answer is very instructive. Jesus took the time to *personally* explain to His disciples what His teaching was *because they asked Him!* The rest of the crowds who heard the interesting word pictures and who marveled at His miracles were content to

---

[34]Luke 8:9.
[35]Matthew 13:36.
[36]Matthew 13:51.

merely hear His words without reflecting on them and without asking Him to personally teach them what they meant. Multitudes of believers today do exactly the same thing. They hear the sermons at church and read the Bible but never ask God Himself, "What do these things mean?" Consequently, they go their way unilluminated—untaught. Their eyes have not been opened.

CHAPTER SEVEN
RESTORING THE UNITY

We have just looked at the glorious security that we can have in Christ Jesus. I hope you have spent some time basking in the noonday sun of that truth. It is foundational for personal peace and joy. Paul brings us face to face, however, with another reality. He shows us that while God wants to reconcile all men to Himself through the gospel, there are great divisions among men. While personal peace with God is possible, peace with men often seems like an illusion. The social setting of the first-century world in which Paul moved was most unappealing. Note Phillips's description of it.

> The enmity between Jew and Gentile [in that first century] was deep, acrimonious, ancient, and enduring. Jews regarded Gentiles as unclean scavenger dogs. Gentiles despised Jews as grasping, canting, religious hypocrites. Jewish ritual laws, especially the laws concerning clean and unclean food, made it virtually impossible for a conscientious Jew to have table fellowship with a Gentile, so social intercourse was practically forbidden. The commercial instincts of the Jews—developed in Babylon, practiced in Biblical times, and brought to a fine art in later ages—made the Jews moneylenders to the world. Gentiles were often obligated to borrow Jewish money, but that did not endear the Jews to them. The Gentiles used the Jews, but detested them.[1]

Though not a pretty sight, in many ways the setting is similar to our own times. Tribal wars, racial tensions, terrorism, and social upheaval are the order of the day in every corner of the globe in spite of peace accords, civil rights laws, and high-level negotiations. Never has there

---

[1]John Phillips, *Exploring Ephesians* (Neptune, N.J.: Loizeaux Brothers, 1993), 71.

been more talk of world peace and international community, and yet never has there been less promise that it will come to pass. It was not always like this.

BACK TO EDEN

After God finished His initial creation of man, He stood back and "saw every thing that He had made, and, behold, it was very good."[2] Every part of the new creation functioned in perfect harmony with every other part. Everything fulfilled God's intention for it.

But the Fall of man destroyed all that. Adam stepped out of the divine path assuming he could improve his life independent of God. Instead his actions put him out of sync with His Creator, and he was disconnected from his own purpose for existence. He chose to live in a fantasy world where he fancied *himself* to be the most important component. He became subject to a divine sentence, a cursed existence, and a personal emptiness—none of which could be remedied until his relationship with his Creator was restored.

But eons before Adam ever drew his first breath, the Creator knew what He would do when this cosmic mutiny came to pass. In eternity past God put in place a plan that would reunite all things to Himself. In that final restoration "in the ages to come"[3] He will again vindicate once and for all the absolute perfection of His character before every created being—holy and evil. Though maligned for centuries by His fallen race, on that great day He will usher into the courtroom of the heavens His primary material witness: the Church. At the sight of its stunning restoration to a state far surpassing man's original creation, the entire universe of created beings will marvel at the wisdom, kindness, and power of the Supreme One, the Creator—and now, the Redeemer.

As we saw earlier, God faced two obstacles with respect to the witnesses for that grand demonstration of His glory. First, the material witnesses were *dead*. Indeed, their just condemnation made them better witnesses in Satan's charges *against* God. Fallen creatures certainly do not testify that God is worthy of the exclusive worship of His creatures.

---

[2]Genesis 1:31.
[3]Ephesians 2:7.

Before they could be credible witnesses, they needed life. They needed to be *redeemed* from the penalties and dominion of their sinfulness.

Secondly, the segment of the creation that God intended to use as material witnesses was *divided*. Those He was intending to gather as spokesmen for His grace—a mix of Jews and Gentiles—were hostile to each other. Again, they were better testimonies for Satan, who contests that God does not merit any special worship. Indeed, it would seem God couldn't even get His own creatures to agree that He was more important than they themselves were. Jews and Gentiles needed to be *reconciled*.

We have already addressed God's provision for the redemption of those "dead in trespasses and sins"[4] in chapter four of our study together. We now want to focus on God's solution to the second obstacle. We want to ponder what He has done to reconcile the warring factions of Jews and Gentiles in order to make them into one unified witness to His everlasting excellence. How will He bring them to realize and demonstrate that they were created for *His* glory?

ONE PATTERN FITS ALL

We do not want to miss the picture God is painting for us here in Ephesians, for *the pattern He used to reconcile Jews and Gentiles must be followed anytime men need to be reconciled to each other.* This plan has to be followed to bring warring factions within the church back into fellowship with each other. The resolution of marital strife must follow the pattern we are about to see.

If we are to restore unity among the brethren, we must see the master plan Paul outlines for us in Ephesians 2:11–3:11. This is a rather lengthy section of Ephesians, but try to capture the flow and message of these verses. As you read this passage, remember that Paul is a Jewish believer writing to a church of Gentile believers. He is letting them in on a most comforting, divine secret—God has included the Gentiles in His plan to display His glory through the Church now and before all creation at the end of the age!

---

[4]Ephesians 2:1.

Wherefore remember, that ye being [formerly] Gentiles in the flesh, who are called Uncircumcision by that which is called the Circumcision in the flesh made by hands;

That at that time ye [Gentiles] were without Christ, being aliens from the commonwealth of Israel, and strangers from the covenants of promise, having no hope, and without God in the world:

But now in Christ Jesus ye [Gentiles] who [formerly] were far off are made nigh by the blood of Christ.

For he is our peace, who hath made both [Jew and Gentile] one, and hath broken down the middle wall of partition between [Jew and Gentile];

Having abolished in his flesh the [hostility], even the law of commandments contained in ordinances; for to make in himself [the two into] one new man, so making peace;

And that he might reconcile both [Jew and Gentile] unto God in one body by the cross, having slain the enmity [in Himself]:

And came and preached peace to you [Gentiles] which were afar off, and to [the Jews] that were nigh.

For through him we both [Jew and Gentile] have access by one Spirit unto the Father.

Now therefore ye [Gentile believers] are no more strangers and foreigners, but fellowcitizens with the saints, and of the household of God;

And are built upon the foundation of the apostles and prophets, Jesus Christ himself being the chief corner stone;

In whom all the building fitly framed together groweth unto an holy temple in the Lord:

In whom ye [Gentiles] also are builded together for an habitation of God through the Spirit.

Chapter 3

For this cause I Paul, the prisoner of Jesus Christ for you Gentiles,

If ye have heard of the [stewardship] of the grace of God which is given me to youward:

How that by revelation he made known unto me the mystery; (as I wrote afore in few words,[5]

Whereby, when ye read, ye may understand my knowledge in the mystery of Christ)

Which in other ages was not made known unto the sons of men, as it is now revealed unto his holy apostles and [New Testament] prophets by the Spirit; [and here is the mystery:]

That the Gentiles should be fellowheirs, and [fellow members], and [fellow] partakers of his promise in Christ by the gospel:

Whereof I was made a minister, according to the gift of the grace of God given unto me by the effectual working of his power.

Unto me, who am less than the least of all saints, is this grace given, that I should preach among the Gentiles the unsearchable riches of Christ;

And to make all men see what is the fellowship of the mystery, which from the beginning of the world hath been hid in God, who created all things by Jesus Christ:

To the intent that now unto the principalities and powers in heavenly places might be known by the [testimony of the] church [what is] the manifold wisdom of God,

According to the eternal purpose which he purposed in Christ Jesus our Lord.

I hope you catch the drama and the wonder in this passage! Here is God's plan of the ages, and you and I who know Jesus Christ as our Savior are a part of the script! Perhaps we should pause here to note the significance of this drama.

No one can have an appropriate appreciation for the enormity of God's power until he has some enlightened understanding of the enormity of the obstacles God has overcome through the blood of His Son. The divine provision and execution of a plan whereby a fallen and cursed creation could be brought to a state completely acceptable to all the perfections of God staggers the mind and thrills the heart! No wonder the inspired apostle proclaims, "O the depth of the riches both of the

---

[5]He speaks here of what he has written in the verses we just saw in 2:11-22.

wisdom and knowledge of God! how unsearchable are his judgments, and his ways past finding out!"[6] No wonder the saints and heavenly creatures cry day and night, "Worthy is the Lamb that was slain to receive power, and riches, and wisdom, and strength, and honour, and glory, and blessing!"[7] What else can they say? Human language breaks down under the weight of the glory! If you do not yet see the wonder of this, beg God to open your eyes to see the astounding beauty of this plan. When you see it, your heart will echo the message of the hymn writer Thomas Kelly.

> Look, ye saints! The sight is glorious:
> See the Man of Sorrows now;
> From the fight returned victorious,
> Every knee to Him shall bow:
> Crown Him! Crown Him!
> Crowns become the Victor's brow.
>
> Crown the Saviour! Angels, crown Him!
> Rich the trophies Jesus brings;
> In the seat of power enthrone Him;
> While the vault of heaven rings:
> Crown Him! Crown Him!
> Crown the Saviour King of kings. . . .
>
> Hark, those bursts of acclamation!
> Hark, those loud triumphant chords!
> Jesus takes the highest station;
> O what joy the sight affords!
> Crown Him! Crown Him!
> King of kings, and Lord of lords![8]

Your heart will yearn to see this wonderful coronation when Jesus Christ finally receives the honor and is praised for everything He is! This is where the whole thing is headed, but for right now there is an impediment.

---

[6]Romans 11:33.

[7]Revelation 5:12.

[8]Thomas Kelly, "Look, Ye Saints! the Sight Is Glorious," in *Worship and Service Hymnal* (Carol Stream, Ill.: Hope Publishing Co., 1957).

THE EXTERNAL PROBLEM: DIVISION

We have looked at an overview of this awe-inspiring plan. Let's look now at its details. As we have seen, the Jewish world of Paul's day was *divided* into two warring groups—Jews and Gentiles. The Jews enjoyed the special favor of God. He had given to them the law and the covenants of promise. It was through their father, Abraham, that all the world was to be blessed. They prided themselves on being in the center of God's plans for the earth and considered all other nations to be "outsiders." The divine exclusiveness of the Jewish belief system, however, corrupted by the pride of these "chosen people," caused them to be despised by the Gentile world. They failed to be the blessing to all nations that God intended for them to be.

Weighing in at the other corner of the ring were the heavyweight champions of the world: the Gentiles. The Greeks, the first-century "insiders," had their own way of classifying people. One was either a Greek or a barbarian—an "outsider."

The Grecian empire had been absorbed into the Roman world by Paul's time and enjoyed all the splendor that human excellence could produce: cultural magnificence, athletic achievement, scientific advancement, philosophical astuteness, and world dominance. The Greeks were proud of their excellence. Within the Gentile community they looked upon themselves as "the beautiful people" and considered anyone to be a barbarian who did not belong to their exclusive ranks of educated, affluent, cultured, first-century yuppies.

God's plan was to make out of these two groups one new group—the Church. He not only had to bring members of these two groups together, but He also had to keep the new body, the Church, unified once He brought them together. What a challenge! But God had a perfect plan that would do just that. We need to know the essential components of His plan so that, first of all, we will praise Him for the wisdom of it when we finally see it with illuminated eyes. Secondly, we need to know this plan because it is the pattern for us when attempting to reconcile warring factions today. Let's begin by looking at the root problem.

THE INTERNAL PROBLEM: PRIDE

The essential problem is that both parties—Jews and Gentiles—had turned God's gifts into barriers through their *pride*. Their spirit was "if you don't have what I have, you are inferior." This stance comes naturally for all of us. Consider this scenario.

Pride in Her Parenting

Julie, a young home-schooling mother, is distraught over a conflict with Shirley, another mother who is the leader of the small home-school group in their church. This group of families periodically bands together to provide outings and activities for their children. The self-appointed leader of the group is Shirley, who has the oldest child in the group. She has two children of elementary school age and a daughter in her early teens. She is an industrious, energetic Christian woman with set and determined ways about the discipline of her children. Shirley has taken it upon herself in recent years to study every conservative book on parenting and has been the local "expert." She and her husband, Tim, who is as involved with the group activities as his job allows, seemed in days gone by to possess a mature way about their parenting that the others definitely admired. Tim is also a deacon in their church, which sponsors the home-school group for its members. All three of their children are well behaved and do exactly what they are told—even cheerfully.

Shirley began insisting, however, that the rest of the mothers adopt her parenting standards and techniques when they attend group activities. She sees this as a defining spiritual issue and will not give any ground on it. When the other mothers do not exact the same kind of behavior and response from their children, Shirley will not let her children associate with the offending children—even on group outings. Her children are told they cannot talk to the "wrongdoers." Of course, these demands are alienating the other mothers from Shirley. Tim appears to know what is going on and seems to be uncomfortable with his wife's demanding ways but hesitates to challenge his wife on these issues.

Up until the last few months when she became more aggressive in keeping her children from the "influence" of the other children, some mothers would call Shirley for advice because she seemed to be doing so well with her own children. They have stopped going to her and, of course, Julie has noticed the distance between Shirley and the others, which makes even normal conversation awkward with her at church. Shirley's exclusive standards and alienating ways are creating a widening rift between her and the other women.

Here we have a mother who would never allow her children to be exposed to anything worldly or tempting. She does not want them deceived by the "lusts of the flesh." She is right on target with her concerns. However, she herself has fallen prey to the "pride of life." She has turned her "gift" of knowledge into a "barrier" by her pride.

The Jews did the same thing. They focused on the externals, which in their pride became a relational "middle wall of partition." If Shirley does not see the subtle pride of her own heart, she will be blinded to the more subtle manifestations of pride in her children in the days ahead. She will continue to be very alert to the obvious external issues she has seen in her studies. But tragically, she will probably lose one or more of her children later because she is oblivious to the ways that pride can destroy the inside of a person who is doing everything right on the outside. When her child falls because of his pride, she will bitterly ask God why He let her fail when she did everything right.

And herein is the principle: *Any gift will divide when it is utilized in pride!* Gifts are given by God to be utilized for His glory. When used in pride, it siphons the glory away from God and directs it to the creature. You may have even wondered why we do not see more wealthy, influential, dynamic personalities converted. God gives the answer in I Corinthians 1:26-29.

> For [consider] your calling, brethren, how that not many wise men after the flesh, not many [powerful], not many [well-born], are called: but God hath chosen the foolish things [in the sight] of the world to confound the wise; and God hath chosen the weak things [in the sight] of the world to [shame] the things which are mighty; and base things [in the sight] of the world, and things which are despised, hath God chosen, yea, and things which are not, to [nullify] things that are: *that no flesh should glory in His presence.*

Paul puts forth the same reasoning when he says in II Corinthians 4:7,

> But we have this treasure in earthen vessels, that the excellency of the power may be [shown to be] of God, and not of us.

The lesson here is that God has made us all of varying "wattages." It is utterly foolish for a 150-watt bulb to proudly compare itself to a

15-watt bulb when *both* are equally inadequate before the sun. A 150-watt bulb who leaves the darkness of the chambers of its own heart to daily step into the sunshine of the King of glory will be duly humbled and will not boast of its gift of 150 watts. It will use its light to be a blessing to others wherever God places it. It will be grateful for the gift it has been given and will seek to keep it burning brightly, but it will not boast in it. The only one who can boast of His glory is the true Light—Jesus Christ.

King on the Hill

God knows that the biggest temptation of fallen man is his pride. And pride can corrupt even the most precious of gifts. One of the telltale signs that pride is at work in a fallen creature is that it manifests itself in "contentions"—power struggles. God says, "Only by pride cometh contention" (Proverbs 13:10).[9] Like children trying to push each other off the top of a huge pile of snow, people—even Christian people—who are walking in pride will push and pull to gain the unspoken title "king on the hill."

These "king on the hill" power struggles have many names. Some of the more popular secular ones in our day are feminism, gay activism, environmentalism, liberalism (both political and religious), racism, and postmodernism. Every group is dissatisfied that the power seems to lie with someone else, and each plays the game of "king on the hill." Without the cleansing and purifying work of Jesus Christ, however, no group can be anything but essentially selfish. Their arguments are reduced basically to "My brand of selfishness is better than your brand of selfishness; therefore, you must give way to my brand." Each group is always either "in power" or "being robbed of power."

Christian Battlegrounds

Power plays are not limited to the unbelieving world. The disciples quarreled over "which of them should be accounted the greatest."[10] Jesus rebuked them for acting like Gentile rulers—people who struggled for power over others. He said this kind of one-upmanship was not

---

[9]See also James 4:1-3.
[10]Luke 22:24.

a part of His plan. His followers were to be looking for someone to serve, not someone to rule.

"Religious wars" have been fought—and continue to be fought—over doctrinal positions, parenting philosophies, educational choices, and Bible translations—to name a few. The Body of Christ can certainly profit from sound biblical teaching in these areas, but we must be ever alert to the pitfall of pride when we have determined what we think the Bible teaches in these areas. *We may hold a truly biblical position, but it can be corrupted if held, taught, and defended in pride.*

In fact, it is this toxic element of pride that Paul addressed in I Corinthians 3. Listen to his pointed rebuke to the church at Corinth for their party spirit:

> And I, brethren, could not speak unto you as unto spiritual [people], but as unto carnal, even as unto babes in Christ. I have fed you with milk, and not with meat: for hitherto ye were not able to bear it, neither yet now are ye able. For ye are yet carnal: for whereas there is among you envying, and strife, and divisions, are ye not carnal, and walk as men? For while one saith, I am of Paul; and another, I am of Apollos; are ye not carnal? (I Corinthians 3:1-4).[11]

Paul never took the time to hammer out the details of their different persuasions. Apparently none were so off base to be heretical or he would have addressed that issue. He certainly did elsewhere.[12] Most likely the divisions were more along the line of who was their favorite "religious personality."

Whatever the differing viewpoint, Paul confronted them with their carnality—the fleshly pride—which was at the root of their envy, strife, and division. He called them "babies"—people characterized by infantile self-centeredness. G. Campbell Morgan comments on this passage in his commentary on the Corinthian epistles. His words are instructive for us.

---

[11]See also I Corinthians 1:10-13.

[12]I Timothy 1:19-20; 6:3-5 (here he also addressed the pride issue); Titus 1:10-16, etc.

Here was the trouble with this Corinthian church. They were carnal, *sarkikos;* they were of the flesh. They were living in the fleshly realm. They had descended to the lower level, and that was mastering their thinking. They were proud of their divisions, their quarrels, and were finding great relief in them. It was fleshly, and not spiritual. There are the two levels of the flesh and the spirit, and everyone is mastered by one or the other in Christian life and experience. I may be living mastered by the lower side of my nature, the fleshly; or I may be living mastered by the higher, which is spiritual, in fellowship with the Holy Spirit of God. These people had degenerated into the lower levels of life. They were not motivated by spiritual values and outlooks, but by carnal and fleshly desires and passions. That is what lay at the root of the whole trouble, and they were rather pleased with their divisions.[13]

So this is a nasty problem. All of us have seen it at one time or another in our homes, churches, places of work, and friendships. Let's look at the solution.

THE SOLUTION: HUMILITY

Step One—Remember the Past

God begins by reminding these Ephesian Gentile believers in 2:12 that at one time before He had intervened, they were

"Without Christ"—They did not have a Messiah who was to deliver them.

"Aliens from the commonwealth of Israel"—They were "outside that circle [the community of Israel] in which God is particularly interested."[14]

"Strangers from the covenants of promise"—There were no special blessings specifically targeted to come their way.

"Having no hope"—Without the promises of God's deliverance they were doomed to pay the eternal punishment for their treason against the Creator.

---

[13]G. Campbell Morgan, *The Corinthian Letters of Paul* (Old Tappan, N.J.: Fleming H. Revell Company, 1946), 27.

[14]D. Martyn Lloyd-Jones, *God's Way of Reconciliation: An Exposition of Ephesians 2* (Grand Rapids: Baker Books, 1972), 169.

"Without God in the world"—Here is the great summary statement of the world's predicament.

I remember the first time these truths dawned on me as a freshman in college. I was reading Ephesians 2 and remember thinking, "I am a Gentile, and unless God had done something drastic, I would be outside His plan forever." As a sinner I had definitely needed salvation, but I had never realized that there was a time when Gentiles did not seem to be part of the deliverance God was providing.

The Old Testament promised that all the nations would be blessed through the seed of Abraham, but that probably brought very little comfort to individual Gentiles who heard that promise. Not until the ministry of Jesus Christ was it made clear that "whosoever will may come." What an amazing thing that He included us Gentiles too!

Paul's reminder here is that before these Ephesian believers got boastful they needed to remember that at one time they did not have any hope—certainty—about their outcome. But Jesus Christ changed all of that! They needed to be humble and grateful.

Step Two—Repent of Your Pride

After we have been reminded about our pitiful condition so that we are duly humbled, God does a second thing. *He calls both parties to repent.* Both have to be reconciled to God.[15] Every reconciliation must begin here. It is not enough to appeal to people to become more kind, to be more patient, or to have more good will. When God begins to reconcile warring parties, He calls upon them to confess their pride and seek forgiveness.[16] Paul details this further in chapter 4.

> And grieve not the holy Spirit of God, whereby ye are sealed unto the day of redemption. Let all bitterness, and wrath, and anger, and [yelling], and [contentious words], be put away from you, with all malice: and be ye kind one to another, tenderhearted, forgiving one another, even as God for Christ's sake hath forgiven you (4:30-32).

---

[15]Ephesians 2:16.

[16]This is the message of Luke 17:3-4, Matthew 5:23-26, and Matthew 18:15-20, where Jesus deals with brothers who sin against each other.

How did God bring the Jews and Gentiles to this place of humility where they would be reconciled to Him and to each other? *He removed the thing in which they boasted.*

The Jewish boast was in the "law of commandments contained in ordinances"—the religious ceremonies and sacrificial rituals—which God had given specifically to their nation through Moses. They had turned these gifts into a figurative "middle wall of partition" that excluded the Gentiles.

God in His wisdom sent Jesus Christ to fulfill all the Jewish laws and ceremonies. All of their rituals were but the shadow—the type—of which Christ was the reality. If a Jew accepted God's next step in the plan of redemption—the once-for-all sacrificial atonement of Jesus Christ—he no longer had any ceremonies in which to boast.

What about the Gentile world? The Greeks, the pinnacle civilization of the world, boasted in their wisdom. They thought they had the world all figured out. But even with all their philosophers and worldly wisdom, they missed the most strategic event of all time. Listen to Paul's pointed arguments through the ears of a first-century Greek who esteemed his wisdom very highly.

> Where is the wise? where is the scribe? where is the [debater] of this world? hath not God made foolish the wisdom of this world? For after that in the wisdom of God *the world by wisdom knew not God,* it pleased God by the foolishness of preaching to save them that believe. For the Jews require a sign, and the Greeks seek after wisdom: but we preach Christ crucified, unto the Jews a stumbling-block, and unto the Greeks foolishness (I Corinthians 1:20-23).

Paul said that the "princes of this world" were so blinded to the significance of the crucifixion of Jesus Christ that "had they known it, they would not have crucified the Lord of glory."[17] So here we have Jesus Christ at the center of all things again. By the crucifixion and resurrection, He stripped away the source of boasting for both Jew and Gentile. He proved the Jewish ceremonies unnecessary and the Gentile wisdom inadequate. No wonder Paul declares that "the foolishness of

---

[17]I Corinthians 2:8.

God [if there ever could be such a thing] is wiser than men; and the weakness of God [again, another impossibility] is stronger than men."[18]

The application for us is very pointed. The only valid posture before the Supreme One is humility. In fact, God Himself says,

> Let not the wise man glory in his wisdom, neither let the mighty man glory in his might, let not the rich man glory in his riches: but let him that glorieth glory in this, that he understandeth and knoweth me (Jeremiah 9:23-24).

God says, "I am not impressed with your wisdom. I gave it to you. I am not impressed with your strength. That came from Me too. Neither am I impressed with your riches, for I gave you the power to have wealth. The only person that impresses Me is a man who truly knows who I am and what that means." To the one who refuses to bow before God but proudly boasts in something else, God often finds a way to remove the thing in which he boasts. We see the pattern clearly in Ephesians 2.

For Christians Only—Before leaving this point of reconciliation through humility, we need to be clear about something else. The world speaks much of peace today, but the Bible makes it clear that there is no peace apart from reconciliation with God. The best the world can hope for is a cessation of hostilities. Negotiators may urge both sides to give a little so they can both win a little. Others counsel that certain boundaries should be set and agreements made to stay within those limitations. As long as both parties honor the agreement, they have peace. Warring spouses draw up informal "truces" for the sake of the children, and a modicum of peace returns to the home. Sometimes peace between disputing groups is mandated by a court order or presidential directive. Sometimes it is bought through blackmail or threats of harm by some subversive element. None of these so-called peace settlements are satisfying, however—and never were intended to be satisfying because God is left out of the picture.

Biblical peace means that previously warring parties have laid down their arms, confessed their pride and evil deeds, received forgiveness, and been restored to a mutual fellowship of love and good will towards each other. Enmity has been exchanged for kindness. Hatred has been

---

[18]I Corinthians 1:25.

replaced with friendship. The new relationship is one of charity, good will, and mutual care. We have already seen it in Ephesians 2:1-10, whereby "children of wrath" become "children of God" because their debt has been paid by a God who is "rich in mercy." *The fundamental character of the relationship has changed—not just the terms of interaction.* It should be obvious that this kind of genuine peace among men is possible only between believers. Even then, because God's ways are not followed, it is not often experienced by those that are Christ's. These first two steps, however, are relatively easy compared to the third we are about to see. Many fail to follow through at this point.

Step Three—Restructure the Relationship

If God's first two steps were not enough to cause us to marvel at His wisdom, the third surely does. Not only does God call folks to remember their past condition and repent of their boasting but now *He calls both parties to become something different.* He doesn't let the Jews remain a separate group and then works out an arrangement whereby Gentiles can be included. Neither does He insist that the Jews become a part of the "Gentile club." Rather, He designed that both of them be a part of something entirely new—the Church! He removes both "clubs" from power and starts a new one. Now they are on equal footing. Neither has the advantage, or the position of power. Both must become something new. Both must live under new operating principles that put Christ and His cause at the center instead of living as if they and their causes are supreme. What an amazing plan!

> That is how Christ makes peace. He does not produce a conglomeration of different people; he produces a new people, a new family, a new household, a new race. The apostle explains that in detail towards the end of the chapter; but here it is in principle. That is how Christ makes peace. To persuade nations not to fight one another is not peace in this sense. Peace is only made in God's way, and in Christ's way, when we all belong to the same family, have the same blood in us, as it were, are members of the same humanity, members of the same body, in this living vital relationship with God. That is the only peace the New Testament is interested in.[19]

How futile it is—even within the church—to form our task forces to see how each population group within the assembly is protected and

---

[19]Lloyd-Jones, *Reconciliation*, 216.

appreciated. Biblical unity within the Body of Christ is not built by accentuating and protecting social, racial, and economic differences but by heralding those things the members have in common. Listen to Paul's admonition in the opening verses of chapter 4.

> Walk worthy of the [calling] wherewith ye are called, with all lowliness and meekness, with longsuffering, forbearing one another in love; endeavouring to keep the unity of the Spirit [i.e., the unity that has already been produced by His calling all of you into the same Body] in the bond of peace. There is one body, and one Spirit, even as ye are called in one hope of your calling; one Lord, one faith, one baptism [i.e., inclusion into the Body], one God and Father of all, who is above all, and through all, and in you all (Ephesians 4:1-6).

If one member treats another with disrespect, he should be challenged about the self-centeredness behind his actions and attitudes. He needs to be confronted about the pride of his heart that puts himself above others. Paul doesn't say, "Now you Cephists need to give some say to the Paulists and the Apollists. We need to set up a task force with equal representation from each faction, which can map out ways to educate the rest about your individual strong points. Perhaps in this way we can get some better appreciation of each other. We want to be sure you all have an equal say and get equal rights." Granted, this is about the best idea the world can come up with, and certainly it is important for us to understand each other's particular struggles, but the Church should have a far greater understanding of the real problem than this reveals. Education is not the answer; Spirit-enabled self-denial that loves God and others at our own expense is.

Paul addressed issues on this level. From the passages we have already looked at, he said essentially, "As long as you act this way, you reveal that you need to start growing up spiritually; you are carnal. You still haven't dealt with your pride, and you have forgotten that God has outlined the things that are important—things you ought to all be agreeing upon in a spirit of meekness and humility. Start walking in a way that demonstrates the high road of Christlike self-denial to which you were called."

When Christian people within a church body won't work together, speak to each other, and serve each other, they need to be confronted about their pride. Then they need to be reminded that they are all fellow heirs, fellow members, and fellow partakers of God's promises in Christ.[20] Paul portrayed them as members of a family relating together, stones in a building being fitted together, and parts of a temple being framed together.[21]

Paul urged them to recognize and celebrate their essential unity. He did not tell them to protect their individual diversities. The world has this entirely wrong, but we should expect that. They refuse to acknowledge God's plans and goals. Everything He does, He does through His redeemed Church and to the glory of His Son.

THE SECOND MYSTERY REVEALED

This idea of the Church—a whole melting pot of both Jews and Gentiles—was an entirely new idea to first-century believers. It was up to this time a "mystery." Remember, *mysteries in the Bible are divine secrets previously unknown at this level of detail.*

God had unveiled this mystery to Paul, who wrote it out in this very epistle we have been studying. Let's pause for a moment to look at all three of the mysteries of Ephesians.

The Mystery of Christ—The divine secret previously unknown at this level of detail is that the *foundation* for all spiritual unity is Jesus Christ (1:1–2:10).

The Mystery of the Church—The divine secret previously unknown at this level of detail is that the *solution* for spiritual unity is the Church (2:11–3:21).

The Mystery of Marriage—The divine secret previously unknown at this level of detail is that the *illustration* of spiritual unity is marriage (5:22-33).

We will look again at each of these in the final chapter of our study, but I want you to get some idea of how central the Church is to the

---

[20]Ephesians 3:6.
[21]Ephesians 2:19-22.

master plan of God. This Body of which His Son is the Head, this Bride of which His Son is the Bridegroom, is the centerpiece of everything He is doing in this age. Paul paints its purposes with broad strokes in the first three chapters of Ephesians. But he also gives us enough details in the final three chapters of Ephesians for us to live it personally in each of our own local church bodies.

There is sadly so much disunity in His Church worldwide that it will never be gathered together in biblical unity until Christ Himself reigns upon the earth again. Many of these divisions are not due to mere carnality but, even more tragically, to doctrinal impurity. As long as groups of God's people choose to abandon His truth and His righteousness in the name of tolerance and for the sake of a surface organizational unity, there can be no true spiritual unity of believers worldwide.

By contrast, however, local churches whose creeds are sound doctrinally can experience a loving spirit of unity among their members whenever carnal pride is not allowed to reign. Though this kind of peace cannot be realized globally among believers, it ought to be experienced locally.[22]

When spiritual unity is not the case in individual families and individual congregations, Spirit-filled pastors must bring their people back to the fundamental realities of Ephesians 1-3 before they will see them practice Ephesians 4-6. To put the cart of practice before the horse of doctrine will lead to frustration on the part of the people—and the pastor. God's plan will work His way! God's people must see that His Church is central to everything He is doing and must begin to cooperate with His program.

Where would we be if God had not engineered a master plan of such astounding wisdom? It is a plan that can solve problems of cosmic proportions, yet it breathes such tender concern that it includes

---

[22]John Phillips in *Exploring Ephesians* says, "This ultimate goal will not be realized until the rapture when all the individual members of the body of Christ will be glorified together with the head. In the meantime, we should not expect the church universal to display this glorious unity and maturity. Denominational differences, doctrinal conflicts, dispositional clashes, and other issues constantly divide the church. However, the goal is certainly achievable within the fellowship of any local church" (p. 120).

individuals like you and me. We have become, in His marvelous wisdom and love, His Bride—the Church! He—and we—long for the day when all the disunity is removed, and we can enjoy His presence in joy and harmony as the Bride with her Groom. We shall fully know what it means to be our Beloved's—and our Beloved will be ours!

TAKE TIME TO REFLECT

1. Think about your own relationships with family members, coworkers, neighbors and acquaintances, and fellow church members. List those in which a conflict still exists.

2. Next examine each conflict and write out how your own pride has contributed to that rift.

3. Are you willing to confess that pride to God and to the other person? Why or why not?

4. Once you have repented of your pride, God wants you to become something different—to restructure the relationship. According to Luke 22:25-27, what specific role does He want you to take in that relationship?

5. List specific ways you can be a servant to the person with whom you have had the conflict.

A WORD TO DISCIPLE-MAKERS

Relational Terrorists

Keep your eyes open to what is happening in the world around you as various groups try to bring about "peace" and "unity." Since the world has left God out, the process of unification has been fatally corrupted in at least two ways. First, the world misdiagnoses the problem; then it misprescribes the cure.

I shall illustrate this by a look at the feminist movement. Understand, however, that the same flaws are inherent in all of the so-called rights movements—gay rights, white supremacists, black supremacists, militia groups, freedom of expression in the arts movements, literary deconstructionism, and any other group that is out of touch with the reality that "the Lord reigneth."[23]

---

[23]Psalm 96:10.

The feminist movement—along with the other groups mentioned above—is gaining an astounding platform in our current culture. *Feminists are rightly concerned about the abuses of male leadership over the years.* Men who have had the positions of authority have often tyrannically abused that power to the injury of those who follow them, or they have passively abdicated that power when they should have been exercising it to protect and provide for those who follow them. I will address those concerns again in chapter eleven.

Feminists have taken the position that the root problem is that the power has resided in the hands of men. For *mainstream* feminists and *evangelical* feminists the solution is for men to share the power with women. For *radical* feminists the solution is to remove the power from men altogether. They want to restructure the family system (with the help of the homosexual agenda), restructure the church (allowing women to pastor), and retool as much of society as possible to shift the balance of power to women.

The point that feminists miss is that the *systems* of the home and the church are not flawed—they are God-ordained. Rather, the *men* who lead the system are fallen—they are self-serving, sinful creatures. The men cannot be "fixed," however, until they are redeemed by the blood of Christ and are walking in the Spirit, as we shall see in chapter nine.[24] Only then will they be able to love God and others rather than themselves.

The feminist movement is destructive on two fronts. First, its proponents cannot produce the peace they desire by jettisoning the ideal structures of the church and home as set forth by God. Whatever they replace those structures with is already doomed to fail.

Second, whatever structure they erect, those in power will still be destructive because the sin-corrupted men in leadership will be replaced with the other sin-corrupted gender. The end result will be far worse

---

[24]I say, "walking in the Spirit" because many Christian men have abused their position of power when they have been "walking in the flesh." Christian men can be just as self-serving as the unsaved when in a fleshly state. Carnal, believing men can be just as tyrannical or just as passive as unbelievers unless they are submitted to *their* authority, Jesus Christ. We shall look at this more thoroughly in Part Three of this study.

than the former because now the whole system is flawed on its two most crucial counts—its structure and its leadership.

To restate the problem, feminists believe the problem is that the power rests with men. The real problem is that the power rests in the hands of *sin-corrupted* men. It is not the system that is flawed; the men who lead the system are fallen.

On the national level radical feminists cannot hope to win the positions of power by reasoned debate and peaceful negotiation because the men they must persuade to step down will not do so without a fight. The only resort left is a form of terrorism—subversive displays of power. They must sabotage their opponents by enraged emotionalism.[25] Studies are recast and facts distorted.[26] For example, the "original sin" of humanity is assumed to be the supremacy of men in leadership. Truth does not matter—only effect. Relativism was the foundation for rejecting the system, and relativism is the means for destroying it. Whatever works for the cause is acceptable.

Sadly, it is just this kind of self-serving mindset that corrupted the *men* in the first place. When the men in leadership abandoned God's ways, the only course was a relativism that justified for them whatever they wanted to do—even the exploitation of women—to get what they wanted. Once again, the real problem is in the fallenness of the leaders, not any flaws in God's system.

Where Will It All End?

As the world continues to fracture into various power groups fed by the subjectivism and relativity of postmodern thinking, a global conflict will erupt that can be suppressed only by the reign of someone with enormous power—the Antichrist. His totalitarianism will be unmatched in human history, and God's people will suffer greatly at his hand. Once his plan to usurp God on every front is deployed and all the watching universe can see the evidence of his treachery, he will be

---

[25]"It is precisely the disconnection between reality and feminist claims that requires constant rage and hatred to keep the movement viable." Quote by Robert H. Bork, *Slouching Towards Gomorrah* (New York: ReganBooks, 1996), 203.

[26]"In articles and books about . . . gender, the trend is to move away from objective research and to report on one's own experiences." Quote by Lynne V. Cheney, *Telling the Truth* (New York: Simon and Schuster, 1995), 67.

deposed by none other than Jesus Christ Himself! Then the glorious plan for reuniting the redeemed creation will be realized. What an amazing scene is unfolding before our eyes!

Do you see now how God's plan for reconciling the warring parties of the Jews and Greeks is so beautiful? It takes both groups out of power and realigns them under God's authority. The world cannot imagine this, nor can they duplicate it. There is no other path to peace.

CHAPTER EIGHT
REJECTING THE FANTASY

A MAN WITHOUT AN "ENGINE"

I mentioned earlier that at the present time I am doing a custom restoration of a '74 Volkswagen bug. The car was given to me with a seized engine. It had been sitting for a couple of years under a tree when someone tried to run it—not realizing it was out of oil. Of course, without lubrication the engine ran for about five minutes before the excessive heat melted the main bearings and warped the case. I had a nice looking car—very little rust and only a few dings—but no engine.

Since I grew up in the home of a mechanic, I had been drilled that the mechanics of a car always had priority over the cosmetics. My dad would not let me do anything to the body of my first car—which was a 1961 VW bug—until we had fixed some problems with the engine. I have carried that same philosophy into the resurrection of this VW as well. I first had the engine rebuilt. I then rebuilt the front-end suspension and reworked the carburetion and ignition systems. Only now, as time and money permit, am I beginning to work on the details of the exterior body and the interior upholstery, head-liner, and carpeting of the car.

A man without God is like an automobile without an engine. He has no life. All a man without God can do is work on the image—the outer part of his life. He is only a shell of what he was originally created to be. Before I fixed the engine, I could have sat in the car and pretended I was going somewhere. I could have turned up the sound system, run the windshield wipers, made motor sounds with my mouth, and imagined all sorts of adventures, but in the end I would have gone nowhere.

This is the picture Paul paints of the man who is "alienated from the life of God."[1] He is estranged—disconnected—from the Source of genuine life. Men in this condition live in the "vanity of their mind." How did man get this way? Paul tells us.

In verse 17 of chapter 4, in one phrase the apostle summarizes the whole problem with the unconverted mindset. He says,

> This I say therefore, and testify in the Lord, that ye henceforth walk not as other Gentiles walk, in the vanity of their mind.

His word choice, "vanity of their mind," is most descriptive. Here he exposes what is the greatest consequence of the Fall upon fallen man: his soul is essentially empty, pointless, and aimless.[2] The main component of life—God in the soul—is gone. The result is a profound emptiness and meaninglessness in every man apart from Christ. We saw this to some degree in chapter one when we discussed despair. We shall expand on it further in this chapter.

THE PATH TO EMPTINESS

In verse 18 there are two phrases that describe the root cause of emptiness. The verse reads,

> Having the understanding darkened, being alienated from the life of God through the ignorance that is in them, because of the [hardness] of their heart.

Paul first says that "the understanding [is] darkened" with the result that he is "alienated from the life of God." The next two phrases describe *how* he came to be alienated from God. Paul says it was "because of the ignorance that is in them" and "because of the [hardness] of their heart." There is a divine logic here that we must follow to see this picture. Look at how this is illustrated schematically and then we must consider its meaning.[3]

---

[1] Ephesians 4:18.

[2] "Mind" here refers to the entire soul of man—intellect, will, and emotions.

[3] Charles Hodge explains the sequence in this way: "The clauses may be taken as they stand . . . : 'The heathen walk in vanity, being (*i.e.*, because they are) darkened as to the understanding, alienated from the life of God through the ignorance that is in them, through the hardness of their heart.' Darkness of mind is the cause of igno-

Darkness in the understanding
↓
Ignorance in the intellect
↓
Hardness in the will and emotions
↓
Disconnection from the life of God
↓
Emptiness in the whole being

LOST IN A CAVE

The picture of Ephesians 4:17-18 is like a couple of spelunkers[4] who have moved some distance into a cave but have accidentally damaged their lights. Consequently, they are plunged into darkness. They know by previous arrangement with team members outside the cave that if they are not back within a designated time their associates will come searching for them. Their best course of action is to sit in the darkness until found. But they stubbornly decide to find their own way out.

Their "understanding" about their surroundings is severely limited. They grope on in "the ignorance that is in them," exposing themselves to great dangers. In the darkness even their sense of direction is affected. They plod on thinking they are heading toward the cave's mouth while they move deeper and deeper into the cavern. They set their wills even more stubbornly. They are determined that they will find the way out on their own. They are too proud to wait for help. So because of the "hardness of their heart" they press on.

At some point in their adventure, the reality of their hopelessness will set in. They can either redouble their efforts to press on in the darkness, perhaps entertaining themselves with songs or jokes to keep their minds off their dire condition. Or they can wait for help.

---

rance, ignorance and consequent obduracy of heart are the cause of alienation from God. This is both the logical and theological order of sequence. The soul in its natural state cannot discern the things of God,—therefore it does not know them, therefore the heart is hard, and therefore it is destitute of holiness" [Charles Hodge, *Ephesians* (Carlisle, Pa.: The Banner of Truth Trust, 1856), 183].

[4]Those who explore and study caves.

If they stubbornly press on, the end result will be their destruction as they become "alienated from . . . life." They unwittingly have cut themselves off from life itself. They are walking "in the vanity of their mind." Their efforts to solve their problem without light are futile, aimless, and empty—vain!

This is Paul's description of the human journey without God. Please think carefully through this sequence. It will help you understand what is happening around you in the world today. How apt it is that God has described the human condition as "darkness." Slowly read the following inspired descriptions of man's predicament, asking God to show you the sobering dilemma.

> But if our gospel be hid, it is hid to them that are lost: in whom the god of this world hath blinded the minds of them which believe not, lest the light of the glorious gospel of Christ, who is the image of God, should shine unto them (II Corinthians 4:3-4).

> And this is the condemnation, that light is come into the world, and men loved darkness rather than light, because their deeds were evil. For every one that doeth evil hateth the light, neither cometh to the light, lest his deeds should be reproved. But he that doeth truth cometh to the light, that his deeds may be made manifest, that they are wrought in God (John 3:19-21).

> Then spake Jesus again unto them, saying, I am the light of the world: he that followeth me shall not walk in darkness, but shall have the light of life (John 8:12).

> [God showed the apostle Paul shortly after his conversion that He was sending him to the Gentiles,] to open their eyes, and to turn them from darkness to light, and from the power of Satan unto God, that they may receive forgiveness of sins, and inheritance among them which are sanctified by faith that is in me (Acts 26:18).

> The way of the wicked [those without God] is as darkness: they know not at what they stumble (Proverbs 4:19).

This is why those in the world, try as they might, have no workable answers to many issues of life. Anytime they try to solve a problem that deals with man's soul—his emotions, will, and understanding—they will get it wrong. They simply have no light; they cannot find their way out of the cave.

To say that is not unkind; it is simply true. And Christians who take their cues from the world on these issues will be walking "in the vanity of their mind" with the same predictable results. The final result of this darkness is always despair, as we saw in chapter one of our study.

THE DOWNWARD PATH

Paul, however, does not just warn us generally with his statement to "walk not as other Gentiles walk." He spells out the particulars that follow when anyone walks in the "vanity of [his] mind." He describes a moral and ethical decline that inevitably follows.[5] In Ephesians 4:19 he speaks of the indulgences that the world uses to overcome the emptiness. He describes them as those

> who being [callous] have given themselves over unto [shameless lusts], to work [every sort of impurity] with [self-gratifying excess].

Paul gets even more specific about their moral pollution in the next chapter. Notice his concern and his descriptions in 5:3-17.

> But fornication, and all uncleanness, or covetousness, *let it not be once named among you*, as becometh saints;
>
> Neither [vulgarity], nor foolish talking [lit., "moron words"], nor jesting [lit. "well-turned"; i.e., words with a twisted, double meaning], which are not [proper]: but rather giving of thanks.
>
> For this ye know, that no [immoral], nor [impure] person, nor covetous man, who is an idolater, hath any inheritance in the kingdom of Christ and of God.
>
> Let no man deceive you with vain words: for because of these things cometh the wrath of God upon the children of disobedience.
>
> *Be not ye therefore partakers with them.*
>
> *For ye were sometimes darkness, but now are ye light in the Lord: walk as children of light:*

---

[5]He has mapped out the same decline in Romans 1.

(For the fruit of the Spirit [consists] in all goodness and right-eousness and truth;)

Proving what is acceptable unto the Lord.

And have no fellowship with the unfruitful works of darkness, but rather reprove them.

For it is a shame even to speak of those things which are done of them in secret.

But all things that are reproved are made manifest by the light: for whatsoever doth make manifest is light.

Wherefore he saith, Awake thou that sleepest, and arise from the dead, and Christ shall give thee light.

See then that ye walk circumspectly, not as fools, but as wise,

Redeeming the time, because the days are evil.

Wherefore be ye not unwise, but understanding what the will of the Lord is.

Sadly, many believers today *are* "partakers with them." Many of these sinful activities *are* "named" among the children of God. Many *do* "fellowship with the unfruitful works of darkness" and would *never* "reprove them." Paul says when this is true we walk as "fools." This mindset is called "worldliness."

GOD'S ATTITUDE TOWARD THE WORLD[6]

The term "worldly" is despised by most contemporary Christians, and yet the believer who is "of the world" and who "loves the world" is a great concern to God and a great hindrance to His program of reuniting all things together in Christ. The worldly Christian is separating himself from God's ways and God's plans. His concerns and lifestyle are contrary to everything God intended for the redeemed race. He is "this-worldly" rather than "otherworldly," and it shows up in choices

---

[6]The term "world" is used in three ways in the Bible: (1) to describe people in general—"for God so loved the world" (John 3:16), (2) to describe the planet earth—"And spared not the old world, but saved Noah" (II Peter 2:5), and (3) to describe the system of values of the unbelieving mindset, which leaves God out—"love not the world" (I John 2:15). It is this third use of the term that we are studying together in this chapter.

that give first place to things of this world instead of things of the world to come.

It is clear that the Scriptures speak much of the pull and debilitating influence of this "world." It is foolish to ignore this powerful influence that constantly targets and strengthens the "flesh." Note carefully these admonitions from the Scriptures.

Now we have received, not the spirit of the *world*, but the spirit which is of God; that we might know the things that are freely given to us of God (I Corinthians 2:12).

Who [Jesus Christ] gave himself for our sins, that he might deliver us from this present evil *world*, according to the will of God and our Father (Galatians 1:4).

But God forbid that I should glory, save in the cross of our Lord Jesus Christ, by whom the *world* is crucified unto me, and I unto the *world* (Galatians 6:14).

For Demas hath forsaken me, having loved this present *world* (II Timothy 4:10).

For the grace of God that bringeth salvation hath appeared to all men, teaching us that, denying ungodliness and *worldly* lusts, we should live [sensibly], righteously, and godly, in this present *world* (Titus 2:11-12).

Pure religion and undefiled before God and the Father is this, To visit the fatherless and widows in their affliction, and to keep himself unspotted from the *world* (James 1:27).

Ye adulterers and adulteresses, know ye not that the friendship of the *world* is enmity with God? whosoever therefore will be a friend of the *world* is the enemy of God (James 4:4).

Love not the *world*, neither the things that are in the *world*. If any man love the *world*, the love of the Father is not in him. For all that is in the *world*, the lust of the flesh, and the lust of the eyes, and the pride of life, is not of the Father, but is of the *world* (I John 2:15-16).

For whatsoever is born of God overcometh the *world:* and this is the victory that overcometh the *world,* even our faith (I John 5:4).[7]

THE EFFECT OF THE WORLD ON THE HEART

We all have within us a sinful nature. It is called the "flesh" in many Bible passages. It is that tendency within us to leave God out of our thinking and to handle life our own way. The flesh is the enemy within us. Satan and the world are the enemies outside of us.[8]

The "world" is defined as those influences *outside* of us that encourage the flesh *inside* of us to leave God out and to live life for ourselves. *The great fantasy of worldliness is that a man can live independently of God.* It is the lie of the serpent to Eve woven into the fabric of the fallen world system. The danger for the child of God is that he can be pulled into the mindset of the world around him. His soul can become so shrouded in darkness that he no longer "sees" the things of God except in momentary lightning flashes of conviction. They appear on the horizon of his soul for a moment. In that flash of conviction the believer is shown some impediment to godliness in his soul and lifestyle. If he ignores it, he is plunged into greater darkness, and he stumbles on. If the conviction is heeded, his light is increased and his path becomes clearer.[9]

We want to look together at the specific ways that the world moves upon the human heart. Most Christians who try to avoid worldliness do so by becoming concerned about the *content* of the messages the world offers—its immorality, materialism, violence, and so forth. But one culture watcher, Kenneth Myers, warns that even greater dangers lurk within the world system.

> A common approach among Christians [is to] worry that the content of popular culture will encourage certain behavior (e.g., disrespect to parents, drug abuse, sexual promiscuity, proclivity to violence, etc.). While these are obviously legitimate concerns, what

---

[7]For more passages on the world, see John 15:19; 17:14-16; I Corinthians 1:27-28; and I Corinthians 2:6-8.

[8]For a more thorough discussion of the flesh, see chapters two through five in *Changed into His Image.*

[9]See Proverbs 4:18-19.

should attract more attention is the effect of consistent exposure to popular culture, whether or not the content is objectionable, on the development of internal dispositions. The habits of mind, heart, and soul—in short the qualities of *character*—that are encouraged or discouraged by the aesthetic dynamics of our cultural activities are at least as important to Christian reflection [emphasis his].[10]

Earlier Myers said,

The erosion of character, the spoiling of innocent pleasures, and the cheapening of life itself that often accompany modern popular culture can occur so subtly that we believe nothing has happened. . . . Popular culture's greatest influence is in the way it shapes *how* we think and feel (more than *what* we think and feel) and how we think and feel about thinking and feeling [emphasis his].[11]

The Wise Man and the Foolish Man

Jesus taught that there are only two basic worldviews: the foolish man, who builds his house upon sand, and the wise man, who builds his house up a rock.[12] He very plainly said that the man who becomes wise builds his life upon "hearing" and "doing" the words of God. They are foundational to the development of Christlikeness—Christian character. The foolish man by contrast ignores God and His Word.

I have devoted chapters eight and nine in *Changed into His Image* to the basic disciplines of hearing and doing, so I will not repeat them here. Since we are learning in this chapter how to reject the fantasy of the world, which says you can make up your own rules and leave God out, I want to devote our time to the two particular "habits of the heart" that characterize the fool.[13] A fool in Scripture is simply someone who leaves God out of his life. These habits of the foolish heart are reinforced by the world around us. They are spelled out for us in James 1:14-15, which says,

---

[10]Kenneth Myers, *All God's Children and Blue Suede Shoes* (Wheaton: Crossway Books, 1989), 76.

[11]Ibid., xiii.

[12]Matthew 7:24-27.

[13]The phrase "habits of the heart" is also from Myers (pp. 72, 76ff, 97, 192).

But every man is tempted, when he is drawn away of his own lust,[14] and enticed. Then when lust hath conceived, it bringeth forth sin: and sin, when it is finished, bringeth forth death.

The picture here is a very discreet portrait of the union of a husband and wife in a physical relationship, which results in the conception of a child. James says, "With every lust there is the enticement to indulge it. When your will—one partner in the union—agrees with your strong desire—another partner in the union—a sin is conceived and born. Grown-up sin leads to death."

The twin disciplines of a wise heart are "hear" and "do." The twin culprits in a foolish heart are "desire" and "indulge." Everything around us in our culture reinforces these two destructive habits of the heart. The most serious flaw in "desiring and indulging" is that God is left out of the process entirely. The world says, "Desire what you want and then go for it—indulge yourself! This is the path to real living!" That practice in the soul is lethal to godliness. It is precisely the opposite of dying to self and denying self. It is spiritual adultery.[15] The proper union occurs when our will agrees with *God's* desires. The result of that union is righteousness.

This, then, is our battle, and we must see beyond the issues of "Does this or that music or movie have good content?" to "What is the impact of this or that element of pop culture upon my inner dispositions? Is it training me to leave God out of my thinking and values? Is it teaching me that all that matters is my happiness and my experiences?"

WHEN DAD COMES HOME

For example, let's look in on how Kevin, a middle-aged father of three, comes home from work. After a pressure-filled day at the job, it is Kevin's practice to return home, change clothes, eat supper, and then

---

[14]"Lust" in the Bible does not always mean sexual desire, although it can mean that. It always means, however, "strong desire." It is up to the context of the word's use to tell us whether that strong desire is good or evil. In this passage, it can be either. Any lust—whether an evil lust like greed or a good lust like the strong desire to see our children turn out right—can be a source of temptation for us. Greed can lead to all sorts of deceptive and destructive actions, and an overpowering desire for our children's success can lead to all kinds of destructive parental excesses as well.

[15]James 4:1-4.

settle down in front of the television to watch ESPN.[16] He figures he owes it to himself after putting his all into his work during the day. He reasons that he isn't neglecting any household responsibilities, and if he is needed by someone, he will shut off the television—although perhaps reluctantly—and will help out.

Other believers may not park themselves in front of the television after a difficult day but may do something else taught by our culture. Perhaps they immediately head for their favorite sport or hobby to relieve the stress. Or perhaps they call a friend, go shopping, put on the headphones to listen to music, play video games, go for a walk, or take a bubble bath.

Now certainly there is nothing wrong with going for a brisk walk, taking a bubble bath, or calling a friend. None of these activities needs to be destructive in itself. Often a physical activity is a great help in relieving muscular tension that has built up during the day, and it expends pent-up energy. Mentally, any change of pace is usually refreshing in itself.

But if these are all we do with the pressures of life, and we never stop to reflect upon what God is doing in us and through us at work through these pressures and through these people, we are in effect leaving God out. We must take the time to ask ourselves,

- "What was exposed about my heart today when I got so agitated at Bill's interruptions?"
- "What lust was ruling in my heart today when I got upset over losing that sales contract?"
- "When I blew up at the kids today, what did that reveal about my heart?"
- "What ways am I leaving God out of my problem solving and struggles today?"

---

[16]Or the History Channel or the Discovery Channel or some other channel, where the content is usually acceptable from a Christian viewpoint. Kevin knows that the content of the premium movie channels—and most other channels for that matter—is laced with unbiblical content. It is important to understand that "what we find beautiful or entertaining or moving is rooted in our *spiritual* life" (Myers, 27). Dr. Bob Jones Sr. put it this way: "What you love and what you hate reveal what you are."

These kinds of questions bring God into the picture and remind us of our fallenness and of our accountability to Him. They show us how much we need God and how far short we come of putting Him first in our daily activities.

While the *content* of the stress-relieving practices described above may not be polluting our minds, what is the *practice* doing to our hearts? The proper kind of reflection may not be the *first* thing we do after a stressful day—taking a walk or watching the news may be a good immediate refreshment—but it is without doubt the most *important* thing we can do about our pressures. If our primary way of handling pressure is to pursue the activities mentioned above, we have left God out. We are practicing worldliness.

This is clearly the message of James 4:13-16.

> [Come] now, ye that say, To day or to morrow we will go into such a city, and continue there a year, and buy and sell, and get gain: [yet] ye know not what shall be on the morrow. For what is your life? It is even a vapour, that appeareth for a little time, and then vanisheth away. [Instead] ye ought to say, If the Lord will, we shall live, and do this, or that. But now ye [boast in your arrogance]: all such [boasting] is evil.

Here is a man who is very proud of his astute plans. He thinks he has things all worked out. His tragic flaw, however, is that God is not in his plans whatsoever. He has made his plans independently of God. This is the "vanity of the mind." This independence from God is the essence of worldliness.

But there is still more. If our stress-relieving practices also include a fleshly *content*, the combination is especially toxic. If the television programming or video game is violent, if the jog is with the neighbor's spouse, if the music is sensual, if the web-surfing includes erotic pictures or romance-filled chats with a newfound acquaintance, if the shopping fuels our greed for a lifestyle we cannot afford or shouldn't emulate, or if the nap in the chair is intended to escape the demands of the wife and children, the effect upon the heart is particularly disastrous.

THE DESIRE-ORIENTED LIFE OF A FOOL

Let's look specifically at the mindset of a worldling.[17] I think you will see how the habits of the heart encouraged by the world are toxic to godly living.

The Worldling Is Easily Distracted

Since life apart from God has no lasting meaning or satisfaction, the worldling must keep himself distracted in order to dull the pain of his emptiness. He does not see his restlessness as a problem, however. He doesn't know that it could be otherwise. Proverbs says,

> Wisdom is before him that hath understanding; but the eyes of a
> fool are in the ends of the earth (Proverbs 17:24).

The heart of the fool is always looking for something to do, something to see, something to experience. He is on a continual quest for adventure and stimulation. Nothing he tries satisfies him for very long. Consequently, he is driven to have something . . .

New—The progress of recent years has generated a degree of affluence and leisure time unknown to previous generations. We can now have diversion at the rate of 250 channels, 123 flavors, high-speed access, 250 horsepower, 2 years without interest, and a 20-percent discount if we are over 50. We wait eagerly for the new season of programming, the new fashions, and the new models—models produced with intentional obsolescence and advertised as "new and improved."

There is no doubt that in many areas, particularly technology, new is better. But what is true for technology is false for truth. We must be careful not to confuse *old*—as in computers with 286 processors—and *permanent*—as in eternal truth. If we throw out the Bible because it is old, confusing it with last year's *Newsweek*, we have made a fatal error. Tragically, that is exactly what is being done today. That shouldn't surprise us, however, because God addressed the same problem with the people of Israel.

---

[17]I use the term "worldling" to describe anyone—lost or believing—who is dominated by the world's fantasy that life can be lived independently of God. He is the one whose values come from the world.

Thus saith the Lord, Stand ye in the ways, and see, and ask for the old paths, where is the good way, and walk therein, and ye shall find rest for your souls. But they said, We will not walk therein (Jeremiah 6:16).

When we are more easily swayed by our peers—and teenagers aren't the only ones susceptible to the problem—than we are by our spiritual leaders and by God's Word, we are worldly. When our biggest goals for the week are to clinch a certain deal or make a certain purchase, we are worldly. When we pore over fashion magazines or stay up with the sports scores or current movies just so we will not be out of step with our associates at school or work, we are worldly. When we spend hours a week in front of the television and scant minutes with our Bible, we are worldly. In all of these things we are allowing the world to tell us what is important. Worldliness is taking our cues from the world; godliness takes its cues from God.

For too long Christians have associated worldliness with externals: wearing the clothing and hairstyles of the latest rock group, television personality, or movie celebrity. While this may truly be a worldly matter because it reflects that we are valuing what the world values—appearances, acceptance, and whatever political statement may be intrinsic in the fashion—there are many more less obvious ways to be influenced by the world. What is *new* is not the only thing a worldling is susceptible to. He is also easily moved by what is . . .

Now—One of those less obvious influences of the world is its encouragement in the habit of impatience. It is fostered by the kind of pace the world encourages. Today we have express lanes, instant relief, easy money, fast food, casual sex, and instant credit. All of these tell us we can have what we want—now!

Impatience is a particularly dangerous habit of the heart because everything worthwhile takes time. Good marriages take time. Spiritual maturity takes time. Financial stability takes time. Effective ministry takes time. Wisdom takes time. People who are not willing to take time cannot have any of the above.

Fast Farming?—I'm glad that my early years of life were lived on a farm. Nothing happens fast on a farm. Fields don't get plowed fast. Seed doesn't get planted fast. Corn doesn't grow fast. Cattle don't fatten fast.

Fences don't get fixed fast. Silos aren't filled fast, and buildings aren't painted fast.

The whole life of farming—at least thirty years ago in South Dakota—was slow-paced. People worked hard, but nothing happened *now*. Furthermore, if you wanted to stay solvent, you didn't worry about your equipment being *new*. The *old* combine was better because it was paid for. Many of the *old* methods were better because they were time-tested. Innovation wasn't scorned, but it wasn't worshiped either. You couldn't allow yourself to be distracted. You had to keep your mind on your work.

Now I'm not saying that we should all go back to the farm, but the culture of the farm automatically taught many values that were in line with biblical thought. Running a farm did not make anyone godly, but it did reinforce the same habits of the heart that it takes to be godly. That is why so many of Jesus' illustrations dealt with agriculture—sowing and reaping, shepherding, vine dressing, and so forth. These pictures not only connected with the agricultural culture of the day but also illustrated the processes at work in both the physical and spiritual realm. They were similar because they have the same Author.

To create a family life that reinforces biblical values today takes as much hard work to engineer as it took to run a farm when I was a boy. And the parents who will not roll up their sleeves to work hard at discipling their children towards God and away from the flow of the godless world will sacrifice their children to the god of this world. Popular culture does not build strong disciples of Jesus Christ.

The Worldling Is Easily Lured
Because the worldling is easily distracted, he is easily lured into temptation. Because his eyes are in "the ends of the earth,"[18] he always sees something he likes better than what he has now. He is taught to *desire*. In fact, the purpose of advertising is to make us unhappy with what we have and make us think that the product being hawked will bring happiness and meaning into our life. The worldling is easily lured because he has no objective, abiding *principles*.

---

[18]Proverbs 17:24.

Most people make their value judgments today based upon one thought: "But I like it!" They do not make principled decisions. They make decisions based upon what will give them the most pleasant experience and what will tingle their sensations. They are happy for you to "like" the old hymns, but they "like" the pulsing, and often sensual, sound of Christian rock. No matter what biblical principles you bring to bear against Christian rock, they are all swept aside in their minds because they still "like" the music.

This relativism—making myself or my group the final word on life—is the most dangerous part of modern culture. God presents enduring and objective truths in the Bible with which we must evaluate every decision of life—even our music. Because of the sinful bent of the human heart what we "like" must be governed by something outside of us!

For example, the world teaches that "beauty is in the eye of the beholder." What is beautiful to the eye, however, may be colored by the wickedness of the heart. The Bible teaches that beauty is in the eye of the Creator, and it is our responsibility to take our cues from Him about what is beautiful and what is not. What is beautiful to God can—and must—become beautiful to us. Notice the words of Philippians 4:8.

> Finally, brethren, whatsoever things
>> *are* true [i.e., accurate, true to fact],
>> *are* honest [i.e., honorable, worthy],
>> *are* just [i.e., right],
>> *are* pure [i.e., uncontaminated],
>> *are* lovely [i.e., pure and beautiful],
>> *are* of good report [i.e., nondestructive];
> if there be any virtue [i.e., moral excellence],
> and if there be any praise [i.e., worthiness],
> think on these things.

This passage says there are some things that *are* true. They don't *become* true because I want them to be. Some things *are* worthy and right. They don't *become* worthy and right because I think they should be so. Some things *are* pure and lovely. They don't *become* pure and lovely because I like the way they look. Some things *are* morally excellent and praiseworthy. They don't *become* those things because I have decided they should be. There are laws of beauty and moral tone in music, art, speech, drama, and literature that cannot be violated without detracting from the glory of God and without destroying our own souls.[19]

God establishes the objective standards for evaluating every part of life. This is part of His sovereignty—His rulership over His whole creation. To ignore His standards is not a matter of "different tastes." It is a matter of mutiny against the Creator.

Granted, these standards are not always easily articulated unless one has done much study in that field. His answers to these foundational issues of life are called wisdom. Though James 1:5 says we can just pray for it and have it, I would suggest to you that the context is talking about "fire extinguisher" wisdom—wisdom for that particular trial. It is also a wisdom that He cannot remind you of in a trial unless you have acquired it previously.[20]

The normal way to get wisdom—whether in God's realm of natural revelation (creation) or in the realm of supernatural revelation (the Bible)—is to search for it diligently. See Proverbs 2:1-11 for instruction on how to gain wisdom and thereby be preserved from the evil around you.

---

[19]It is outside the scope of this book to discuss these standards for every area of life. I would commend to you, however, *Christian Education: Its Mandate and Mission*, edited by Dr. Ron Horton and published by Bob Jones University Press, 1992. A philosophy committee made up of members of the administration, the seminary faculty, and the various academic disciplines of the University labored for ten years to produce this work. The result was a landmark treatise applying God's eternal principles to every major academic discipline taught at Bob Jones University and providing the philosophical basis for the entire line of textbooks published by BJU Press for Christian schools and for home education. Especially noteworthy for the current discussion are the chapters on "The Christian Teaching of Music," "The Christian Teaching of Art," and "Christian Educational Censorship." The book is worthwhile reading for laymen as well as teachers because it skillfully applies the principles of God's Word to everyday parts of life.

[20]The mindset for many of us in life is the same mindset we had in school. We would not prepare adequately for an exam but would fervently pray for the Lord to help us on the test. He cannot help us recall anything we have not studied. Nor will He give us answers in a trial when we have not prepared ourselves for trouble ahead of time.

Just as a child who has not worked out a budget and tried to stay within it has no concept of how to make wise decisions with his money, so believers who have not taken the effort to discover God's principles for music, art, literature, drama, and so forth will have no concept of how to make wise decisions in those areas either. They will be driven, like the child with a dollar in his pocket, to spend it arbitrarily on what they like. Because they are not evaluating their choices by God's wisdom, they are left without principles and must live entirely by sensation and emotion.

THE INDULGENT-ORIENTED LIFE OF A FOOL

Being hammered with what is *new* and what is *now* teaches the heart to lust. It creates strong desires of staggering proportions—desires absolutely out of sync with setting our affections on things above.[21] In order to *fulfill* the desires it has been taught by the world, the human heart must defy God, who has established objective standards for mankind. The natural product of relativism is rebellion against authority. God is not first. The relativist sets his own rules based upon what *he* likes. If he doesn't *like* it, he will not do it.

He is defiant to the *created order* in nature. The worldling is defiant against God's standards of beauty, order, and design. We have already touched on this in the previous paragraphs, but more needs to be said.

The original creation didn't clash and resonate with dissonance. Those tensions came as a result of the Fall. It is our duty as God's creatures made in His image to discover and reflect *His* nature and model *His* works. That doesn't mean, however, that an artist cannot paint something dark and foreboding, for that is a real part of the fallen creation. It certainly shouldn't be the constant pattern for his works, however. That would most likely indicate a heart that has not experienced deliverance from the darkness of the world. Though David's psalms often began on a note of discouragement because of some oppression he was experiencing from his enemies, he always ended them on a note of joyful hope in the God of Israel, who did all things well. The inspired balance is instructive.

---

[21]Colossians 3:1-3.

The worldling misses the mark when he makes "self-expression" the goal for his creativity. We are to express God's values and standards in our work. To use the creative powers He has given us for mere self-expression is a prostitution of those powers. Though we do not always have to copy someone else, what we call "originality" must be in complete harmony with the laws by which God has ordered His universe.[22]

In imitating God and His works, we would do well to remember that God isn't sloppy. He isn't garish and morose. He doesn't come dragging on to the scene late. God isn't haphazard and careless. His excellencies must become the standard for our works as well.

The worldling is also defiant to the commanded order. God is clear in His Word about morality, integrity, and other expressions of godliness. The world draws the heart away from these by editing God out of the picture altogether.

For example, modern critics who disagree with Paul's teachings on the woman's role in the church or his call to separate from the world dismiss the inspired instructions and commandments, calling Paul a product of the culture of his day. Others bolder simply assert that Paul was wrong. Here are men without "God at the center," living life as if God didn't exist and had not spoken. This is again the essence of worldliness.

The result of the foolishness of the world is death. Everything dies when removed from the light of God. This is the reason that despair is so rampant in our times. People's souls are empty. It cannot be any other way when God is left out of the picture. This is why Paul admonishes us to "walk not as other Gentiles walk, in the vanity of their mind." In the next chapter we shall examine God's method for bringing about the needed changes in a believer's heart that will result in Christlikeness rather than conformity to the world.

---

[22]For more help in this area, see Christian Education, mentioned in a previous footnote. Also see Art and the Bible: Two Essays by Francis A. Schaeffer (Downers Grove, Ill.: InterVarsity Press, 1973) and Modern Art and the Death of a Culture by H. R. Rookmaaker (Wheaton: Crossway, 1994).

TAKE TIME TO REFLECT

1. How do you unwind from a stressful day?

2. Is serious reflection upon what is going on in your heart during pressured times part of the habits of your heart? If so, write out when and how you go about this self-appraisal.

3. What messages in the world around you are encouraging you to desire things the world deems of value—pleasure, possessions, prestige/power?

4. What parts of your environment encourage you to indulge your desires?

5. What strategies are in place in your life to keep yourself reminded that you must learn to suffer, sacrifice, and submit if you are to be useful to Christ?

A WORD TO DISCIPLE-MAKERS

Discipleship Themes of a Biblical Worldview

If we are truly discipling our children and converts, we will be showing them not mere specifics of what items should be "edited" out of their worldly indulgences. We will be teaching them by our own life and passion the excellencies of another world.

First John 2:16 is an inspired account of what *the world* values: "the lust of the flesh, and the lust of the eyes, and the [boastful] pride of life." Our Lord emphasized some very different matters with His disciples from those the world hawks today. I shall not develop each one but merely chart the contrasting themes and let you develop them on your own.

- Lust of the flesh (desiring *pleasure*) vs. a willingness to *suffer* for Christ
- Lust of the eyes (desiring *possessions*) vs. a willingness to *sacrifice* for Christ
- Pride of life (desiring *power/position*) vs. a willingness to *submit* for Christ

Jesus went to great lengths to model and teach the themes of suffering, sacrifice, and submission to His disciples. And the apostles echoed them as well, teaching that all of these were to be done, not for the sake of the virtues themselves but for the Lord Christ. Devotion to Him gave them a "cultural weightlessness" whereby they were unaffected by the pull of sensual pleasure, material possessions, or earthly power and position. They lived closer to another Star in the heavenlies, whose gravitational pull was far greater than the pull of the world.

If God saw fit to give them gifts of pleasure, possessions, or power while on this earth, these gifts were received thankfully, used responsibly, and held loosely. The presence or absence of the gifts was a means to live out before a watching world and a worthy God the realities of what—or rather who—truly mattered to them. The disciples and apostles didn't view themselves as savvy Christian consumers on holiday at a mall. Their Master taught them that they were soldiers on assignment in occupied territory. There was a war raging, and what they did mattered—eternally. They lived for a world yet unseen, except by the eye of faith through the telescope of biblical revelation. They saw that they existed to be "living advertisements" that the God of heaven was the first and the greatest!

The world certainly does not stress these themes. The popular music, the current movies, and the never-ending advertisements do not say, "Learn how to suffer well." "Sacrifice is a 'must have' quality in your life." "Don't forget that the mark of maturity is submission." These themes are totally incongruous with pop culture. While we may recognize this when we stop to think about it, what we do not recognize is how much we ourselves have been influenced by popular culture. The result is that we more readily identify with desiring pleasure, possessions, and power than we do with the call to suffer, sacrifice, and submit.

Our culture says, "Sometimes you have to bend the rules." "You don't have to become anybody's doormat." "If you can dream it, you can have it." "Make it happen." "You are the master of your own universe."

Dr. Bob Jones Sr., founder of Bob Jones University, contrasted the world's view and the Bible's perspective this way.

> The Christian philosophy is a philosophy of self-denial, self-control, and self-restraint. The satanic philosophy is a philosophy of 'live as

you please'; 'have what you want'; 'don't let anybody tell you what to do'; 'it's your life, you have got a right to live it.'[23]

Loving the world—living as if it is all that matters—is a danger to be avoided at all costs. What is the remedy for worldliness?

> There are two ways to displace from the human heart its love of the world—either by a demonstration of the world's vanity, so as that the heart shall be prevailed upon simply to withdraw its regards from an object that is not worthy of it, or by setting forth another object, even God, as more worthy of its attachment, so as that the heart shall be prevailed upon not to resign an old affection which shall have nothing to succeed it, but to exchange an old affection for a new.[24]

---

[23]*Chapel Sayings of Dr. Bob Sr.* (Greenville, S.C.: Bob Jones University, n.d.), 8.

[24]Thomas Chalmers, *Twenty Centuries of Great Preaching: An Encyclopedia of Preaching*, vol. 3 (Waco: Word Books, 1971), 300, as quoted by Don Kistler in the study guide for *The Fear of God* by John Bunyan (Morgan, Pa.: Soli Deo Gloria Publications, 1999), 211-12.

CHAPTER NINE
RESPONDING TO THE SPIRIT

A FAREWELL DINNER

The event could not be considered one of those festive *bon voyage* parties celebrating some young executive's departure from home to a more prestigious career elsewhere. The intimate gathering of friends in the dining room took on a tone more like that of a tearful good-bye to a bed-ridden loved one about to step out of this life into the next. The guests at this private affair could sense that something of great importance was unfolding before their eyes, but they could not imagine what it was. Their host was speaking to them as if this dinner were their last together, but they did not feel the liberty to ask too many questions. His final words to them were filled with tender warmth, careful instruction, and fatherly warnings about what would happen to them after he went away.

Fortunately, the speech of their host was recorded by one of those present, and we are privileged to have the exact conversation of Jesus Christ with His disciples at what has come to be called the Last Supper.

John, the Beloved, captures the moments in great detail in chapters 13-16 of his Gospel. My heart is always warmed and energized when I read this passage. I love to read it out loud when I am alone. I concentrate better when I read the Word out loud. I picture myself in that small band of followers hearing these words for the first time. But I have an added benefit that the original twelve did not have on that night. I have Acts and the Epistles, which provide the needed commentary to His words—words that must have sounded very mysterious to the original disciples that night. I always walk away from that setting with a renewed vision of what it means that I, too, am a disciple of Jesus Christ.

In those parting hours in the Upper Room He spoke much of His coming departure and warned them that they would not understand everything now but would later. He tenderly affirmed His continuing love for them and repeatedly reminded them that their love for each other would be the mark that they were His true followers. Jesus affirmed His deity, assuring them that if they had seen Him they had indeed seen the Father to whom He was going. He also left them with the certain expectation that there would be a time when they would be with Him again.

What is especially instructive for us in these final words are the promises He made to them about "another Comforter"—one who was like Him and whom He would send to disciple them in His place. Read carefully these passages, which are scattered throughout His final conversations with them.

> And I will pray the Father, and he shall give you another[1] Comforter, that he may abide with you for ever; even the Spirit of truth; whom the world cannot receive, because it seeth him not, neither knoweth him: but ye know him; for he dwelleth with you, and shall be in you. I will not leave you comfortless: *I will come to you* (John 14:16-18).

> These things have I spoken unto you, being yet present with you. But the Comforter, which is the Holy [Spirit], whom the Father will send in my name, he shall teach you all things, and bring all things to your remembrance, whatsoever I have said unto you. Peace I leave with you, my peace I give unto you: not as the world giveth, give I unto you. Let not your heart be troubled, neither let it be afraid (John 14:25-27).

> But when the Comforter is come, whom I will send unto you from the Father, even the Spirit of truth, which proceedeth from the Father, *he shall testify of me*: And ye also shall bear witness, because ye have been with me from the beginning (John 15:26-27).

---

[1]The Greek word for "another" here means "another of the same kind."

It is expedient for you that I go away: for if I go not away, the Comforter will not come unto you; but if I depart, I will send him unto you. And when he is come, he will reprove the world of sin, and of righteousness, and of judgment: of sin, because they believe not on me; of righteousness, because I go to my Father, and ye see me no more; of judgment, because the prince of this world is judged. I have yet many things to say unto you, but ye cannot bear them now. Howbeit when he, the Spirit of truth, is come, *he will guide you into all truth:* for he shall not speak of himself; but whatsoever he shall hear, that shall he speak: and he will shew you things to come. *He shall glorify me:* for he shall receive of mine, and shall shew it unto you. All things that the Father hath are mine: therefore said I, that he shall take of mine, and shall shew it unto you. *A little while, and ye shall not see me: and again, a little while, and ye shall see me,* because I go to the Father (John 16:7-16).

These passages provide the clues we need to discern what kind of ministry Jesus intended the Holy Spirit to have once He Himself left the earth. Much confusion exists today about the role of the Holy Spirit, but those wrong perceptions can be clarified if we understand what Jesus is saying in the passages we just looked at.

THE HOLY SPIRIT'S MINISTRY

Some believers think the Spirit's primary ministry is to provide the *power* of the Christian life. The Bible certainly teaches that it is His power that enables us to battle the flesh[2] and minister to others through our spiritual gifts,[3] but that is not His primary ministry.

Others teach that the Holy Spirit's foremost activity is to develop *holiness* in the believer's life.[4] There is no doubt that it is the Spirit who produces the fruit of Christlikeness within us. But sanctifying us is not His primary ministry either.

---

[2]Galatians 5:16-17.
[3]I Corinthians 12-14.
[4]Galatians 5:22-26.

Still others emphasize His *teaching* role.[5] Though there is no doubt it is the Spirit whose anointing[6] enables us to understand the Word and helps us discern spiritual things, even this function is not His primary role.

All of the functions discussed above are a part of the Holy Spirit's ministry to us, but none of them by themselves is His primary ministry. *The Holy Spirit's principal ministry is to make real to us the* presence *of our Master, Jesus Christ.*[7]

Jesus Christ is central to everything God has ever done on the earth and to everything God would continue to do once Jesus Christ left earth to go to the Father. Through the presence of the Holy Spirit today, Jesus continues to call disciples to Himself, teach and instruct them, empower them for service, convict them of sin, and enable them to take on His own character. The passages we saw above very clearly teach that the Holy Spirit's ministry is to represent Jesus Christ as the present Comforter and that He is to speak to us of Christ.

> The Spirit's message to us is never, "Look at me; listen to me; come to me; get to know me," but always, "Look at *him,* and see his glory; listen to *him,* and hear his word; go to *him,* and have life; get to know *him,* and taste his gift of joy and peace."[8]

HOW DOES THE SPIRIT SHOW US CHRIST?

If the Holy Spirit's principal ministry is to make real to us the *presence* of our Master, Jesus Christ, what means does He use to do that? What can we expect to experience when He is at work in this way?

Although, as we read the Scriptures, it is important for us to concentrate on the setting of the narrative before us and to make every effort

---

[5]II Corinthians 3:18.

[6]I John 2:27.

[7]John 15:26; 16:13-16.

[8]J. I. Packer, *Keep in Step with the Spirit* (Grand Rapids: Fleming H. Revell, 1984), 66. Again, I must caution the reader. While this book presents one of the best overviews of the Holy Spirit's ministry I have seen, it does contain implications and applications that must be read with great caution. Dr. Packer has taken ecclesiastical positions in recent years that cannot be endorsed by Fundamentalists, but his theological contributions are sometimes quite valuable and biblical. His works, though often insightful, must always be read with great discernment.

to take the words of God personally, the Holy Spirit's mission of making Christ's presence real to us is more than granting to us a sort of "sanctified imagination." It is more than just our pretending that we are involved in the scene we are reading and somehow feeling its ambience. Please understand there is nothing essentially wrong with trying to mentally capture the sense and sensations of the passage before us. We would profit much more from a mindset that acknowledged that the Word of God was written to us just like it was written to and about real people centuries ago. This is helpful but not enough.

Neither must we believe that the Holy Spirit's mediation of Jesus Christ's presence to us will come by the divine activation of some sixth sense whereby we feel an eerie—or even comforting—"presence" in the room. Various novels and movies have generated almost a medieval superstitiousness regarding the spirit world today. People imagine they have felt the presence of demons in the room with them. Others feel they have felt the presence of Christ with them in the same way. There is neither biblical example nor instruction to support their experience. Granted, when the Holy Spirit does reveal Christ to us in the manner we shall see next, His presence is indeed made vividly real to us. The method He uses, however, must not be thought of as some kind of spiritual radar that can sense the presence of spirit beings—good or evil.

The method the Holy Spirit uses to make us aware of the abiding presence of Jesus Christ with us is simply *illumination*. I have discussed this at length in chapter five of this book and in *Changed into His Image*.[9] Nonetheless, I want to recap some previous points here so that we can understand this ministry of God's Spirit.

We must not think that Bible reading alone changes a man. God's Spirit must personally show the realities of God to that man as he ponders the Scriptures. This divine work is called "illumination."[10]

> In Matthew 16:13 Jesus asked His disciples, "Whom do men say that I the Son of man am?" They replied that some thought He was John the Baptist and that others thought He was one of the prophets—perhaps Elijah or Jeremiah. He asked them a more pointed question

---

[9]Berg, 144-53.
[10]Berg, 144-45.

in verse 15: "But whom say *ye* that I am?" Peter answered with a powerful statement of reality: "Thou art the Christ, the Son of the living God" (v. 16). Jesus' reply to Peter is instructive to us at this point in our study. Our Lord said, "Blessed art thou, Simon Bar-jona: *for flesh and blood hath not revealed it unto thee, but my Father which is in heaven*" (v. 17).

Jesus said in effect, "Peter, you have experienced something that is not common to all men. You cannot learn what you learned by natural means. My Father Himself showed you this truth. He opened your eyes and you were illuminated."

Here is how C. H. Spurgeon described illumination when commenting on Psalm 36:9, "In thy light shall we see light."

> Purify flesh and blood by any educational process you may select, elevate mental faculties to the highest degree of intellectual power, yet none of these can reveal Christ. The Spirit of God must come with power, and overshadow the man with His wings, and then in that mystic holy of holies the Lord Jesus must display Himself to the sanctified eye, as He doth not unto the purblind [blinded] sons of men. Christ must be His own mirror. The great mass of this blear-eyed world can see nothing of the ineffable glories of Immanuel. He stands before them without form or comeliness, a root out of a dry ground, rejected by the vain and despised by the proud. Only where the Spirit has touched the eye with eye-salve, quickened the heart with divine life, and educated the soul to a heavenly taste, only there is He understood.[11]

A. W. Tozer expresses the same thought this way:

> For millions of Christians . . . God is no more real than He is to the non-Christian. They go through life trying to love an ideal and be loyal to a mere principle. . . . A loving Personality dominates the Bible, walking among the trees of the garden and breathing fragrance over every scene. Always a living Person is present, speaking, pleading, loving, working, and *manifesting Himself whenever and wherever His people have the receptivity necessary to receive the manifestation.*[12]

---

[11]Charles Haddon Spurgeon, *Morning and Evening* (Peabody, Mass.: Hendrickson Publishers, 1991), 619.

[12]A. W. Tozer, *The Pursuit of God* (Camp Hill, Pa.: Christian Publications, 1993), 46.

It remains for us to think on [these truths] and pray over them *until they begin to glow in us.*[13]

If we cooperate with Him in loving obedience, *God will manifest Himself to us, and that manifestation will be the difference between a nominal Christian life and a life radiant with the light of His face.*[14]

THE EFFECTS OF ILLUMINATION

Truth that is illuminated by the Holy Spirit has three primary effects upon the believer. These collectively provide a *certainty* about spiritual things that assure him of their *reality*. Truth does not *become* reality when illuminated. It was always real. Illumination makes the fallible and finite creature *unmistakably aware* of the reality. It provides the measure of *assurance* of truth that we discussed in chapter six. Let's look briefly at the three primary effects of illumination.

Illuminated Truth Moves the Believer Intellectually

When God's Spirit opens the eye of a believer to some portion of the Word of God, the believer sees afresh the *validity* of the truth.

He is moved to have a steadfast confidence, an inner assurance. He says to himself, "This is right; I must believe it." An illuminated man is divinely persuaded that he has seen something from God and that what he has seen is right. He will boldly defy every assault of hell and will burn at the stake if necessary before he will deny the truth of what he has seen and knows to be true.[15]

Jesus promised His disciples in the Upper Room that the coming Comforter would "testify of me."[16] In other words, "He will show the validity of everything I have said about Myself. You will know it is right, and you will know that you must believe it." That certainly was the case. When the Comforter came to indwell and empower these men at the Day of Pentecost, they turned the world upside-down with their confident proclamation that Jesus Christ is the Messiah and the coming Judge and King.

---

[13]Ibid., 56.
[14]Ibid., 58.
[15]Berg, 148.
[16]John 15:26.

This assurance did not come because they had spent three and a half years with him. That "real life experience" was not enough to remove their doubts and calm their fears. Witness their anxieties after His resurrection. It was not until He "opened . . . their understanding, that they might understand the scriptures"[17] and until the Spirit of God descended upon them at Pentecost that they went forth with great boldness and confidence. Being an eyewitness of His miracles and His teaching was not enough. The death-defying conviction with which they preached His gospel to the world came from a Spirit-taught, illuminated understanding of Jesus Christ.

Illuminated Truth Moves the Believer Emotionally

An illuminated believer viewing the glory of God sees the *beauty* of the truth. He declares, "This is beautiful; I must praise it!" The Word becomes attractive to him and he finds himself admiring it. It may even be breathtaking. There is a new loveliness and worthiness about the truth to him. He cherishes it and delights in its splendor.[18]

Such also is the effect upon a believer when He sees the beauty and glory of His lovely Lord—Jesus Christ. He is not merely a truthful teacher sent from God. He is not only a fulfillment of centuries of messianic prophecy. He will appear, rather, as the one who has loved us with everlasting love, the one who has tenderly drawn us to Himself though we have run fast and hard away from Him. We will see the beauty of His patience, the glory of His holiness, and the wonder of His love to us. He will no longer appear to us as a portrait hung on the wall of our hearts—like a picture of a distant ancestor who brought our family over from the Old World to America centuries ago. He will be a living, ever-present Spouse to us—our Groom become Husband—who lovingly provides, protects, and leads us—His Bride—into ever-increasing delight and security.

In 1674 Jeremiah Burroughs addressed this when he said,

Above all things in the world, the Word of God has the most of the glory of God in it. Though it's true, a soul for a long time, while it is in darkness, sees nothing of this, but when God's good time is come

---

[17]Luke 24:45.
[18]Berg, 150.

to work graciously upon the heart, God opens to this heart such a divine luster shining in the Word that it never saw before, which makes the heart now to stand in awe of it more than ever it did before.[19]

It is this lack of illuminated awareness of Jesus Christ that lies at the root of the believer's doubts and fears. There is no fear when we are aware that Christ is in the boat with us. No matter how fierce the winds or tumultuous the waves, the ever-present Christ is our shelter, and our hearts can rest. This factor alone ought to drive us to beg the blessed Spirit of God to show us our ever-present Savior.

Illuminated Truth Moves the Believer Volitionally

When God's Spirit illumines the mind with truth, the believer is shown the *urgency* and the *responsibility* of the truth. He cries, "This is compelling; I must do it!" He is energized and motivated. He immediately wishes to become a witness of these things. He has something to testify about—he has seen God! The prophet Isaiah, when he saw God, exclaimed, "Here am I; send *me*" (Isaiah 6:8). The apostle Paul, upon beholding the glory of God, asked, "Lord, what wilt thou have *me* to do?" (Acts 9:6).[20]

The entire Book of Acts is the living testimony of this truth. These first-century believers did not expend their energies and eventually their lives taking the gospel to every creature because they had spent three and a half years under the teaching of Jesus Christ. The memories of lessons learned and miracles worked grow dim with the passing years. The mind grows fuzzy about the details of His sermons, and the emotions forget the former experiences of supernatural intervention. The Spirit of God, however, by illuminating their minds, could keep the truth fresh and real and the memories of Jesus Christ clear and energizing. This is still His work today. *We, His disciples today, can know the power and presence of Jesus Christ just as vividly as His original disciples.* It is this kind of Holy Spirit intervention in our lives that is so desperately needed in our day. These are the *effects* of illumination. I shall not spend any time here speaking of the *means* of illumination

---

[19]Jeremiah Burroughs, *Gospel Fear* (1647; reprint, Morgan, Pa.: Soli Deo Gloria Publications, 1991), 9.

[20]Berg, 152.

since I have addressed that elsewhere in this book.[21] We turn now to its *content*.

THE CONTENT OF ILLUMINATION

We have seen in brief overview *how* the Holy Spirit shows us Jesus Christ through illumination. We want to look now at *what* in particular we can expect Him to show us about our Savior. In the past several days I had the opportunity to sit down and read from Acts through the Revelation out loud. As I read through these inspired books, I had the sense that these were the words of the Master at whose feet I was sitting while He taught me His ways. As a disciple of Jesus Christ I was *hearing* His words, and the incumbent responsibility was now for me to *do* them.[22]

When I read the Old Testament and the gospel accounts, I sense that I am listening to Jesus Christ Himself tell me how it all started. When I read the Acts of the Apostles I hear Jesus Christ telling me how His followers went everywhere preaching His death, burial, and resurrection for the redemption of men.

It is obvious, by the way, from Acts that His followers had one preoccupation—Jesus Christ! He was central to their lives and ministry. They preached for Him, suffered for Him, and died for Him. Life for them revolved around a risen Savior, who confirmed their words and their works by manifestations of His Spirit. The Holy Spirit was operative in various ways throughout the birth and infancy of the Church but always enabling men to see and respond to Jesus Christ.

> The essence of the Holy Spirit's ministry, at this or any time in the Christian era, is to <u>mediate the presence of our Lord Jesus Christ</u> . . . [creating] an awareness of three things. The first is that Jesus of Nazareth, the Christ of the Scriptures, once crucified, now glorified, is *here*, personally approaching and addressing me. The second is that he is *active*, powerfully enlightening, animating, and transform-

---

[21]See "Pile on the Firewood and Pray for the Fire" and "A Word to Disciple-Makers" in chapter five of this book and chapter six of *Changed into His Image* for help on the means whereby we experience illumination from God.

[22]"Hearing" and "doing" are the basic disciplines required of a disciple of Jesus Christ. See Matthew 7:24-27 for the words of our Lord Himself about their importance, and refer to chapters eight and nine of *Changed into His Image* for a more complete development of these twin disciplines.

ing me along with others as he stirs our sluggishness, sharpens our insight, soothes our guilty consciences, sweetens our tempers, supports us under pressure, and strengthens us for righteousness. The third is that in himself as in his work he is *glorious*, meriting all our worship, adoration, love, and loyalty of which we are capable [italics his; underscoring mine].[23]

How deficient it is for us who preach to view a passage of Scripture as a mere text to be outlined and exposited. Every text is a portion of a discourse from Jesus Christ Himself to His followers. There is a personal message from the ever-present Master in them. We must be Spirit-sensitized to hear the *Person* in the text—not merely find and obey the principles contained in it. We must never let the Christian life drift from a relationship with Jesus Christ into merely keeping religious rules—however important those rules may be.

The Christian's Interpreter

We have many wonderful international students at Bob Jones University. They bring a refreshing variety to the student body, and their burden for the lost in their homeland is infectious. Many of them stay on the campus year-round since they cannot afford to return to their country at Christmas or during the summer and since immigration laws do not permit them to work anywhere but at their college while in the United States.

Sometimes their parents are able to come to America for their graduation. It is a time of great excitement as mother and father are reunited with their son or daughter to share in the festivities. We who have taught their children especially enjoy meeting the parents of these international students. In a few cases, however, the parents do not speak English, so the graduating student must interpret for them when he introduces them to us.

If the parents are believers, they are full of praise to the Lord for what they have seen accomplished by the Lord in their child's life. They are grateful for the opportunity the Lord has given their child to come from across the globe to prepare for the Lord's service. The conversation is delightful and sometimes filled with tears for all of us.

---

[23]Packer, 55.

In these situations we converse with the parents but their words and ours are mediated by an interpreter, their child. It is the child's responsibility as he interprets to make us aware of his parents' words and to teach us their meaning if the phrases are not familiar to American ears. It is also the student's role to communicate our words to his parents in ways that his parents will understand. In reality, we are carrying on a conversation with his parents though we cannot understand each other directly.

Of course, this illustration has many flaws when illustrating the Holy Spirit's role as a spokesman for Jesus Christ and as an interpreter for us. The main point, however, is valid—that an interpreter's responsibility is to make known accurately and unobtrusively the words and heart of someone else.

This is the primary responsibility of the Holy Spirit with respect to Jesus Christ. The Master has written down His words through the Agent of His Spirit. That same Spirit teaches the meaning of those words, bringing to us the comfort, rebuke, and instruction that we need at that moment from the Master.

But the Holy Spirit does something else a student interpreter does not do. When a student interprets for his parents, his parents are visibly present. We know they are real because we can see them. Jesus Christ is present at all times, but we cannot see Him. It is the Holy Spirit's wonderful mission to make us aware of the presence of Jesus Christ. The Holy Spirit shows us Jesus Christ is *here*. He, by His illuminating work, assures us the truth of the Lord's words, "I am with you alway"[24] and "I will never leave thee, nor forsake thee,"[25] so that *we know with divine assurance that we are in the presence of Jesus Christ and that He Himself is speaking directly to us through His Word.* Here's how John the apostle put it.

> And we know that the Son of God is come, and hath given us an understanding, that we may know him that is true, and we are in him that is true, even in his Son Jesus Christ. This is the true God, and eternal life (I John 5:20).

---

[24]Matthew 28:20.
[25]Hebrews 13:5.

Is His presence a living reality to you? Do you have any internal assurance that Jesus Christ is always with you? Or are you fighting loneliness, bitterness, fear, and resentment? All of these are the symptoms of a life being lived without a Spirit-taught, conscious awareness of Jesus Christ. Martyrs of old did not go to the stake trying to convince themselves of God's help by repeating, "God is with me. God is with me. God is with me." They did not have to talk themselves into believing this truth. They *knew* He was present with them. The Spirit had taught them so. With amazing confidence they knew the words of their God to be true when He said,

> But now thus saith the Lord that created thee, . . . and he that formed thee, . . . Fear not: for I have redeemed thee, I have called thee by name; thou art mine. When thou passest through the waters, *I will be with thee;* . . . when thou walkest through the fire, thou shalt not be burned; neither shall the flame kindle upon thee. For I am the Lord thy God, the Holy One of Israel, thy Saviour. . . . Fear not: *for I am with thee* (Isaiah 43:1-5).

They experienced as they burned what the hymn writer knew when he penned, "The flame shall not hurt thee; I only design thy dross to consume, and thy gold to refine." They knew their God was with them. They knew the presence of Jesus Christ.

The Spirit shows us not only that Christ is *here* but also that He is *active*. He is actively calling us into fellowship with Christ by showing us the impediments to that fellowship. The Spirit convicts of sin that separates us from God. He is actively transforming our character by producing His fruit in our lives—the likeness of Christ—as we repent of our sin, mortify our lusts, and meditate upon the Word, which reveals the Lord Jesus to us.

Again, the Acts of the Apostles is a most powerful testimony of this *active* role that Jesus Christ played in the lives of the members of the early Church. As I read through Acts aloud, I highlighted in my Bible every time the name of Jesus Christ was mentioned in their sermons and in their discourses with each other. These men and women knew beyond any shadow of doubt that Jesus Christ was with them and that He was actively calling out from the Gentiles a people for His name through their efforts.[26] They saw Him at work actively preparing darkened souls like that of Saul of Tarsus to receive the light of the gospel. They watched Him call together thousands at a time to form His new Body, the Church. They observed Him actively give divine grace to the first martyrs as their blood was spilt for His testimony. This was a generation of believers whose experience testified to the living and active Lord, Jesus Christ. They loved Him, listened to Him, obeyed Him, worshiped Him, proclaimed Him, and many died for Him. They didn't do this simply because they believed some stories about Him—though many had friends and relatives who had seen the risen Christ.[27] *They had personally seen the living Christ through the ministry of the Holy Spirit though many of them had never seen Him in the flesh.*

They did not die for a cause, however noble it was. They died for a Lord they had seen to be *glorious*. The Holy Spirit showed them His beauty, His love, His tenderness, His great power on their behalf, His multifaceted wisdom, His pity for the world, His hatred for evil, and the glories of His coming kingdom, where they would reign with Him.

It is precisely because most present-day believers do not have a Spirit-taught, illuminated awareness of the presence of Jesus Christ—that He is here, that He is active, and that He is glorious—that we do not see today the kind of zeal and devotion of the early Church.[28] So how is it that the Church does not experience this powerful ministry of the Holy Spirit? Let's return to our study of Ephesians for the answer.

BACK TO EPHESIANS

As we have seen earlier, one of the backdrop themes of the first three chapters of Ephesians is the work of the Holy Spirit.[29] Paul outlines in chapter 1 the preliminary work God has done in us by sealing us with the Spirit. Paul also tells us that the Spirit is the earnest—the down payment—within us. We see, therefore, that the indwelling presence of the Holy Spirit in the believer at salvation is the underpinning for

---

[26]Acts 15:14, et. al.

[27]I Corinthians 15:5-8.

[28]Happily, notable exceptions exist in select, local assemblies in America and in some foreign countries.

[29]Ephesians 1:13-14, 17; 2:18, 22; 3:5, 16.

His continued work of sanctification throughout the believer's life. As I mentioned earlier, there are no commands whatsoever in Ephesians 1-3. Once we move into chapters 4-6, however, we are faced with many, including two regarding the Holy Spirit.

In 4:30 Paul commands us to "grieve not the holy Spirit of God, whereby [we have been] sealed unto the day of redemption." And in 5:18 he instructs us to be "filled with the Spirit." The title of this chapter is "Responding to the Spirit," underscoring the need for us to have the proper response to these two commands in order for Him to be free to show us Jesus Christ.

First Command: Grieve Not the Holy Spirit of God (4:30)
The full command from Jesus Christ through His apostle is

> Grieve not the Holy Spirit of God, whereby ye are sealed unto the day of redemption.

This command comes after Paul's admonition for us not to walk "as other Gentiles walk, in the vanity of their mind."[30] We have already looked in the last chapter at the degeneracy that follows when men walk in darkness. Paul declares by contrast, "But ye have not so learned Christ; if so be that ye have heard him, and have been taught by him, as the truth is in Jesus."[31] Paul says, "I taught you before that the way of Jesus Christ was a way of light, not a way of darkness."

Then the apostle goes on to discuss how Christians can be just like Gentiles in their speaking, thieving, and anger, and he urges them to "put off" these elements, which were characteristic of their former lifestyle. In verses 20-24 he says the reason believers should distance themselves from these things is that they are not the things we learned from Christ. Then in verse 30 he says they also grieve the Spirit of God. When we do not live like Christ, we grieve His Spirit.

Notice that Paul does not say, "When you steal, you violate the church standards" or "when you lose your temper, you violate our code of conduct." Both of these cases may be true, and not necessarily wrong, but this kind of thinking easily degenerates into externalism. Externalism

---

[30]Ephesians 4:17.
[31]Ephesians 4:20-21.

occurs anytime someone keeps the rules or is encouraged to keep the rules without any regard to the relationship he should have with the one who gave the rules.

Literally, Paul writes, "Stop continuing to grieve the Spirit, the Holy One." He is saying, "Stop living in such an insensitive way! You are grieving the Spirit—the *Holy* Spirit at that—the one who lives in you; the one whose presence indicates that He is safe-guarding you eternally for a special relationship with Jesus Christ."

We grieve the Spirit—we grieve Jesus Christ—when we continue to practice sin. To "grieve" Him means to disappoint Him, to hurt Him. Since the Spirit of God is holy, He does not pout or whine or get angry when He is hurt, but He genuinely aches inside when He sees our sin. He dwells within us to make us aware of Jesus Christ. When we sin, we are acting as if Jesus Christ doesn't matter. The hurt the Spirit feels is much like the hurt we may feel when someone we love ignores us and pretends we aren't even present.

The Grief of a Broken Heart—Dr. Bob Jones Sr. used to tell of a country boy who left the farm to go to college at his widowed mother's insistence. She wanted her son to have an education. In addition to keeping up with the farm, she took in laundry from some of the city people to make extra money for her son's education.

When he got to college, the boy got caught up in the fast life of his friends. He passed his classes but lived for the pleasure of the weekend parties. He seldom wrote home, seldom opened his Bible, and seldom visited his poor mother.

Finally, the days were approaching for him to graduate. She found out the day of his graduation, put on her best dress, and took the train to the town of her boy's college. She watched him walk across the stage to get his diploma. Her heart burst with pride for her son as she wiped the tears from her eyes with her best Sunday handkerchief. After the ceremony she made her way to her boy through the crowd. She found him talking with his friends and started over to him. Embarrassed by his mother's plain dress and obvious country look, he quickly herded his friends off in another direction, ignoring his broken-hearted mother.

This is what it means to grieve someone who loves you. Here is a boy who knew his mother was present but treated her as if she didn't matter. There wasn't any law at his college that said, "Thou shalt talk to thy mother and treat her with honor when she comes for graduation." He didn't violate a college rule, but he violated a mother's love. He selfishly sought his own interests even when it hurt her deeply.

If he had loved his mother as he ought, it wouldn't have mattered to him whether his friends liked her dress or her country ways. He wouldn't have cared that her skin was parched dry and brown by the hot sun on their small farm. He would have been proud that she wanted to share in this day, and he would have gratefully handed her the diploma and said, "Mother, this really belongs to you. You made this possible. I will forever be grateful." He would have kissed her cheek and embraced her in loving gratefulness.

Our hearts can feel the ache in this mother's heart, but we seldom stop to consider the grief we bring to Jesus Christ. We need to start realizing that Jesus Christ is here. He is just as present with us now as He was with His disciples in Galilee. *To ignore Jesus Christ is to grieve Him.* It is a personal offense to live our lives as if He weren't even around. When we ignore Him, we also grieve His Spirit, whose ministry it is to penetrate our insensitivity and make Jesus Christ real to us.

"Grieve not the Spirit" is Paul's first command in Ephesians regarding the Holy Spirit. There is yet another command regarding the Spirit in this book, which sheds additional light on our relationship with Jesus Christ.

Second Command: Be Filled with the Spirit (5:18)
Many believers who are trying to live better Christian lives try merely to follow some formula for Spirit-filling or for discovering and deploying their spiritual gift and never once think of how Jesus Christ is to be the central component in their pursuits. The teaching they have received is incomplete and their efforts are often confused and unfruitful. Paul's exact words in Ephesians 5:18 are "And be not drunk with wine, wherein is excess [i.e., wastefulness]; but be filled with [i.e., controlled by] the Spirit."

The word "filled" here is not speaking of possessing a certain *quantity* of the Spirit as we might speak of a glass "filled" with water. It expresses, rather, the idea of "control," as when we speak of someone being "filled with rage." We mean by that phrase that anger is such a dominant part of his life at that moment that he is controlled by it. We might speak of someone being "filled with fear" or "filled with lust" in the same way. The person described as "being filled" with these passions is so consumed by the fear or lust that his behavior is noticeably affected.

Paul compares being filled with the Spirit to being drunk with wine. A man who is filled with wine to the extent of drunkenness behaves differently when he is under the influence than when he is sober. He is transformed into a destructive, wasteful person. The alcohol affects every part of the man's life, but in a destructive way. That is why Paul says the effect of drunkenness is "excess" (literally "wastefulness").[32]

The control of the Spirit will produce something very much the opposite of drunkenness. A person under the control of alcohol is excessive, disorderly, wasteful—of time, money, and energy. His thinking is impaired and his morals are desensitized. Since alcohol is a depressant—not a stimulant—it blunts a man's perceptions and faculties. He is left without his higher reasoning powers and operates more on base instincts. He becomes animalistic.

The Spirit of God does just the opposite. A Spirit-filled Christian is not out of control; he is orderly. He is not wasteful; he is productive for God and a blessing to others. His moral sensibilities are quickened. All of his natural powers are energized to a new level of usefulness. These are the effects of God in the soul. The "fruit of the Spirit"[33] borne out in these ways makes him more Christlike.

This control of the Spirit of God is what Paul refers to in Romans 8:14 when he says, "For as many as are led by the Spirit of God, they are the sons of God."

The apostle is not teaching in this verse that we should expect the Spirit of God to give us mystical leadings and nudgings, and thereby direct our lives. That is not what Paul is talking about at all. This verse is in the context of Romans 6-8, which speaks of the work of sanctification that God is trying to work out in our lives—a process

---

[32]Berg, 187-88.
[33]Galatians 5:22-23.

initiated and orchestrated by the Spirit of God. He is leading in this process. He is the divine Leader calling attention through His convicting voice to the times when we are intent upon going our *own way*. He leads us into an understanding of the Scriptures and leads us into "paths of righteousness"[34] that will reflect Christ's life in us. Those who experience this kind of leadership—away from sin and toward Christ's likeness—"are the sons of God."[35]

The Holy Spirit's leadership away from our flesh and toward the ways of Jesus Christ is exactly what Jesus Christ did with His disciples when they were here on this earth. He corrected them, instructed them, and encouraged them. The Holy Spirit does the same thing to us on behalf of Jesus Christ now.

Being filled—or controlled—by the Spirit means that we have the frame of mind and heart that is willing to be led to become something we are not. The filling of the Spirit is parallel to the abiding in Christ of John 15. It is the submissive and yielded heartedness of one who is coming to Jesus Christ to *hear* His words and *do* them. It means that we continually submit to the control of the one who dwells within us as the representative Agent of Jesus Christ Himself.

Galatians 5:16 tells us, "Walk in the Spirit, and ye shall not fulfil the lust of the flesh." The Greek word "walk" here is *peripateo*, which means to "go about, walk around."[36] The stress in this word is that our daily lifestyle should be characterized by a sensitivity to the Spirit of God—to what He is teaching us about Jesus Christ in the Word and to what He is convicting us about as Jesus Christ continues to refine us.

In the same chapter, verse 25 uses a different Greek word, which is also translated "walk" in our English versions. It says, "If we live in the Spirit, let us also walk in the Spirit." Here the word "walk" is *stoicheo*. This word means "to be in line with." Figuratively, it means "agree with, follow."[37] These two words capture the entire flavor of being "filled with [i.e., controlled by] the Spirit." Our daily lifestyle—our

---

[34]Psalm 23:3.

[35]Berg, 7-8.

[36]William Arndt and F. Wilbur Gingrich, *A Greek-English Lexicon of the New Testament and Other Early Christian Literature* (Chicago: University of Chicago Press, 1979), 654.

[37]Ibid., 777.

walking around—is to be in agreement with the Holy Spirit as He makes the words and the ways of Jesus Christ known to us through the Word and through His conviction.

It is a mistake to take the command "be filled with the Spirit" as a spiritual formula or ritual that is repeated over and over to invoke some kind of special power or coveted blessing. It is a command to stay in the submitted relationship of a disciple to the Master. It calls for a heart that is yielded to the control of someone else—Jesus Christ. It is the same attitude of heart Paul described in Ephesians 3:16-17 and I discussed earlier in chapter six of this book. Paul prayed that the Ephesians would allow Jesus Christ to "house-down" in their hearts—be allowed to be the resident Master instead of the tolerated Guest. Those whose lives were characterized by this kind of Spirit-control were said to be "full of the Holy Ghost."[38] Responding to the Spirit—hearing and doing His words—was a lifestyle issue for them.

THE TRAINING OF THE TWELVE . . . AND MORE[39]

We have many advantages over the original twelve disciples. Their knowledge of Jesus was far more incomplete than ours. Their view of His mission was sketchy, and their efforts were often flawed. Yet because they sincerely loved their Master and genuinely desired to understand and carry out His wishes, Jesus was longsuffering with them and used their efforts to advance His program. They were willing and eager to "hear" and "do" the words of the Master. The wonderful result was a first generation of disciples who penetrated their world with the good news that Jesus Christ had come to save sinners.

Do you remember Jesus' promise to His disciples regarding the Spirit? He said that when the Spirit is come "greater works than these shall he do; because I go unto my Father."[40] That promise is still operative in those disciples today who will let the Holy Spirit teach them that Jesus Christ is present, that He is powerfully at work in our midst, and that

---

[38] Acts 6:3-5; 7:55; 11:24.

[39] This subject heading is borrowed from a classic Christian book by the same title. A. B. Bruce's *Training of the Twelve* (1894; reprint, Grand Rapids: Kregel Publications, 1971) is perhaps the most comprehensive and heart-warming study available of Jesus' ministry to His disciples.

[40] John 14:12.

He is wondrously glorious to know and experience. May God make us earnest, single-minded disciples of our Lord Jesus Christ as we respond to His Spirit.

TAKE TIME TO REFLECT

1. The Holy Spirit's principal ministry is to make real to us the presence of our Master, Jesus Christ. How is He doing that in your life?

2. Jesus Christ is walking in the midst of His churches just like He is pictured in Revelation 2 and 3. As He walks in the midst of your church, what strengths and what weaknesses does He see— what might be the contents of a letter He would write to your assembly? Reread Revelation 2 and 3 if you need some ideas.

3. Describe the last time the Holy Spirit "interpreted" a Scripture passage to you, making it real to you.

4. Is Jesus Christ special or glorious to you in any way? If so, in what way(s)?

5. Is Jesus Christ dwelling in you as the resident Master or the tolerated Guest? If not as the resident Master, what is keeping you from coming to that position of yieldedness and surrender?

A WORD TO DISCIPLE-MAKERS

Is There a Difference Between Human Virtues and Christian Character?

There is a renewed interest in character development today—even in the public sector. Some educators and even some public officials have taken up the cause of character education for the nation's youth. Former U.S. Secretary of Education William Bennett penned a bestseller entitled *The Book of Virtues*, further fanning the flames of concern. Some current non-Christian and Christian parenting curricula present a renewed emphasis upon rearing morally responsible children.

While Christians can be thankful for any effort that attempts to upgrade the moral fabric of our society, it is crucial that we realize that developing human virtue in our children and in ourselves is not the same as developing Christlikeness in us. *Although it is impossible to have Christlikeness without the processes of discipline that develop human virtues, it is entirely possible to have certain human virtues without any semblance of godliness*. It is important that we understand both the similarities and the differences.

Human Virtues

By human virtues I mean qualities such as responsibility, honesty, loyalty, charity, generosity, courage, compassion, punctuality, cheerfulness, helpfulness, dependability, initiative, obedience, and fair-mindedness. These qualities are admirable in saved and unsaved alike.

Human virtues, however, can be developed by anyone. An unsaved man can follow God's universal laws, whether scientific, social, or moral, and benefit from them. The capacity to develop virtue is one of the aspects of the residual, marred image of God in man.[41] A lost businessman can be honest. A lost employee can be loyal. A lost philanthropist can be charitable. A lost soldier can be courageous. A lost student can be punctual.

The cultivation of admirable virtues is possible for every man because of God's common grace to all men. Jesus said of the Father, "He maketh his sun to rise on the evil and on the good, and sendeth rain on the just and on the unjust."[42] The psalmist said, "The Lord is good to *all*: and his tender mercies are over *all* his works."[43] God in His goodness to all His creatures makes certain blessings available to all, whether the creature is righteous or unrighteous.

The development of human virtue simply requires discipline. The old adage captures this well: "Sow a thought, reap an action. Sow an action, reap a habit. Sow a habit, reap a character." A person who will submit himself to the instruction and accountability of wise elders and will discipline himself—or allow himself to be disciplined by others— will with enough practice develop certain commendable qualities. This is how U.S. military academies can develop men and women of character. This is how parents who are willing to take the time to discipline and train their children can be rewarded with virtuous children.

---

[41]Genesis 1:27; James 3:9.
[42]Matthew 5:45.
[43]Psalm 145:9.

Society is certainly improved when its citizens possess moral character, but God is not necessarily impressed. The motive of the unregen-
erate heart—and the carnal, believing heart—is always self-serving.
Its charitableness, and even its courage, are inextricably intertwined
with the self-centeredness of the proud heart that leaves God out. A
prime biblical example is Saul of Tarsus. Before his conversion Saul
was loyal, courageous, dependable, and certainly a model of initiative,
but Jesus Christ Himself testified that Saul's efforts were at odds with
God Himself.[44]

While we can rejoice at whatever good we can see in man and his
works around us—good art, good music, good literature, just laws, and
fair courts—we as believers cannot be content with moral virtue alone.
And certainly, we must not confuse these human virtues with Christlikeness.

Children may leave Christian homes and graduate from Christian high
schools and colleges with certain commendable qualities and still not
be godly.

Christian Character—Christlikeness

Christlikeness is another term for the "fruit of the Spirit."[45] That term
alone teaches us that the "fruit" we are speaking of is developed by the
Spirit of God. Unlike human virtues, the fruit of the Spirit is produced
only by the life of God in the believing and yielding soul. There is
something supernatural going on. Think of it this way.

A family on vacation might be able to build a lifelike sand sculpture of
a dog at the beach, but it would take an act of God to make the dog
sculpture live. It is the same with Christian character. You can develop
certain qualities that look like godliness, but only God can transform
them into the fruit of His Spirit.

Sanctification—the process of developing Christlikeness—is a dual responsibility. That means that we do something—with God's help—

---

[44]Acts 9:5.

[45]The list of qualities in Galatians 5:22-23 is representative, not exhaustive.
Other passages outlining godly qualities include the Beatitudes in Matthew 5:1-12,
the qualities of love in I Corinthians 13:4-8, the great virtues of II Peter 1:3-11, and
the characteristics of wisdom in James 3:17-18.

and at the same time He works. It is all of God ultimately, but He has mandated that we cooperate with Him. To cooperate with God, we must practice God-dependent self-denial. Self-discipline alone isn't enough. It must have a God-ward focus so that the motive is right and so that the source of strength is God-dependent, not self-dependent. *God does not bless any work that is not His own.*

Jesus made it clear to His disciples that He wanted them to bear much fruit, but He was also clear that they could not do this on their own. He said,

> Abide in me, and I in you. As the branch cannot bear fruit of it-self, except it abide in the vine; no more can ye, except ye abide in me. I am the vine, ye are the branches: he that abideth in me, and I in him, the same bringeth forth much fruit: for without me ye can do nothing (John 15:4-5).

Without the God-dependent, disciplined effort of the disciple to abide in the Vine by meditating upon His words and interacting generously with the Lord Himself, there will be no fruit. This God-dependent, dis-ciplined effort puts him in a position for the Vine to do His divine work in the soul. Without abiding, there would be no opportunity for him to benefit from the gracious supply of the Vine Himself.

This abiding is the same action as walking in the Spirit. It is a *conscious* yielding to God. A Spirit-filled walk is not the result of following a formula for being Spirit-controlled. It is the glad surrender of the heart to God. It is yielding to another Master, saying no to ourselves. The re-sult of this abiding and Spirit control is the fruit of the Spirit.

This God-ward focus of dependence must be a part of any discipling ef-fort if we are to see Christlikeness formed in those with whom we are working. It is not enough to develop human virtues in our children, students, church members—or in ourselves. The "sand sculpture" of character will live as Christlikeness only as the disciple is *responding to the Spirit.*

PART THREE

DISPLAYING THE GRAND REALITY OF GOD

CHAPTER TEN

LIVING IN THE FEAR OF GOD

TWIN TOWERS AND THE TOWERING GOD

I am writing this chapter on a Saturday, four days after Islamic terrorists on separate commercial flights turned three domestic jetliners into guided missiles, destroying the twin towers of the World Trade Center in New York City and a portion of the Pentagon in Washington, D.C. As I write, our hearts are heavy with sorrow, and our minds are filled with the gut-wrenching images of the destruction we saw on our television screens on that fateful Tuesday, September 11, 2001.

We watched dust-covered citizens emerge from the area of the collapsed buildings looking like mummies resurrected from ancient tombs. We choked back our own emotions as we considered the awful horror that swept over the thousands trapped inside the buildings in those final moments. And we shared in the jubilance of those who found that their missing loved ones were alive. Their tears and lingering hugs testified of immense joy in the midst of agonizing terror. The emotions and reactions of the victims and survivors on that day are instructive to us as we consider not what it means to be trapped in the twin towers but what it means to walk in godly fear before the God who towers over all things.

A FRIGHTENING VULNERABILITY

Think with me about the people trapped inside the buildings in those final moments of horror as they realized the inevitability of their destruction. They experienced intense vulnerability in the face of overwhelming destructive powers—the consuming power of flames and the crushing power of tons of crumbling concrete and steel. Some in those final moments of terror decided to jump to their destruction rather than face the encroaching flames. Others called or e-mailed loved ones to say their final good-byes and then waited for the inevitable. All hope of escape had vanished. All that was left for them in the final moments was terror. We were spared the final screams of those engulfed in the inferno. If in our minds we put ourselves in their place during those last moments, our hearts shudder at the thoughts of such horror and agony. We can't begin to imagine the terror in their souls nor the pain in their bodies.

Their experiences are in many ways parallel to what it means to experience the "fear of God." In the tower tragedy and in what it means to fear the Lord there is a sense that you are facing a power far greater than you and that you are very much at risk in your present situation.

Anyone who has seen the funnel cloud and heard the roar of an approaching tornado or felt the severe lashings of hurricane winds understands the frightening vulnerability that is a part of the fear of the Lord. When a man is brought face to face with some aspect of God's *greatness*, he is dwarfed by the immensity of a Being with far greater powers than his own.

A sinner who has just become aware of his sin and his judgment by God if he has no atonement, or a believer like King David, whose sin has just been exposed, is also experiencing the frightening vulnerability that is a part of the fear of the Lord. Whether you see God's greatness in powerful natural displays or experience His greatness when considering His powerful judgments on sin, the effect is the same. Jeremiah testifies,

> Forasmuch as there is none like unto thee, O Lord; thou art great, and thy name is great in might. Who would not fear thee, O King of nations? (Jeremiah 10:6-7).

But Jeremiah was not the only Bible character struck with godly fear upon seeing the greatness of God. The Scriptures are peppered with such accounts.

Vulnerability Before a Mysterious Hand
Belshazzar, king of Babylon, was entertaining his lords in a drunken feast. He arrogantly commanded that the temple vessels from

Jerusalem be brought into the banquet hall, where he invited his guests to use them while drinking toasts to "the gods of gold, and of silver, of brass, of iron, of wood, and of stone."[1] Then something happened to drain the party of its festive atmosphere.

> In the same hour came forth fingers of a man's hand, and wrote over against the candlestick upon the [plaster] of the wall of the king's palace: and the king saw the part of the hand that wrote. Then the king's [face] was changed, and his thoughts [frightened] him, so that the joints of his [hips] were loosed, and his knees smote one against another (Daniel 5:5-6).

Though he was the king of the known world, this was a power far greater than he had reckoned with before. He knew he was being out-ranked and was at great risk.

Finally Daniel was brought into the banquet hall to interpret the handwriting on the wall. Daniel interpreted the writings. He said, in effect, "Your days are up. You have been weighed on the scales and found deficient. The Medes and Persians will divide your kingdom."

That night Belshazzar was killed by the invading forces of the Medes. He experienced the frightening vulnerability to a power greater than himself—an essential component in the fear of the Lord.

Vulnerability Before a Smoking Mountain

The children of Israel had faced a similar situation years before at the foot of the mountain in the wilderness of Sinai. God was going to give the law to Moses on two tablets of stone, and He wanted the people to understand that what was happening was of divine origin and was not a fanciful idea from Moses. God prepared an enormous display of His power. It had its intended effect.

> And the Lord said unto Moses, Lo, I come unto thee in a thick cloud, that the people may hear when I speak with thee, and believe thee for ever. And Moses told the words of the people unto the Lord. And the Lord said unto Moses, Go unto the people, and sanctify them to day and to morrow, and let them wash their clothes, and be ready against the third day: for the third day the

---

[1] Daniel 5:4.

Lord will come down in the sight of all the people upon mount Sinai. And thou shalt set bounds unto the people round about, saying, Take heed to yourselves, that ye go not up into the mount, or touch the border of it: whosoever toucheth the mount shall be surely put to death: there shall not an hand touch it, but he shall surely be stoned, or shot through; whether it be beast or man, it shall not live: when the trumpet soundeth long, they shall come up to the mount. And Moses went down from the mount unto the people, and sanctified the people. . . . And it came to pass on the third day in the morning, that there were thunders and light-nings, and a thick cloud upon the mount, and the voice of the trumpet exceeding loud; *so that all the people that was in the camp trembled* (Exodus 19:9-16).

Here again we see the frightening vulnerability of people who are brought face to face with a power that is in another league. They are experiencing a part of what we call the fear of the Lord.

Vulnerability in the Local Church
The New Testament presents a similar effect upon the early church when Ananias and Sapphira lied about their contribution from their land sale. Peter charged Ananias with lying to the Holy Spirit, who killed Ananias on the spot. The immediate effect of his death was that *"great fear came on all them that heard these things."*[2] His wife's subse-quent death had the same effect: "And *great fear came upon all the church,* and upon as many as heard these things."[3] Once again, people faced with a power far greater than themselves realized their frighten-ing vulnerability and feared the Lord.

Vulnerability: A Common Theme
Similar experiences are reported through both Testaments. Every time a man or woman faced an angel—a messenger from God—the effect was the same. Each fell on his face fearing for his life. When the high priest went into the holy of holies once a year on the Day of Atone-ment, he knew he was about to face a Presence in that room of im-

---

[2]Acts 5:5.
[3]Acts 5:11.

mense power and purity. He felt very keenly his vulnerability before the shekinah glory of God.

When a man is aware that he is in the presence of the living God, the only appropriate response is to put his face in the dust. It is true that the once-for-all atonement of Jesus Christ for us has changed our vulnerability regarding eternal condemnation. But our forgiveness has not abolished our need to fear the Lord. The writer of Hebrews exhorts us to "serve God acceptably with reverence and godly fear."[4] Peter also tells us that since we will answer to the Father, who "without respect of persons judgeth according to every man's work, [let us] pass the time of [our] sojourning here in fear."[5] Later he states very bluntly, "Fear God."[6] The New Testament is replete with references that exhort us to fear God.[7]

But while this sense of vulnerability must be present anytime we are aware of who God is and who we are, there is another aspect of the fear of God that injects great hope and gladness into our experience of the fear of the Lord.

A JOYFUL SECURITY

At the start of this chapter I likened the frightening vulnerability of fearing God to the horrible vulnerability the victims of the terrorist attacks felt when *trapped* inside the Word Trade Center.

The experience for those who *escaped*, however, was far different. As they made their way down the stairways, they experienced along with the rising *fear*, a growing *hope*—a hope borne out of an increasing awareness that they might be able to escape the seemingly inevitable destruction. Once outside and reunited with friends and loved ones, their hope broke into overpowering *joy* and uncontrollable sobs as they realized how close they had come to death. The reality of their safety hit them with waves of *gratefulness* though mingled with a lingering *heaviness* at the loss of friends and coworkers. All of this was overcast

---

[4]Hebrews 12:28.

[5]I Peter 1:17.

[6]I Peter 2:17.

[7]In addition to the passages cited above, see Acts 19:17; Romans 3:18; II Corinthians 7:1; Ephesians 5:21; 6:5; Hebrews 4:1; 11:7; 12:21; I Peter 2:18; 3:2; and 3:15.

with a sense of *awe* at the unthinkable destruction they had just witnessed.[8]

Those who escaped the terrorist attacks with their lives not only saw the *greatness* of the danger but also experienced the *goodness* of deliverance. This is the closest an unbeliever can come to understanding the components that make up the fear of the Lord. The believer, however, has an awareness of the *greatness* of an even more terrifying danger—eternal judgment—and has experienced an even more thrilling *goodness* when he tasted the deliverance of God in salvation.

As a rescued sinner contemplates his once-desperate condition, in addition to the fear of judgment, he experiences a hope, joy, gratefulness, heaviness, and sense of awe similar to that the survivors of the terrorist attacks felt on that dreadful day in September. This mixture of emotions when considering the greatness and the goodness of God in His actions towards us completes the picture of what the Bible calls "the fear of the Lord."

The fear of the Lord is truly multidimensional and cannot be defined in one brief statement. It does, however, seem to contain several key thoughts that we must attempt to put in order. We can say that the fear of the Lord is *the awe and reverence left over when the frightening vulnerability before the greatness of God is mixed with the joy of security upon experiencing the goodness of God.*

The sense of vulnerability—the essence of fear—remains because His greatness is overpowering. Yet the awareness of His goodness injects a joyful sense of security—the essence of hope—into the picture. The result is a mixture of an energizing, respectful, and jubilant awe that propels the believer into worship and service for the God of heaven.

This was the experience of Isaiah in the well-known scene of chapter 6. He said,

---

[8]I use the word "awe" in its true sense: "An emotion of mingled reverence, dread, and wonder inspired by something majestic or sublime" (*The American Heritage Dictionary of the English Language*, s.v. awe). Unfortunately our culture has trivialized the word by using its derivative "awesome" to describe everything from the taste of a soft drink to the deafening music of a rock concert—experiences hardly sublime enough to inspire reverence, dread, and wonder in anyone.

In the year that king Uzziah died I saw also the Lord sitting upon a throne, high and [exalted], and [the train of His robe] filled the temple. Above it stood the seraphims: each one had six wings; with [two] he covered his face, and with [two] he covered his feet, and with [two] he did fly. And one cried unto another, and said, Holy, holy, holy, is the Lord of hosts: the whole earth is full of his glory. And the posts of the door moved at the voice of him that cried, and the house was filled with smoke.

Then said I, Woe is me! for I am [fit for destruction]; because I am a man of unclean lips, and I dwell in the midst of a people of unclean lips: for mine eyes have seen the King, the Lord of hosts. Then flew one of the seraphims unto me, having a [burning] coal in his hand, which he had taken with the tongs from off the altar: and he laid it upon my mouth, and said, Lo, this hath touched thy lips; and thine iniquity is taken away, and thy sin purged. Also I heard the voice of the Lord, saying, Whom shall I send, and who will go for us? Then said I, Here am I; send me (Isaiah 6:1-8).

Here the prophet saw the stunning majesty and glorious perfections of God. His reaction was to cry out because of his vulnerability at being a mere creature—and an unclean one at that—before the transcendent glory of his Creator. He also experienced the mercy of the King as he was cleansed from his sin. The result was a man who was energized to live in glad surrender to the Creator-God. Though the phrase is not used in this passage, Isaiah experienced here the "fear of the Lord."

This fear of God—this sense of God's greatness mixed with His goodness—is present in every believer from the moment of salvation,[9] though often in a severely underdeveloped fashion. Its maturity is dependent upon how much the believer has personally seen the greatness and the goodness of God from his study of the Word.

The seeming absence of the fear of God in today's believer is due to the blindness of God's people to their own sinfulness along with their ignorance of who God is. *Growth in the fear of the Lord is directly proportionate to our knowledge of His perfections*—His unstoppable power, His

---

[9]Jeremiah 32:38-41.

piercing holiness, His unchangeable love, His undeserved mercy, His unsearchable wisdom, and so forth. Jonathan Edwards addressed this very issue.

> The more you have of a rational knowledge of divine things, the more opportunity will there be, when the Spirit shall be breathed into your heart, to see the excellency of these things, and to taste the sweetness of them.[10]

John Bunyan also addresses the necessity of a more full knowledge of God.

> This fear of God flows from a sound impression that the Word of God makes on our souls; for without an impression of the Word there is no fear of God. . . . For as man drinks good doctrine into his soul, so he fears God. If he drinks in much, he fears Him greatly; if he drinks in but little, he fears Him but little; if he does not drink it in at all, he does not fear Him at all.[11]

The diligent, prayerful study of the Scriptures gives us opportunity to be taught by the Spirit what our great God is like. But we must also depend upon the Spirit of God to teach us not only what God is like but also that this El-Shaddai—God Almighty—is *here!*

The victims and survivors of the disaster on September 11 had known before that week that fires in skyscrapers posed great dangers to those inside. They had previously understood that to be inside a building when it collapsed would surely mean death. That knowledge may have sent shivers through their bodies when they momentarily thought upon these facts in days or years past as they rode the elevators up the towers. But most of them quickly dismissed those thoughts from their minds because they were too uncomfortable. What sent the mixture of emotions through their beings on that awful Tuesday was that all of those possibilities were *here!* They were not "what ifs" but present realities!

Another way of describing the fear of God, therefore, is the *awareness of the powers of the ever-present God.* To fear God, you must be aware

---

[10]Jonathan Edwards, "Christian Knowledge," in *The Works of Jonathan Edwards,* vol. 2 (1834; reprint, Peabody, Mass.: Hendrickson Publishers, 2000), 162.

[11]John Bunyan, *The Fear of God* (Morgan, Pa.: Soli Deo Gloria Publications, 1999), 76-77.

that He has infinite *powers*—awe-inspiring attributes like omnipotence and comforting attributes like compassion—and that this Infinitely Powerful One is *present!* That awareness can be either a comfort or a terror to you. Let me illustrate it this way.

IT DEPENDS ON WHICH SIDE OF THE LAW YOU ARE ON!

Suppose you are driving down the interstate, and as you crest a rise in the highway you notice a patrol car just ahead—seemingly half buried in the tall grass of the median. Even if you are a law-abiding citizen and are driving the speed limit, you still double-check your speedometer just to be sure that what he is "seeing" on his radar scope is acceptable. You instinctively know that if you are breaking the speed limit you are vulnerable.

What creates that sense of vulnerability? You know that he is *present* with the *powers* to enforce the law. He has many powers at his disposal: the power of his gun, the power of government backing, the power of communication to backup units, and so forth. You may never have thought much about those powers before, but now the reality of him exercising those powers if you are speeding strikes fear in your heart because of his *presence*. If you are breaking the law, his *presence* and *powers* make you feel exceedingly uncomfortable. And they should!

On the other hand, suppose that you work at a store in a local mall, and you are the last employee to leave late in the evening after you have closed the store. You walk outside to your car, which you have parked on the far side of the lot to leave the closer spots for the customers. As you walk toward your car in the darkness, you notice three men who come out of the shadows of the mall complex and start towards you. The street lights are little comfort to you as the men increase their speed when they see you walk faster. You know they will reach you before you reach your car. Your heart races as you consider your vulnerability. There is no use screaming because there is no one around to hear you. The men are about ten yards behind you, and you still have about twenty yards to go to reach your car.

Just as you break into a run and the men do the same, a police officer in a squad car pulls around the corner. As soon as he sees your predicament, he turns on his flashing lights and his siren and heads straight for you. A second patrol car comes from the other direction and heads for the men. The men are detained, and you are asked to sit inside the patrol car while an officer gets a citizen's report from you. He explains that their units received a call a few minutes earlier that a burglary was in progress in one of the stores. They suspect that these men are the culprits and were looking for a car to steal to get away.

To the thieves, the *presence* and *powers* of uniformed police officers in squad cars bring an unsettling vulnerability—fear. To you, the *presence* and *powers* of those same officers bring instant relief and joy. You now sit in the squad car, perhaps still shaking from the experience, but with a new respect and admiration for the devotion of these officers to the laws of the land and to its citizens. The response to the *presence* of such *powers* is dependent upon which side of the law you are on.

THE ESSENCE OF MAN

Living and growing in the fear of the Lord are absolutely essential if a man is to be restored to the kind of life God intended for him to live. They are not optional for man's true happiness; they are central to it. The Book of Ecclesiastes, after a sobering discussion of God's greatness and man's finiteness and fallenness, ends with a pointed conclusion in 12:13-14.

> Let us hear the conclusion of the whole matter: *Fear God, and keep his commandments:* for this is the whole duty of man. For God shall bring every work into judgment, with every secret thing, whether it be good, or whether it be evil.

This is an intriguing passage because it summarizes "the whole duty of man." We have a sense as we reflect upon it that we are examining something very foundational to the quality of our existence. In fact, that is exactly the case. "The whole duty of man" means it is the essence—the "'manishness' [sic] of a man and 'womanliness' of a woman."[12] A man cannot be totally complete until this element of godly fear—which was lost in the Fall—is restored. Paul describes unbelievers with the phrase "There is no fear of God before their eyes."[13] As I have mentioned in chapter eight, a man without God is like a car

---

[12]Walter C. Kaiser Jr., *Ecclesiastes: Total Life* (Chicago: Moody Press, 1979), 125.
[13]Romans 3:18.

without an engine. Without this godly fear all a man can do is work on his external image because the "engine" that is to drive him is malfunctioning. *Godliness is the core of manliness.* It is the essence of man as God intended him to be. Matthew Henry expressed it this way:

> Of all things that are to be known this is most evident, that God is to be feared, to be reverenced, served, and worshiped; this is so the beginning of knowledge that those know nothing who do not know this.[14]

Bunyan, in his classic work on the fear of the Lord, says the same thing.

> This fear of the Lord is the pulse of the soul, and as some pulses beat stronger and some weaker, so with this grace of the fear in the soul.[15]

It is crucial that we as believers study what God has to say to us about the fear of the Lord because the extent to which we fear the Lord is the measure of our personal godliness. In fact, godliness is a synonym for the fear of the Lord. The Scriptures are replete with the theme that mature believers are those who fear the Lord.

When Jethro, the father-in-law of Moses, instructed Moses to deputize spiritually minded leaders to share his administrative burden, he commanded Moses to choose "able men, such as fear God."[16] Israel's kings were required to be "just, ruling in the fear of God."[17] God described Job's spiritual maturity as "one that feareth God,"[18] and the psalmist declares that the man "that feareth the Lord" is one "that delighteth greatly in his commandments."[19] Isaiah prophesied that one of the sevenfold characteristics of the coming Messiah would be His "fear of the Lord."[20]

The New Testament continues the theme. Luke described the spiritually vibrant first-century church as a body of people who were "walking

---

[14]Henry, vol. 3, 470.
[15]Bunyan, 173.
[16]Exodus 18:21.
[17]II Samuel 23:3.
[18]Job 2:3.
[19]Psalm 112:1.
[20]Isaiah 11:2.

in the fear of the Lord."[21] And Paul himself admonishes us that if we are growing Christians we will be "perfecting holiness in the fear of God."[22] The Scriptures are clear, therefore, that *spiritual maturity is characterized by the fear of the Lord.* This is why in years gone by a mature believer was called simply "a God-fearing man."

Once again, Matthew Henry provides a wonderful summary to help us understand the blessedness of coming to this kind of maturity.

> Most people think that they are happy who never fear; but there is a fear which is so far from having torment in it, that it has in it the greatest satisfaction. Happy is the man who always keeps up in his mind a holy awe and reverence of God, his glory, goodness, and government, who is always afraid of offending God, and incurring his displeasure, who keeps his conscience tender, and has a dread of the appearance of evil, who is always [watchful] of himself, distrustful of his own sufficiency, and lives in expectation of troubles and changes, so that, whenever they come, they are no surprise to him. He who keeps up such a fear as this, will live a life of faith and watchfulness, and therefore happy is he, blessed and holy.[23]

As we can see, the fear of the Lord is not a characteristic that makes a man dull and dreary. We saw in Isaiah's case that the effect is just the opposite. It energized him to action—repentance, worship, and service.

Though some people question whether a Christian should be afraid of God, it should not be difficult to understand that it is entirely appropriate to fear God. In fact, a believer who is walking in the Spirit and enjoying the presence of God *delights* in the fear of the Lord!

Notice how the psalms repeatedly link rejoicing and happiness with fearing the Lord.

> Praise ye the Lord. Blessed is the man that feareth the Lord, that delighteth greatly in his commandments (Psalm 112:1).

> Blessed is every one that feareth the Lord; that walketh in his ways (Psalm 128:1).

---

[21]Acts 9:31.
[22]II Corinthians 7:1.
[23]Henry, vol. 3, 566.

Behold, that thus shall the man be blessed that feareth the Lord (Psalm 128:4).

Proverbs goes so far as to say that "the fear of the Lord is a fountain of life."[24] Later it says that it "[leads] to life."[25] Over and over we see that God puts it front and center as the characteristic of a man who is truly alive—actually living the way he was intended to live. That is why I say it is "the essence of man." Without the fear of the Lord a man is crippled and incomplete. Like a car without a functioning engine he can only be pulled and pushed by other forces.

BUT SHOULD WE REALLY *FEAR* GOD?

Some believers are still not convinced that fearing God is appropriate. They protest, "But we shouldn't fear God. He is a God of love. Isn't He depicted as a kind and loving Father?" They cannot conceive that they should fear someone they should love. They cannot fathom that love and godly fear can exist together. Yet Moses unmistakably weds them.

And now, Israel, what doth the Lord thy God require of thee, but to fear the Lord thy God, to walk in all his ways, and to love him, and to serve the Lord thy God with all thy heart and with all thy soul, to keep the commandments of the Lord, and his statutes, which I command thee this day for thy good? (Deuteronomy 10:12-13).

I have no trouble seeing how these elements can exist together because of the experiences I had with my own father. Some of those experiences I shall never forget.

I received the most memorable spanking of my life when I was about eight years old. We lived on my grandfather's three-thousand-acre cattle farm, where dad was the mechanic. He kept dozens of pieces of large machinery working. Being a conscientious mechanic, he did not like for a piece of farm equipment to be left out in the weather if there was some place to pull it inside out of the elements. He felt the same way about the bicycles and toy trucks of his three sons. We had to take

---

[24]Proverbs 14:27.
[25]Proverbs 19:23. See also 22:4.

them into the garage every night so that rust could not attack the axles of our toy trucks and tractors or the sprockets and chains on our bikes.

One evening as he was coming into the house for supper just after dusk, he passed my bicycle out in the yard. As he was taking off his jacket in the porch, he called to me and asked me why my bicycle was still outside. In a very smart-aleck tone I answered with my own rendition of Philippians 4:13, "Because I can do anything I want through Christ who strengthens me."

My father had a strong aversion for rust, but I found he had an even stronger dislike for arrogant perversions of the Scriptures. I thought I would die before the spanking ended! I saw my life pass before my eyes—being so young I had to watch several reruns of my life before the spanking was over. I shall never forget the experience.

He also had no tolerance for his sons cutting up in church. I liked to sit with the pastor's son, who was my age. He had to sit on the front row where his father could watch him, so I often sat with him. I remember times when we boys were acting up, and my father did not hesitate to march up in the middle of the song service to remove me from my place. He did not take me back to sit with the rest of the family until we had made a trip downstairs, where I would receive a spanking for my disobedience to him and my disrespect for the Lord's house.

I can honestly say that in those younger years, I feared my father. He knew how to raise boys, and when we pushed him we met with firm resistance. But when I say I feared him that does not mean I didn't love him or he didn't love me.

I always felt safe around Dad—unless I knew I had some correction coming to me. He was never capricious in his demands or unfair in his discipline. I always deserved what I got, and I knew it. I remember sitting next to him in church when I wasn't sitting with my friend and leaning my head against his arm and shoulder while the pastor preached. I still remember the smell of his wet wool suit jacket—still not completely dry from the snow falling outside as we came in. I felt comfortable and safe with him.

When I got into my teen years and was away from home more—at high school and later at an evening job—my contact with him diminished.

I no longer feared him as I should have, and my rebellion broke his heart. He could no longer spank me, but he often reminded me of God's ways and of how I was walking off the path. But I didn't care; I was home so very little, and I was so headstrong. I know he and Mom prayed much for me, and when I went off to BJU, where God turned me around, their hearts rejoiced as they saw God work in my heart. I begged their forgiveness, and I feared my dad once more. This time I didn't fear a spanking, but I feared violating his love and breaking his heart again.

John Bunyan in his masterpiece on the fear of God calls this the difference between a "slavish fear"—the fear that a slave would have for a hard master—and a "sonlike fear"—the fear a son would have for a loving father. In the sinful bitterness of my teen years I painted in my mind a picture of my father as a hard taskmaster. I did that by minimizing in my mind his strengths and accentuating his weaknesses and failures. The result was a slavish fear that was nourished by my willful disbelief about my father's genuine love for me. When properly fearing my father, I trembled at the thought of disobeying him but delighted in the security of being his son. Bunyan further instructs us in these matters.

> Would you grow in godly fear? Then labor always to keep your evidences of heaven and your salvation alive upon your heart; for he who loses his evidences of heaven will hardly keep slavish fear out of his heart, but he who has the wisdom and grace to keep them alive, and apparent to himself, will grow in godly fear. . . . Would you grow in this fear of God? Then set before your eyes the being and majesty of God; for that begets, maintains, and increases this fear.[26]

And again, we are brought back to the basics of seeking and maintaining a right view of God. It is the only exercise that can foster a proper fear of God. Let us look at one more facet of this topic before moving on to the applications of the fear of God to our relationships of life.

---

[26]Bunyan, 156-57.

CREATED FOR HIS GLORY

As I rebuilt my VW bug, I must confess that there were times at the beginning of the project that I was tempted to rebuild the engine with the necessary components to add significantly to its horsepower.[27] I could say that something from my teen years stirs within me, but that would be blaming the present urges on some nostalgic emotions of years gone by. There were really other, darker elements at work if I am honest with myself.

So what was really driving that urge? Or to broaden the question, "Why does a teen—even an older, fifty-year-old 'teen' for that matter—want the fast car?"

Quite simply, it is the pride of life. It is the desire to be noticed, to have some glory for himself, to make a statement, to be known as the person with the fast car, to stand out when the light turns green. It is the desire to *show* something: his own qualities—perhaps qualities such as superior mechanical ability, superior driving skills at the "starting line," or a superior bank account to finance such endeavors. More likely, he has subscribed to the pitiful belief that if his *car* is superior to other cars *he* is superior to other car owners. Though any thoughtful believer can see the fleshly motives driving such misguided perspectives, it is sometimes hard to be honest with yourself when you are in the middle of the situation. Pride's intoxicating effect always impairs good judgment.

By this time, you are probably wondering what this topic has to do with the fear of the Lord. I want to make my final—and perhaps my most important—point before leaving this chapter, so stay with me a bit longer.

I think you can see that if a car owner is going to get any glory to himself for his fast car, his car must have a high performance engine under the hood. That engine is the component that makes the statement the driver wants to make—though we must admit, the statement is an unworthy one when considering automobiles. No matter how nice the

---

[27]With the proper combination of larger pistons, stroker crankshaft and rods, hotter cam and so forth, a VW engine can generate 150-200 horsepower—a significant increase from its stock 65 horses.

car looks on the outside, without the high performance engine, it isn't going anywhere fast. Consequently, the driver is not going to have anything to *show*. He will just have to blend into the traffic with all the other uninteresting drivers on the street. Cars aren't people—although some of us affectionately give them names[28]—but if they did have personalities, a car with a poorly running engine would not be happy either.

I made the point earlier that the fear of the Lord is like an engine in the car. It is the essential component of man. Without it, all a man can do is work on his image. Without a maturing fear of the Lord a man has little godliness—he has nothing for his Owner to *show*. He cannot fulfil the purpose for which he was created. God gets little glory from his life because the "engine" driving him is so pathetic. And the man himself isn't happy because his "engine" isn't running well.

We were created so that God would have something to show about Himself. He can take trashed buckets of rust and make them into show material that leave their mark at the speed trials as well. Well-restored and highly performing entries demonstrate His glorious capabilities. Drawing attention to ourselves so that others will esteem us is an evidence of our pride. We are not worthy objects of the worship of others, but God *is* worthy of worship. We detract from *His* glory when we are poor examples of His workmanship.[29]

We were "created for *His* glory." Our well-tuned, highly performing "engines" of godliness are the means whereby He gets the glory due to Him. Without a mature godliness in our lives, He has little to show, and we are not happy "cars" either.

Over the years I have worked with Dad on various engines—everything from lawn mowers to motorcycles to Volkswagens and farm equipment. The sound of an engine turning over and continuing to fire when we finally started it again was a rewarding experience—even if it ran roughly at first. We then knew that probably the hardest part of the work was over. Now we could work on fine-tuning its performance.

---

[28]My daughters have affectionately named my bug "Herbie."
[29]Ephesians 2:10.

Once you have come to know Christ as your Savior, the "engine" of your soul begins to fire. It has been "dead in trespasses and sins."[30] You come alive as a creature. Though you may not have known what to call the phenomenon, you have begun to "fear the Lord." You began to be the kind of creature God originally intended you to be. You are no longer a flat, two-dimensional creature existing only in time and space, driven by your self-centered lusts.[31] An eternal, third dimension was reborn, and you are now driven by things you see in another realm. The "engine" is running—perhaps roughly, but it is running!

CHANGED INTO HIS IMAGE

The process of fine-tuning the roughly running engine of the soul by beholding God and growing in godliness is called sanctification. I have devoted an entire book, *Changed into His Image: God's Plan for Transforming Your Life*, to the study of how we change and grow in likeness to Christ. It could be considered a "Fine-Tuning Manual" for the Christian life.

Obviously, I cannot duplicate its contents here. Many of its themes have been reintroduced throughout this book as the occasion warranted. If your mind is not yet clear about the "nuts and bolts" of becoming like Christ, I urge you to diligently study the doctrine of sanctification. It is God's plan of how you grow in the fear of the Lord—the godliness that characterizes Jesus Christ.

Once the God-ward component of your soul has been installed at salvation, you can begin living the way God intended you to live. I want you to think of the following two chapters as a "Driver's Manual" to help you apply what we have been studying about fearing the Lord to the principal relationships of your life.

TAKE TIME TO REFLECT

1. What attributes of God are a part of His *greatness*?
2. What attributes of God are a part of His *goodness*?
3. In what ways do you feel vulnerable when you think about God's *greatness*?

---

[30]Ephesians 2:1.
[31]Ephesians 2:2-3.

4. In what ways do you feel secure and full of hope when you think about God's *goodness*?

5. What does it mean to have an awe of God? How is that demonstrated in your life? Can you say that you actually fear God?

A WORD TO DISCIPLE-MAKERS

The Cure for Fear

Our society is seeing a growing incidence rate of anxiety disorders. Unfortunately, the church is not lagging very far behind in the anxiety of its members. Many believers seem to have little consciousness that their worry and fear are violations of God's commands to "be [anxious] for nothing"[32] and to "fear thou not."[33] Many who continue in their unchecked fears soon find themselves under the bondage of obsessive-compulsive disorders, panic disorders, gastrointestinal disorders, sleep disorders, generalized anxiety disorders, and the like.

There is no denying the reality of the symptoms experienced in each of these disorders. The shortness of breath and increased heart rate of a panic attack are very real—and extremely disconcerting. The "obsessive" thoughts that bombard the mind and the seemingly overpowering urge to repeat certain rituals to relieve the discomfort of OCD is also real. And just as real is the crippling pain of anxiety-related gastrointestinal sufferers. The pain is not "in their head"—it is felt very acutely in their body—but the underlying cause *is* in the way they think about the vulnerabilities of life. The cause is an unbiblical approach to their fears. Proverbs speaks well to the issue when Solomon says, "The fear of man bringeth a snare: but whoso putteth his trust in the Lord shall be safe."[34]

Though the psychiatric world has gone to great lengths to catalog the constellation of symptoms of these problems, and has rightly called them "anxiety" disorders, it can offer no satisfying and lasting solution. That is understandable because the world dismisses all that God says about anxiety. And sadly, believers who ignore God's diagnosis of and cure for anxiety can turn only to the world's feeble attempts to blunt

---

[32]Philippians 4:6.
[33]Isaiah 41:10.
[34]Proverbs 29:25.

the brain with medications while trying to adjust their lifestyle to avoid uncomfortable vulnerabilities. Though this is all the world can do, the believer has a much more satisfying solution—the fear of God. Jeremiah Burroughs, when commenting on Isaiah 66:2, "to this man will I look, even to him that is [humble] and of a contrite spirit, and trembleth at my word," has these comments:

> "[Godly] fear and trembling at the Word is that which will settle the heart and strengthen the heart against all other fears. It will swallow up other fears that are greater. . . . But that it has a virtue in it to strengthen the heart, to make it stand out against all other fears, this is that which is the gracious trembling at the Word. For instance, a heart that trembles at the Word; though he was afraid then, yet when it comes to outward losses and afflictions in the world, such a heart is not much afraid there.[35]

Believers who are living anxious lives are not living in an immediate awareness that God is powerful, that He cares intensely about them, and that He is present with them now. Their ignorance of God's love and power leaves them with such a low view of Him that they often have some rather unholy thoughts about God.

Their constant sinning against the Lord through their worry has placed a relational distance between them and God so that they do not have any sense that He is near or that He wants to help them. Since they do not know God well and are distant from Him because their sin has broken their fellowship with Him, it is hard for them to understand how knowing God will bring any rest to their souls. Yet this is exactly Jesus' meaning when He says,

> Come unto me, all ye that labour and are heavy laden, and *I will give you rest*. Take my yoke [of fellowship] upon you, and learn of me; for I am meek and lowly in heart: *and ye shall find rest unto your souls*. For my yoke is [custom-made for you], and my burden is light (Matthew 11:28-30).

There can be no "wisdom" to solve life's dilemmas when we ignore the very foundation of that wisdom—the fear of the Lord. Solomon said it this way,

---

[35]Jeremiah Burroughs, *Gospel Fear* (1647; reprint, Morgan, Pa.: Soli Deo Gloria Publications, 1991), 42.

The fear of the Lord is the [starting place] of wisdom: and the knowledge of the holy is understanding (Proverbs 9:10).

When we see life's uncertainties from God's perspective and see God Himself clearly, we do not fear. Let me illustrate it this way.

Tinkerbell, the Cat

I grew up on a farm and was always around animals. That was not true for my daughters, who grew up on a university campus, especially since we have not ever had any pets except goldfish. When my parents eventually moved to Greenville, S.C., where we live, they brought with them a huge Siamese cat named Tinkerbell.

Our family traditionally went to Grandma and Grandpa's home on Thursday evenings for dinner. My two oldest daughters—about four and six years of age at the time of this scenario—loved to go to their home but would not get out of the car to go into the house until they had been assured that Tinkerbell was *not* in the house. For some reason the cat scared them. I can partially understand that because Tinkerbell was large and they were quite small. The cat could look quite ferocious to them up close.

Think of it this way. It would be very much like an adult being told to walk up to a full-grown lion while someone says, "Pet the kitty." Most of us would have second thoughts about the invitation. I think my daughters felt the same way.

The only time they felt safe to "pet the kitty" was when I held Tinkerbell in my lap. They would gingerly reach out their little hands, stroke Tinkerbell's fur, and run away calling to their mother, "Mommy, Mommy, I pet the kitty! I pet the kitty!"

My question is this: "Why did they feel safe petting Tinkerbell when he was on my lap but would not go near him otherwise?" The answer is in some things they *knew* about their dad. They knew I was bigger than the cat. They knew I loved them and would protect them, and they knew I was right there ready to help if needed. I know that all three of those elements were part of their thought processes because when my father, their grandfather, put Tinkerbell in his lap and asked them to "come pet the kitty" they would not do it.

They could see that their grandpa was bigger than the kitty. They could see that Grandpa was near and ready to help. Their fears were not calmed, however, by his size and his nearness. The missing element was that at four and six years of age they had not been around their grandfather enough to know that he, too, loved them.

Most believers will not doubt that God is powerful. Nor will they doubt that He is present all the time, though they may feel distant to Him. What they are not sure of is that God loves *them*. In fact, a very powerful God who does not especially care for you is a source of even greater fears.

There is no cause for living in constant fear—and anxiety is just a form of fear—when you have been taught by God Himself from the Word that He is powerful, that He is present, and that you are secure because *He loves you!* A review of the teachings of chapters two through six of this book will bring His love into greater focus if you need help seeing the unchanging love of our wonderful God for you.

God never promises to remove our fears. Instead, He repeatedly *commands* us to "fear thou not."[36] His command is usually followed by a reminder about something that is true of His nature. Meditation upon that aspect of who He is will cause our hearts to rest if we will believe it. For example, in Isaiah 41:10 God says, "Fear thou not; *for I am with thee.*" A person who refuses to meditate upon God's ever-present care for him will have a hard time obeying the command not to fear. In other places He tells him not to fear because He has promised to save him and has wonderful plans for him though he is in the midst of His chastening now.

Believers, of all people, should not be anxious folks. Our constant worry is a reflection of our low view of God and of our continued disobedience in handling our trouble our own way. It reveals an absence of a maturing fear of the Lord.

---

[36]See Isaiah 41:10; Jeremiah 30:10; 46:28; Zephaniah 3:16-17.

CHAPTER ELEVEN

RULING IN THE FEAR OF GOD

WOUNDED HEARTS

Theresa's Story[1]

The scenes are not uncommon. A woman in her early forties sobs out her story as she seeks help from a godly woman in her church. Her husband, Joel, has not shown any real spiritual depth for their entire twenty years of marriage. He is actively involved in service opportunities at their church, but at home he is spiritually colorless. He will lecture their teens—two sons and a daughter—about being irresponsible or rebellious but doesn't make any attempt to seriously disciple them. He rules them by the force of his quick-tempered personality and his power to ground them or assign them work details. His way of handling people and problems is by controlling them with more force.

Theresa has begged Joel to be gentler with the children. She has watched the light go out in their eyes. They have given up trying to please their father out of any sense of devotion. They do so now simply to escape his wrath and restrictions. Her heart breaks as she sees them hardening their wills against him and against God.

To make matters worse, the boys are having trouble at school. In junior high they both acted up quite a bit, but now in high school the stakes are higher. Both of them have been suspended once for continued

---

[1]Please keep in mind that the illustrations you encounter in this text have been greatly changed "to protect the guilty." Names and details have been altered so that no situation, as it is printed, represents any actual individual in my acquaintance. While I do not wish for anyone's personal identity to be exposed, I would hope that all of us would see ourselves often in the various scenarios so that biblical truth can be more readily understood and applied.

disrespect to teachers and even to the principal himself. The next time could mean expulsion.

In addition, she has watched her daughter become very sensual. Joel thought her tight skirts and blouses were "cute" in junior high and even commented to his daughter about how "grown-up" she looked as her body filled out. Her dress now in high school is no longer "cute." It is downright seductive, and the boys at school and in the youth group have noticed. Theresa is worried about where this will lead, but Joel dismisses her concerns as prudish.

Theresa also confides that the marriage itself is on shaky ground. She has even threatened to leave Joel. His simple reply is "Where would you go, and how do you intend to finance your expedition?" The light has gone out in her eyes as well. She has lost all hope that he will ever change. She has pleaded with him to go with her to the pastor for counseling. Joel insists that there is nothing wrong with his life and tells her that if she would be more submissive to him the children wouldn't be having so many problems either. He has forbidden her to see the pastor. She has dutifully complied with that specific request, but now out of desperation is talking with a woman in the church she deeply respects for her godliness.

Robin's Story

Robin's husband, Phil, is very much the opposite of Joel. While Joel is *quick*-tempered and controlling when handling problems, Phil is *quiet*-tempered and complacent. Robin and Phil have been married ten years and have two elementary-aged children. Samuel, the older, is seven and is autistic. Kendra is five. They determined that because Samuel required so much care they could not have any more children after Kendra was born. Until recently Kendra has been an "easy" child to raise. She has been cheerful, helpful, and obedient to her mother, who must spend much of her day attending to Samuel's needs.

Robin has tried to deal with her growing bitterness to Phil, who does-n't help with Samuel when he is home. He fancies himself to be an Internet day trader in his time at home and spends many hours every evening at his computer playing the stock market. He plays with Kendra when she pesters him enough, but he is totally uninvolved with Samuel. Robin has asked Phil if he resents Samuel or if he is afraid to interact with him because of his special needs, but Phil denies there is any problem. He merely comments that Samuel responds best to her and leaves it at that.

Phil and Robin haven't had a serious spiritual discussion since their first year of marriage. He says he reads his Bible while on his break at work, but Robin has never seen him open his Bible at home.

One year ago she was ordering some clothes online and found pornographic URLs in the browser history of their computer. She confronted Phil about it, but he laughed it off and said he was playing a joke on someone at work. He never could explain how his viewing pornography could be used as a joke, but he insisted she didn't have to worry about him. Nonetheless, she checked the browser history in the days ahead and found he had accessed many additional links.

Talking with Phil about it again was useless. He tried to make her think that because he had gone to some sites the first time, he had been put on some kind of mailing list that automatically put those links in the browser history. Again, she didn't know enough about computers to prove him wrong, but later she learned that his explanation was a lie.

Robin began to have some physical problems of her own. A spastic colon now makes her life miserable, and her spirits are heading deeper and deeper into despair. Samuel still needs constant attention. Kendra, sensing the tension in the home and her mother's despair, is growing increasingly irritable herself. Phil is the only one who hasn't changed. He is still resolutely distant from the family.

Joel and Phil

Our hearts go out to Theresa and Robin. We sympathize with the crushing burdens these women bear because their husbands have misused headship—as in the case of Joel—or have abandoned headship—as in the case of Phil. Though Joel and Phil are the main cause of their family's hopelessness, if they were to ever be honest with themselves, they would have to admit that they have been losing hope too.

Joel sees his ill-temperedness and has tried various tactics to help himself get it under control. The bare facts staring him in the face show him that he is losing his family, and he doesn't know what to do. His pride is still too strong for him to humble himself before his wife and children to ask their forgiveness. He reasons that even if he did he would turn around and mess up again.

He still refuses to see the pastor. He has seen some chinks in the pastor's armor when he worked on a special projects committee at the church and doesn't feel that he should have to "spill his guts" to someone who doesn't have his act together either. So Joel continues in his frustration while his anger and heavy-handedness tears his family apart.

Phil, too, in his more sober moments knows that his growing pornography addiction is going to catch up with him in some way. He knows Robin is taxed to her limit caring for Samuel, but it is easier simply to lose his troubled thoughts in his stock trading and pornography than to deal with the problems at home. He solaces himself with the thought that he is providing for his family financially through his trading efforts. Deep down he knows he is failing but won't allow himself to think about it much. He avoids such uncomfortable thoughts just as he avoids uncomfortable responsibilities.

GOD'S PRESCRIPTION FOR FAILING RULERS

God has a solution for Phil and Joel that not only will breathe hope into their own souls but also will bring hope to their wives as well. As you might guess from the title of this chapter, that solution is the fear of the Lord.

Second Samuel 23:1-5 is called "the last words of David" because he spoke them after he had crowned Solomon as his successor shortly before his own death. David under inspiration wrote from his experience.

> He that ruleth over men must be just, *ruling in the fear of God.* And he shall be as the light of the morning, when the sun riseth, even a morning without clouds; as the tender grass springing out of the earth [like sunshine] after rain (vv. 3-4).

King David knew that to be "just"—to fulfill all responsibilities within a particular relationship—a man must be "ruling in the fear of God." Neither Joel nor Phil is "just" because they are not fulfilling their responsibilities in their homes. They are placing little value on the spiritual development and well-being of their wives and children and

236

placing high value upon their own image and pursuits. They are unjust and will stand before the Righteous Judge one day to give an account of why they squandered valuable time and energy on meaningless and/or sinful pursuits while ignoring significant responsibilities in their homes.

The following discussion and accompanying diagram should help us understand more fully what components make up the fear of the Lord and how they apply to Christians who have leadership responsibilities.

It perhaps bears mentioning that the truths of this chapter are not for fathers and husbands only. They apply to women as well when they have been given positions of leadership as mothers over children in the home or supervisors over people in the workplace and so forth. A fleshly mother can be just as much a tyrant to her children as a fleshly father. A fleshly mother can be just as negligent in her responsibilities to care for and chasten her children as a fleshly father.

The same biblical expectations are in place for college students who have a position of leadership in a campus organization or in a dormitory room. They apply to a high school student who leads a team at teen camp, supervises a car wash activity, organizes a senior-class fundraiser, or leads the soccer squad in exercise drills in the coach's absence.

These truths are also in force in the workplace when men or women oversee the labors of others. They must not fail to use their power to advance the mission of the organization, but neither may they become abusive, tyrannical, harsh, condescending, critical, impatient, or un-feeling towards those they lead. The apostle Paul is clear in Ephesians and Colossians that these principles apply to masters in the labor force. It is essential that we understand how these truths apply whenever any of us has been given a position of sovereignty—rulership—over others.

Furthermore, these truths are important to both men and women for these additional reasons. The unmarried woman needs to know what a God-fearing man looks like so that she will know which men qualify for marriage. Married women who have God-fearing husbands can rejoice that they have such men. Married women who do not have God-fearing husbands can better know how to pray for their husbands. Parents with sons can instruct those sons in the ways of God so that they will become God-fearing men one day, and parents with daughters can prepare their daughters to marry a man only if he is indeed a God-fearing man. The truths we are discussing are, therefore, universal to everyone. Let's look specifically at God's remedy for failing rulers.

Biblical Sovereignty

As we saw in chapter two, "The *grand reality* is God. His eternal existence and absolute supremacy are the most central fact of the universe. He is *first* of all!"[2] "Grand" means simply the greatest, most significant. The fact that God exists eternally as our Creator and man is simply His creature is illustrated in the left box on the diagram below. It is the distortion and ignorance of that ultimate—grand—reality that is at the root of all our troubles. It is at the root of the troubles for Phil and Joel too.

"The Grand Reality *Principle*" is the application of "The Grand Reality" to our lives and is illustrated in the box on the right. The fact that God is the Creator automatically puts Him in the position of supremacy from which He derives His sovereignty over all He has created. That sovereignty—His "right and might to rule"—is His by virtue of His *greatness*—all the intrinsic powers of His nature that grant Him infinite power, infinite wisdom, infinite presence, infinite stability, and so forth. It is never experienced, however, apart from His *goodness*—His infinite love, compassion, mercy, and grace.

The Grand Reality

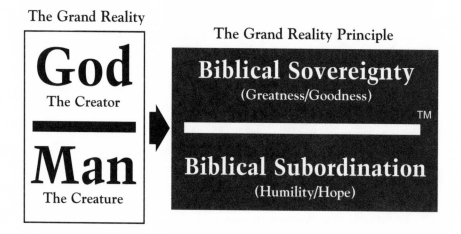

------

[2]See page 28 of this book.

When God assigns to a man the "sovereignty"—rulership—over his family as a father, over his church as a pastor, or over his fellow creatures as a manager, that man has been granted by God the "greatness" of power. That power must be exercised, however, with the same "goodness" that is characteristic of God Himself. When it is used in this manner, David says that ruler is welcomed like a cloudless morning.[3]

How can an ill-tempered man like Joel or a complacent, laid-back man like Phil exercise his sovereignty in a way that his wife will welcome? In both cases these men have accepted a position of sovereignty but have not yet been rightly subordinated under *their* sovereign—God Himself. They cannot rule, therefore, in the fear of God.

Biblical Subordination
The telltale signs that a man has rightly seen God's sovereignty over him as a creature are that he is duly *humbled* and at the same time that he has great *hope*. Joel and Phil are missing both. Note these two elements in the right-hand box in the diagram above.

The *humility* will be manifested in a continued sense of dependence upon God and a regular practice of repentance before God and others he has wronged. It will breed a tenderness and gentleness in him that tempers his fleshly tendencies to run from problems or to handle problems with a heavy fist.

The *hope* will be displayed in his courage and boldness to carry out difficult responsibilities. He will not have to use carnal, excessive force to gain cooperation because his confidence to bring about change rests not in his own powers but in the promised involvement and blessing of God in his labors.

THE TRADEMARK OF THE FEAR OF GOD
The result of this blend of humility and hope is a tender aggressiveness and an aggressive tenderness in a man's dealings with others. *His own subordination under God will temper how he exercises sovereignty over others.* John Bunyan notes, "where the fear of God . . . is not growing, no grace thrives, nor is duty done as it should be."[4] He states further, "the

---

[3]Note in Leviticus 25:14-17, 36, and 43 the warnings against mistreatment of others because of the fear of the Lord.

[4]Bunyan, 145.

world will not be convinced by your talk, by your ideas, and by the great profession that you make, if they see not therewith mixed the lively impressions of the fear of God."[5]

You will notice in the right-hand box a small ™. That symbol stands for "trademark." The dictionary defines a trademark as "a distinctive sign by which a person or thing comes to be known."[6]

By placing ™ inside the box, I want to underscore the truth that if a man is truly living in the fear of God his life has this distinctive quality: He exercises his sovereignty with greatness *and* goodness, which engenders humility *and* hope in his followers. This is why David said that those who rule in the fear of God will be welcomed like a cloudless morning. Notice Matthew Henry's comments on II Samuel 23:3-4.

> [Rulers] must rule in the fear of God, that is, they must themselves be possessed with a fear of God, by which they will be effectually restrained from all acts of injustice and oppression. Nehemiah was so, *ch. v. 15. So did not I, because of the fear of God;* and Joseph, Gen. Xliii. 18. They must also endeavor to promote the fear of God, that is, the practice of religion, among those over whom they rule. The [leader] is to be the keeper of both tables [of the law], and to protect both godliness and honesty.
>
> [The happy result will be that] he that rules *in the fear of God, shall be as the light of the morning, v. 4.* Light is sweet and pleasant, and he that does his duty shall have the comfort of it; his rejoicing will be the testimony of his conscience. Light is bright, and a good [leader] is illustrious; his justice and piety will be his honour. Light is a blessing, nor are there greater and more extensive blessings to the public, than [leaders] that *rule in the fear of God.* It is like *the light of the morning,* which is most welcome after the darkness of the night, . . . which is increasing, shines more and more to the perfect day; such is the growing lustre of a good government. It is likewise compared to the tender grass, which the earth produces for the service of man; it brings with it a harvest of blessings [italics his; underscoring mine].[7]

---

[5]Ibid., 149.

[6]*The American Heritage Dictionary of the English Language,* s.v. "trademark."

[7]Henry, vol. 2, 1015.

GOD'S RULE FOR RULERS

With this overview of the Grand Reality and its principle behind us, let us look more carefully at God's rule for how rulers ought to rule. David captures this rule in the words we have just looked at: "He that ruleth over men must be just, ruling in the fear of God."

When God gives any believer a position of *sovereignty*—by that I mean a position of rulership—he must exercise that rulership in a way that reflects his own *subordination* under God. Notice these warnings to New Testament masters.

> And, ye masters, do the same things unto them, forbearing threatening: *knowing that your Master also is in heaven; neither is there respect of persons with him* (Ephesians 6:9).

> Masters, give unto your servants that which is just and equal; *knowing that ye also have a Master in heaven* (Colossians 4:1).

> My brethren, be not many masters [i.e., don't be ambitious to be teachers], knowing that we shall receive the greater condemnation [i.e., stricter judgment] (James 3:1).

> The elders which are among you I exhort, . . . feed the flock of God which is among you, taking the oversight thereof, not by [compulsion], but willingly; not [out of greed for gain], but [eagerly]; neither as [lording it over] God's heritage, but being [examples] to the flock. And *when the chief Shepherd shall appear*, ye shall receive a crown of glory that fadeth not away (I Peter 5:1-4).

These passages warn those in leadership that they will have a very strict accountability before the Master in heaven. Because of that accountability, the use of oppressive threats and unjust treatment are forbidden by God Himself. The leader's response to those in his charge must be one that reflects his own subordination under God. Even pastors, God's under-shepherds, are accountable to the Chief Shepherd. *No one who has been granted authority is free to use that authority in ways not authorized by God Himself. He must use his authority to accomplish God's purposes in God's manner.*

For example, a police officer has been issued a badge and a gun. The gun enhances his personal "might." The badge authorizes him—gives him the "right"—to use that gun for certain purposes with certain limitations. He can fail his duty in two basic ways.

An unruly officer can use his "right and might" to feed his own twisted ego by intimidating civilians. When he stops a motorist for speeding, he can brandish his gun and insist that the driver get out of his car and put his hands on the car while the officer frisks him. If the motorist resists in some way, he can further antagonize him by sticking the weapon in his ribs while threatening to shoot if he doesn't stand still. If the motorist further resists him, he can handcuff him and throw him on the ground face down and perhaps kick him in the ribs. All the while the fact that he is wearing a badge and waving a gun puts him at a decided advantage over the motorist, who must—at least for now—comply out of fear for his life. We would call this misuse of power "police brutality."

An officer acting in this way has forgotten that he has an authority over him who has the "right and might" to hold him accountable for his flagrant *abuse* of power.

On the other hand, it is possible to have an officer who has been issued a badge and a gun but *fails* to use it when he should. He can hear the dispatcher over his police radio tell him of an armed robbery in progress at a mall a couple of blocks away. He delays his arrival, however, because he is listening to a ball game on the radio and doesn't want to miss the pitches of the final inning. Or perhaps he delays his arrival because of his own personal fear of being shot if he interferes. When he does finally arrive at the scene, the thieves have escaped and the storeowner has been fatally shot.

He too is in serious trouble with his superiors. He has not abused his authority by applying excessive force. Rather, he has neglected to use his authority when he should have. Both of these officers have miserably failed their duties because *they selfishly placed their own interests above the interests of those who authorized them.* It should not be difficult to see the many applications of these two excesses to a father's leadership in the home, but let's look at an illustration that may help us better understand the kind of headship God has given a man in his home.

THE CHIEF GREENHOUSE KEEPER

In two closely related passages in Ephesians Paul gives fathers and husbands some very clear directives.

Directives to Husbands

Husbands, love your wives, even as Christ also loved the church, and gave himself for it; that he might sanctify and cleanse it with the washing of water by the word, that he might present it to himself a glorious church, not having spot, or wrinkle, or any such thing; but that it should be holy and without blemish. So ought men to love their wives as their own bodies. He that loveth his wife loveth himself. For no man ever yet hated his own flesh; but *nourisheth and cherisheth* it, even as the Lord [does] the church (Ephesians 5:25-29).

Directives to Fathers

And, ye fathers, provoke not your children to wrath: but bring them up in the *nurture and admonition* of the Lord (Ephesians 6:4).

Here is the primary mandate given to the head of the home. He is to promote the change and growth—the sanctification—of his wife and children. *His home is a greenhouse for growing spiritual plants.* His authorization from God as the head was given primarily for this purpose. He is the climate-control agent. He is to determine what each individual plant needs to grow. He regulates the temperature and humidity of the atmosphere. He checks for diseases and properly treats them. He ties up the new shoots and prunes the extraneous ones. He fertilizes the soil and waters the beds. He replaces the broken glass in the greenhouse windows and seals the cracks that allow winter air to penetrate the room. He has been authorized and empowered to do whatever is necessary to grow healthy plants.

It would be a tragic misuse of his powers if he neglected the care of the plants and turned a portion of the greenhouse into a hunting lodge, entertainment center, crash pad, or office for his side business. Yet this is exactly what many Christian men do with the "greenhouse" of their own home. It becomes many other things but does not become a healthy environment for the growth of Christian "plants."

He may protest that it is his home and he can do with it what he wishes. His Master has other ideas about it, however. In fact, the Lord Himself told a parable about a house-steward like this.

> Who then is that faithful and wise steward, whom his lord shall make ruler over his household, to give them their [rations] in due season? Blessed is that servant, whom his lord when he cometh shall find so doing. Of a truth I say unto you, that he will make him ruler over all that he hath. But and if that servant say in his heart, My lord delayeth his coming; and shall begin to beat the menservants and maidens, and to eat and drink, and to be drunken; the lord of that servant will come in a day when he looketh not for him, and at an hour when he is not aware. . . . And that servant, which . . . prepared not himself, *neither did according to his will*, shall be beaten with many stripes (Luke 12:42-47).

This steward was given a job to do. He was to make sure the other servants had what they needed to get their jobs done. But the steward in charge treated them roughly and used his newfound authority to take it easy. He spent his time pursuing his own drunken pleasures while neglecting his responsibilities. Jesus' rebuke was quite stout. The unfaithful steward would be severely beaten.

Sadly, so many husbands and fathers neglect their greenhouse responsibilities of growing spiritual "plants" and use their authority and headship to pursue their own interests. They become stumbling blocks to their families. Jesus' words to them are also appropriately stout.

> But whoso shall offend one of these little ones which believe in me [i.e., cause one of these little ones to stumble; make it hard for him to walk as he should], it were better for him that a millstone were hanged about his neck, and that he were drowned in the depth of the sea (Matthew 18:6).

A husband and father has not been given authority by God so that he can get his wife and children to do what *he* wants any more than a police officer can use his badge and gun to get citizens to do what *he* wants. A husband and father can use his headship to accomplish *only* God's purposes for his wife and children.

That may mean he has to put his foot down at times to control the greenhouse climate by censoring music and movies that are brought into the home or by forbidding the children to play with certain friends who are corruptive. It may mean that he has to use his power to spank his child or to bring to bear some other form of chastening so that the child learns he cannot step off the path of obedience to Mom or Dad. It may mean that he must insist that the children take music lessons until a certain age or that they limit their work in town as a teen so as not to interfere with their church attendance or participation in the summer youth mission team. These are all part of wise "greenhouse keeping" but must be done to fulfill the Master's purpose, not the father's dreams. Furthermore, the Master prescribes the *manner* in which the father administers his correction. He must do so with a self-restraint, love, meekness, and gentleness that demonstrates the control of the Spirit in his own life.[8] *Any use of his power for his own ends or in a wrong spirit is an abuse of power!*

Jesus Himself was such a testimony of humble restraint of His powers. Listen to John's statement about Jesus.

> He was in the world, and *the world was made by him,* and the world knew him not. He came unto his own, and *his own received him not* (John 1:10-11).

He had every "right" and He possessed the "might" to throw His weight around—after all, He made it all—but His use of authority evoked humility and hope in His followers. Why? Because as the Messiah, He had upon Him the "spirit . . . of the fear of the Lord."[9] He exercised His *greatness* with a God-approved *goodness.* Jesus' use of authority is the trademark of the God-fearing person.

FLESHLY HEADSHIP

We have already looked at two extremes illustrated by two contrasting sets of leaders—Joel in contrast to Phil and an overbearing police officer in contrast to an uninvolved one. I want to revisit each of these fleshly styles of headship one more time. We want to recognize

---

[8]Galatians 5:22-23.
[9]Isaiah 11:2.

them so clearly that we will notice them at first glance when they creep into our headship.

Self-Serving Authoritarianism

When a leader is oppressive and uses his authority in a demeaning, self-centered way, he is operating in an authoritarian manner. This means *he pleases himself by controlling others more than God intends—too strictly—or by ruling others in a spirit God forbids—too harshly*. It is the "spirit of Saul" we find throughout I Samuel. King Saul capriciously threw spears at David while David played his harp for him,[10] threw a spear at his own son,[11] chased the exiled David through the wilderness,[12] and even sentenced his own son to death for violating a command his son never heard.[13] The end result was that Saul drove his own son Jonathan away from himself and further cemented Jonathan's relationship with Saul's own perceived enemy, David. The "Sauls" of life manifest their pride by *controlling* problems and people.

The parallels to this today are innumerable. I remember an incident here at the University in which a young lady had to be disciplined. She readily repented and accepted the consequences with a broken spirit. She had stepped off the path of obedience to God's moral laws and knew it. She was relieved that her sin was discovered and that she could now put it behind her. She was encouraged that the people dealing with her wanted to help her grow through the chastening so that she could in due time taste "the peaceable fruit of righteousness."[14] Her father's response unfortunately was typical of an increasing number of Christian men who operate with self-serving authoritarian manners. He was demanding and abusive with the dean of women. When the dean of women finished the phone conversation, the student apologized for her father. She said, "My dad is a manipulator. He thinks he can push everybody around and get whatever he wants." Here is a modern-day father attempting to control problems and people in the spirit of Saul—the spirit of the flesh.

---

[10]I Samuel 18:10-11.

[11]I Samuel 20:30-34.

[12]I Samuel 22-24.

[13]I Samuel 14:23-45.

[14]Hebrews 12:11.

I have often seen heavy-handed fathers who thought they were "teaching a lesson" to their sons, but instead, merely made their sons more bitter. As a result the sons sought out like-minded companions who led them farther down a path of destruction. All the while the authoritarian dad salves his own conscience by rationalizing that he is just doing his job. *The sad part is that a father who is ruling with this kind of iron fist doesn't even realize that he is actually teaching by example that it is OK to disobey authority.* Dad himself is disobeying God's commands to "restore such an one in the spirit of meekness; considering thyself, lest thou also be tempted."[15] His son logically—though unbiblically—reasons, "If Dad doesn't have to obey *his* authority, why do I have to obey *mine?*" The boy has a point—on the human level! Dad needs to heed I Timothy 4:15-16.

> Meditate upon these things; give *thyself* wholly to them; that thy profiting may appear to all. Take heed unto *thyself*, and unto the doctrine; continue in them: for in doing this thou shalt both [spare] *thyself*, and them that hear thee.

Dad is modeling rebellion before his son's eyes. He is not "ruling in the fear of God." The Puritans saw the fear of God as a bridle that kept a man in check. Remove the bridle and the horse runs wild. The fact that news periodicals carry regular articles dealing with male rage is a sad commentary on the state of our nation.[16]

Even more tragic is that this controlling man is increasingly common within the church. He may be the most faithful man in the congregation. He would never miss church! Everyone knows his high standards for music, dress, and punctuality. He can quote the Scriptures to back up his views, but ironically, no one—including his children—wants to follow him. There is something in him that repulses other people. It is the absence of the proper fear of God. If he ruled in the fear of God, he would be welcomed like a cloudless morning.[17]

---

[15]Galatians 6:1.

[16]Susan Faludi, "Rage of the American Male." *Newsweek*, August 16, 1999, 31, is one such example. Unfortunately, it misses the mark of the real cause for the rise in anger—self-centeredness—and sees other problems as the source.

[17]II Samuel 23:3-4.

Self-Serving Permissivism

On the opposite end of the spectrum are the Phils—those laid-back leaders who don't get involved. Their pride manifests itself not by *controlling* problems and people but by *avoiding* problems and people. *They please themselves by allowing more than God intends—too tolerant.* Their passivity promotes a permissive leadership style that neglects spiritual responsibilities.

Permissive leaders are often "approval junkies," mainlining the acceptance of others. They cannot have anyone upset with them. Their motto is "peace at any cost." This is the spirit of Eli, who would not rebuke the debauchery of his sons. God told the boy Samuel,

> For I have told [Eli] that I will judge his house for ever for the iniquity *which he knoweth;* because his sons made themselves vile,[18] and *he restrained them not* (I Samuel 3:13).

Permissive leaders are not using their God-given authority to control the climate of the greenhouse. Nor do they take action to keep out wintry drafts, insects, or other predators. They do not want to be involved. Their pride may manifest itself in sheer laziness (i.e., today's "couch potato"), fear of disapproval, uncertainty because of ignorance, or any number of other ways. The result is the same: the plants are malnourished, diseased, unproductive, and ugly.

In both Joel and Phil, pride is destroying the plants in their greenhouse. *Leadership isn't about controlling others as much as it is about controlling our own lusts—our own pride.* Giving in to it is lethal to ourselves and to the plants in our greenhouse.

For those who see themselves in these scenarios, there is much hope! We will discuss that hope in the next chapter, where we will look at the results of lining ourselves up under God's sovereignty—where we learn to walk in the fear of the Lord.

---

[18]According to I Samuel 2:22, "they lay with the women that assembled at the door of the tabernacle of the congregation."

TAKE TIME TO REFLECT

1. List all the positions of "sovereignty"—rulership—that God has given you (i.e., husband, mother or father, grandparent, church responsibility, work supervisory role, civic leadership, etc.).

2. In what ways do you attempt to *control* people and problems when you are not ruling in the fear of God?

3. In what ways do you attempt to *avoid* people and problems when you are not ruling in the fear of God?

4. King David said in II Samuel 23:3, "He that ruleth over men must be *just*, ruling in the fear of God." In what ways do you have difficulty being "just" when you are fearing men rather than fearing God?

5. In the leadership roles in which you have the responsibility for the spiritual growth of others, how would you rate your effectiveness as a "greenhouse keeper"? Rate yourself on a scale of 1 to 10 (1 = very ineffective at facilitating spiritual growth; 10 = very effective at facilitating spiritual growth). Explain your rating.

A WORD TO DISCIPLE-MAKERS

Let's Not Fail the Women

While it is easy for pastors to grow frustrated with controlling men like Joel and passive men like Phil, we must not ignore their plight. They are "overtaken in a fault" and must be restored "in the spirit of meekness."[19] Restoring a "greenhouse keeper" to his rightful responsibilities is much more effective than trying to keep all his plants alive by marshaling help from others to support and nurture them while he continues to create an atmosphere destructive to growth.

The wives of these men—the Theresas and the Robins—live with these men day in and day out and after a period of time lose hope. Some bail out of the marriage. Others stay in and nurture a family of bitter children. A small minority of spiritually minded women suffer in a Christlike manner and are a rich blessing to their children and to others. They pay a high personal price for their godly submission and will be richly rewarded by their Lord, Jesus Christ.

---

[19]Galatians 6:1.

In most cases these women have at one time or another made their plight known to a spiritually minded man in the church—often the pastor. My grievance is that so little is done to help them. They are often told, "Check up on your own life and ask yourself, 'What am I doing to provoke his wrath?'" Or "There isn't anything I as your pastor can do about this until your husband wants to submit to counsel. In the meantime, you will have to look to God for strength while you suffer through this."

I readily acknowledge that the wife may need to ask herself if she is biblically submitting to her husband. She certainly does need to look to God for strength. But those words aren't enough! The apostle James warned believers not to send needy people off with mere words of comfort when they also needed active intervention on their behalf.[20] *While the wife is attending to her own soul before the Lord, the pastor should be attending to her husband!*

Here is a woman who is suffering at home by a husband either abusing his power or else failing to use his power for the good of the family. Now she comes to another man, her pastor, who becomes a derelict leader as well. He either uses his power to further oppress her with platitudes about submission—which she may need to hear, but as I said, they aren't enough—or neglects to use his power of being a shepherd to confront her husband. Now *both* spiritual leaders in her life have betrayed her! Where is she to turn?

The pastor may reason, "Well, she is always whining anyway. I'd hate to have to live with her myself." While we may have a child in our home who is more prone to whining than the others, we still would not let his older brother beat up on him. We would have to address both problems—his perpetual whining and his bullying brother.

This is the time to get *both* of them in the office and hear *both* sides of the issue. This is not a time to take any sides—except *God's* side. It is usually not effective for the pastor to say, "Well, Theresa, I'll talk with Joel and see what I can do." What usually happens in those cases is that Joel—who is an excellent manipulator—confesses to "not loving his wife like he should," and the pastor goes away satisfied. But at home

---

[20]James 2:15-16.

nothing changes, and the pastor never checks up with Theresa to see if things are better. Joel has brushed off the pastor by his "good ole boy" talk with the pastor, and Theresa is no better off. In fact, she is worse. Why should she ever attempt to solicit the pastor's help again?

I have seen these scenes repeated so often it makes my heart ache. Men who are not walking in the fear of God need to be lovingly confronted by men who *do* fear God! There need to be some Nathans who will lovingly rebuke the kings of today's homes who are covering violence and immorality.

When Theresa in a spirit of meekness tries to approach Joel about his offenses towards her and is brushed aside, she has every right—and every responsibility—to follow Matthew 18 and bring others into the picture. That means that spiritually minded men of the church and, especially, the pastor need to be ready to intervene and, if necessary, put him out of the church if he refuses to be reconciled to his wife.[21]

That confrontation, however, needs to be done by a God-fearing man who can bring humility and hope into the situation for the wayward husband. It will not work for a controlling, fleshly pastor or deacon to confront a controlling, fleshly husband. That will bring only more corruption into the process. The men involved must be Spirit-filled men who are bold but humble and who can speak of coming judgment but with a confident hope.

A most instructive account of biblical leadership is recorded for us in Nehemiah 5. When Nehemiah returned to Jerusalem, he found a very demoralized population. Many factors contributed to their discouragement, including the oppression from previous city governors and from the wealthy. Nehemiah denounced the self-centeredness of these rulers and demanded that they relieve the burdens upon the people. He said, "It is not good that ye do [these things]: *ought ye not to walk in the fear of our God?*" (5:9).

Though he was entitled to certain privileges, Nehemiah refused to benefit from the perks of his office. His reason? "*Because of the fear of God*" (5:15). Nehemiah's fear of the Lord was at the heart of his

---

[21]For additional help on the proper steps of church discipline, see Jay E. Adams, *Handbook of Church Discipline* (Grand Rapids: Zondervan, 1986).

remarkable leadership in the midst of great opposition. Every leader should seriously study the Book of Nehemiah.

The controlling Joels and the passive Phils need to be restored to usefulness. They need to be reconciled to God and to their wives and families. They need to be discipled and held accountable for change and growth.

This is biblical Christianity in action, but the church needs God-fearing men to carry it out. May God in His mercy raise up a generation of godly men who do not fear men because they rightly fear God!

CHAPTER TWELVE

SUBMITTING IN THE FEAR OF GOD

WHAT'S WRONG WITH THIS PICTURE?

Think with me about several common scenarios. In each case the problem can be addressed as a "submission" problem—and, indeed, it is. The lasting solution, however, will not be found in merely insisting on obedience to authority. The fear of the Lord must be nurtured before a right response is forthcoming.

- Jessica, who is fifteen years old—and pregnant—has just run away with her seventeen-year-old boyfriend, leaving her parents a note that she is tired of their restrictions.

- Theresa, the wife of Joel, whom we met in the last chapter, has just announced to Joel that she has been consulting with her attorney. She is leaving Joel—and the children he has destroyed through his controlling ways. He will have to pick up the pieces of their lives on his own. She also announces that she has been greatly helped throughout this ordeal by a divorcé at work and that she will be moving in with him immediately.

- New government regulations require that particular safeguards be set up in work areas where certain chemicals are stored. Bill, a worker in the chemical storage area of a manufacturing company, thinks the regulations should be enforced in his department. His supervisor, Steve, tells him that the "higher-ups" have decided they don't have to follow the new regulations since the chemicals they store—though similar to the ones on the list—are not specifically mentioned in the regulations. Bill, who has always prided himself in being a "black and white kind of guy," is furious. He immediately goes into a tirade about the insensibility of the shop owners to the safety of their workers. He denounces what he perceives to be their "anything for a buck" philosophy and threatens to quit.

- Pastor Philips has just had another conversation with the youth director, Pastor Jake. Pastor Jake is not being careful about the kind of music he is using with the youth group. His selections are increasingly leaning towards Christian rock. Jake defends his actions by citing certain parents—and their teens—who are happy with his "fresh ideas." He says he really doesn't see music as a moral issue and says, "After all, it is the heart attitude that counts with God—not adherence to man-made standards."

- Phil, the passive, Internet day-trading, pornography-indulging husband of Robin, whom we met in the last chapter, has just been taken to the emergency room of the hospital because of a suicide attempt. Robin had finally sought help from their pastor, who had been seeing Phil about his selfish and sinful ways. The pastor has met with him three times, compassionately offering help but firmly threatening church discipline if he doesn't turn from his sin. Phil, rather than face his sin or face the church, decided to take his life. Fortunately, Robin got up in the middle of the night to get a drink of water and heard the car running in the garage. She found Phil slumped over the steering wheel—almost dead from the carbon monoxide fumes.

So, what's *really* wrong with these pictures? Certainly biblical submission is missing in each scenario. Jessica's lack of submission to her parents and their standards is very obvious. Theresa's divorce threat, Bill's obstinance at the chemical storage area, Jake's undermining of his pastor's wishes, and Phil's stubbornness to be reconciled with God and his family are all evident as well.

In each case the authorities involved have every right—and the responsibility—to insist that their wishes be followed. But in each case the underling—the one under authority—displays an obvious arrogance that insists *his* way is right. Some, like Phil, also display obvious despair. A loss of hope may be present in the other situations as well, but in Phil's case the despair is most clearly evident.

The fear of God is missing in each subordinate's view of the situation. Had it been there they would all have been able to bring into the situations both *humility* and *hope*. Look at our diagram again.

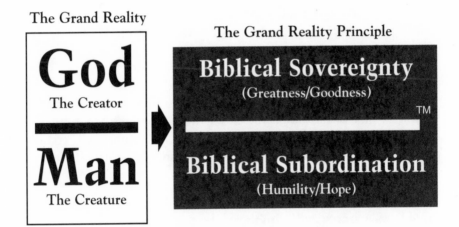

It certainly is easier to submit to authorities who exercise their powers—their "greatness"—with an obvious concern for others—"goodness." It is much harder to yield to authorities who are passive or tyrannical. So how can we *humble* ourselves under our authorities without losing *hope* that all is lost and that nothing will improve? Again, the answer is the fear of the Lord. More than a quarter of the references in the Bible that deal with the fear of the Lord speak of it in the context of obedience.

This is a difficult area for all of us. It is for that reason that I am addressing it at the end of this book. If a man has a hard view of God, he will have a hard view of authorities. If you are not yet "rejoicing in the Grand Reality," as we discussed in Part One, you need to return to those chapters often, asking God to give you a high view of Himself. Without it, you will not respond biblically to authority.

Jesus commented on the maturity of the faith of the centurion based strictly on the man's understanding of authority.[1] To the extent that we fear the Lord, we will respond biblically to our authorities. We might begin our obedience to our parents, teachers, and other leaders with a

---

[1]Matthew 8:5-10.

"slavish fear," but it takes a mature fear of the Lord to respond to them with *humility* that sees God as over all and with a *hope* that is rooted in a robust trust in the Lord. That certainly must be our goal. *This chapter more than any other will reveal your view of God's sovereignty, His love for you, and your trust in His wisdom.* But before we look at how we can make the proper responses, let's look more closely at the two most common failures.

FLESHLY SUBORDINATION

In the last chapter we looked at two ways that rulers can be fleshly. We saw that some rulers *control* problems with a self-serving authoritarianism. We also looked at those who *avoid* problems with a self-serving permissivism. Though the leadership styles are almost opposite each other, the underlying motive of serving self is the same.

Just as there are opposite fleshly ways for ruling, there are opposite fleshly ways for responding to those who rule over us.

Self-Serving Defiance

The response most familiar to all of us is straightforward disobedience to authority. This person pleases himself by *opposing* his authority. It is the spirit of the prodigal son, whose pride demanded more *freedom*. This boy came to his father with the demand "Give me the portion of goods that falleth to me."[2] He wanted life on his own terms.

If we are honest with ourselves, this is the natural bent for all of us. This is why Isaiah said, "We have turned every one to his *own* way."[3] It just seems right to our sinful natures that life should be lived on our terms. But God's Word is clear. When left to our own ways, we destroy ourselves. That is the whole thrust of Romans 1. God does not have to bring any kind of special judgment upon selfish people. All He has to do is let them have their *own* way, and they will self-destruct.

> Most people today have the idea that they are not free unless they are making their own decisions. The fallacy of this line of thinking is seen by reflecting on the condition of our society. We have more people making more decisions about their own lives than at any

---

[2]Luke 15:12.
[3]Isaiah 53:6.

other time in the history of civilization, yet we have some of the worst civil and personal problems that we have ever seen. You see, the practice of making decisions is not necessarily helpful unless the decisions are *wise*—that is, they are in line with God's scheme of life. If they are not *wise* decisions, they add even more corruption to the decision maker's life and to the society he touches. Remember this: *The same pride in a man that demands the right to make its own decisions will pollute every decision that man makes.* That is why we are told in Proverbs 4:23, "Keep [watch over; guard] thy heart with all diligence; for out of it are the issues of life."[4]

Dirty Dishes or a Dirty Heart?—Many years ago Kevin (not his real name), a graduate assistant, came to see me for advice. He was the supervisor of the dishwashing operations in the dining common here at the University. Since the dining common feeds several thousand faculty, staff, and students three meals a day, you can imagine how many thousands of trays, glasses, cups, and tableware must be washed daily!

Kevin had a problem because a new shift manager had just been hired, and the new manager had told Kevin that they must change the flow for the dishwashing operations. Kevin told me, "Dr. Berg, I have worked as a dishwasher since I was a freshman. I have been washing dishes longer than anyone at the dining common—ever! I know dishwashing! This plan won't work. It will cost us money because it is inefficient. It is poor stewardship."

When I asked him what he had done about it, he said he had talked with the dining common manager, who told him they would do it the way the shift manager wanted to do it. I listened to him for thirty minutes as he described the details of the situation. I asked him many questions, trying to lead him to come to the right responses on his own. He finally summarized his concern again and exclaimed, "What do you think of that!?" I replied, "I guess God is more concerned about cleaning up your dirty heart than He is about cleaning up dirty dishes."

He admitted that his attitude wasn't the best but protested that this was poor stewardship of God's money. I reminded him that God trashed the whole earth once to make a statement about human hearts and asked him, "Was that poor stewardship?"

---

[4]Berg, 43-44.

My point here is that *so often we think the issue we are arguing over with our authorities is more important than the issues of our own heart responses.* Jesus Christ didn't die for dishes or whatever issue seems to be at stake at the moment; He died to forgive the sins of rebellious and unbelieving hearts. Kevin is demonstrating self-serving defiance.

God is not silent about this issue. Please read the following passages reflectively, asking God to show you *His* view of submission to authority. Remember that Paul and Peter are writing their epistles during first-century Roman rule under Nero. Many in their audiences were under Nero's rule, and, as slaves, were under the rule of hard masters as well.

> Let every soul be subject unto the higher [authorities]. For there is no [authority] but [from] God: the powers that be are [established by] God. Whosoever therefore resisteth the [authority], resisteth the ordinance of God: and they that resist shall receive [unto] themselves [condemnation]. For rulers are not a terror to good works [i.e., you don't have to be afraid if you are doing right], but to the evil. Wilt thou then not be afraid of the power [i.e., do you want to be unafraid of authority?] do that which is good, and thou shalt have praise of the same: for he is the minister of God to thee for good. But if thou do that which is evil, be afraid; for he beareth not the sword in vain: for he is the minister of God, a revenger to execute wrath upon him that doeth evil. Wherefore *ye must needs be subject, not only for wrath* [i.e., to escape the anger of your authority], *but also for conscience sake* [i.e., conscience toward God, who commands you to obey authority]. For this cause pay ye tribute also: for they are God's ministers, attending continually upon this very thing. Render therefore to all their dues: tribute to whom tribute is due; custom to whom custom; fear to whom fear; honour to whom honour. Owe no man any thing, but to love one another: for he that loveth another hath fulfilled the law (Romans 13:1-8).

Servants, *be obedient* to them that are your masters according to the flesh, with *fear and trembling,*[5] in singleness of your heart, as unto Christ (Ephesians 6:5).

---

[5]"It is not the fear of man, but the reverential fear of God of which the apostle speaks, as what follows clearly proves" (Hodge, 268).

Servants, *obey* in all things your masters according to the flesh . . . in singleness of heart, *fearing* God (Colossians 3:22).

Exhort servants to be *obedient* unto their own masters . . . that they may adorn the doctrine of God our Saviour in all things (Titus 2:9-10).

Servants, *be subject* to your masters *with all fear;* not only to the good and gentle, but also to the [unreasonable] (I Peter 2:18).

In the same manner, Peter and Paul address wives.

Likewise, ye wives, be in subjection to your own husbands . . . *with fear* [towards God] (I Peter 3:1-2).

Wives, *submit* yourselves unto your own husbands, *as unto the Lord* (Ephesians 5:22).

Wives, *submit* yourselves unto your own husbands, as it is fit *in the Lord* (Colossians 3:18).

The same admonition is given to children.

Children, *obey* your parents *in the Lord:* for this is right (Ephesians 6:1).

Children, *obey* your parents in all things: for this is well pleasing *unto the Lord* (Colossians 3:20).

At the same time, all masters, husbands, and fathers are commanded to remember *they too have a Master they must obey!* They must rule in the fear of God—with an awareness of His presence and authority over *their* lives.

Husbands, love your wives, *even as Christ also loved the church,* and gave himself for it. . . . Let every one of you in particular so love his wife even as himself (Ephesians 5:25, 33).

And, ye fathers, provoke not your children to wrath (Ephesians 6:4).

Husbands, love your wives, and be not bitter against them (Colossians 3:19).

Fathers, provoke not your children to anger, lest they be discouraged (Colossians 3:21).

And, ye masters, do the same things unto them, [giving up] threatening: knowing that *your Master also is in heaven;* neither is there respect of persons with him [i.e., God is not impressed with your earthly position over others] (Ephesians 6:9).

Masters, give unto your servants that which is just and equal; knowing that *ye also have a Master in heaven* (Colossians 4:1).

My brethren, be not many masters [i.e., don't be ambitious to be teachers], *knowing that we shall receive the greater condemnation* [i.e., stricter judgment] (James 3:1).

Likewise, ye husbands, dwell with [your wives] according to knowledge, giving honour unto the wife, as unto the weaker vessel, and as being heirs together of the grace of life; that your prayers be not hindered (I Peter 3:7).

The basic thrust of these verses cannot be misunderstood. They were clear to first-century citizens, masters, slaves, husbands, wives, and children who made up the early church. They should be equally clear to us if we let them say exactly what the Lord intended. *A God-fearing believer will submit to his authorities.* He will not be disobedient, demanding more freedom. But self-serving defiance is not the only kind of fleshly response to authority.

Self-Serving Deference

"Deference" means "courteous yielding."[6] A *self-serving* deference means that we yield to our authorities—not because we see God in the picture and want to please *Him*—but because it gets us what *we* want. We saw that self-serving defiance was the spirit of the prodigal son, who was demanding more freedom. Self-serving deference is the spirit of his elder brother, who was demanding more recognition and appreciation for doing right.

While the apostles called for slaves to be obedient to their masters, they warned them not to obey merely for the praise of their masters.

---

[6]*The American Heritage Dictionary of the English Language,* s.v. "deference."

Paul called slaves who responded in this way "men-pleasers" who gave just "eyeservice." These slaves worked hard only when they were noticed. Their responses were just as self-serving as the responses of those who were disobedient. Notice the fuller discussion of the passages we have already seen.

> Servants, be obedient to them that are your masters according to the flesh, *with fear and trembling,* in singleness of your heart, as unto Christ; *not with eyeservice, as menpleasers;* but as the servants of Christ, doing the will of God from the heart; with good will doing service, as to the Lord, and *not to men:* knowing that whatsoever good thing any man doeth, the same shall he receive of the Lord, whether he be bond or free (Ephesians 6:5-8).

> Servants, obey in all things your masters according to the flesh; *not with eyeservice, as menpleasers;* but in singleness of heart, *fearing God:* and whatsoever ye do, do it heartily, as to the Lord, and *not unto men;* knowing that of the Lord ye shall receive the reward of the inheritance: for ye serve the Lord Christ. But he that doeth wrong shall receive for the wrong which he hath done: and there is no respect of persons (Colossians 3:22-25).

> Servants, be subject to your masters *with all fear;* not only to the good and gentle, but also to the [unreasonable]. For this is thankworthy, if a man for conscience toward God endure grief, suffering wrongfully. For what glory is it, if, when ye be buffeted for your faults, ye shall take it patiently? but if, when ye do well, and suffer for it, ye take it patiently, this is [well-pleasing to] God. For even hereunto were ye called: because Christ also suffered for us, leaving us an example, that ye should follow his steps: who did no sin, neither was guile found in his mouth: who, when he was reviled, reviled not again; when he suffered, he threatened not; but committed himself to him that judgeth righteously (I Peter 2:18-23).

This self-serving deference is John Bunyan's "slavish fear"—the opposite of sonlike fear. The slave obeys because he is afraid not to. He bristles at having to obey, but obeying is better than the war that follows if he doesn't.

To summarize, neither self-serving defiance nor self-serving deference pleases God. Both put self before God and others. Both show a view of the situation that is void of the fear of God. Both eventually lead to despair.

All of us recognize them both because we all have used them both. We are all quite flexible in our selfish responses when walking in the flesh. But there is a liberating answer from both: the fear of the Lord.

GOD'S PRESCRIPTION FOR DISCOURAGED AND DISOBEDIENT FOLLOWERS

Both of the self-serving responses we have looked at lack *humility*. The self-serving defiant subordinate draws a line in the sand and declares that it is "his way or no way." The self-serving deferent subordinate likewise pursues his own way—"give the boss what he wants and you can have what you want." Both of these are mutinous substitutes for God's way: "Obey them that have the rule over you, and submit yourselves."[7] Both self-serving responses must be confessed and forsaken for a believer to walk in the Spirit.

Both of these responses destroy *hope*. Self-serving defiance eventually destroys all hope because God has so "wired" His universe that it works against disobedience. A disobedient man alienates himself from God. That distance from God spawns darkness in his soul.[8] No matter what he does to lighten up his life, he ends up in despair.

Self-serving deference eventually destroys hope as well. No matter how much a person submits, if submission is not done in the power of the Spirit with a submissive heart to God, the individual becomes very weary in his service. He either resigns himself to a robotlike existence under his authority or grows increasingly frustrated in his forced submission. In either case, in the long run he loses hope and becomes very discouraged.

As we have seen already, seeing God's sovereignty in the situation—both His greatness and His goodness—is the main characteristic of biblical subordination. We may not have a master/husband/father, and

---

[7]Hebrews 13:17.
[8]Ephesians 4:17-19.

so forth who is kind toward us, but we have a kind heavenly Father, who is the Master of the masters, the Lord of the lords, and the King of the kings. It is because *He* is all-powerful and *He* is all-loving and *He* is all-wise that we can bow in submission to our earthly authorities. They are all under *His* control.

If you will remember, we learned in the earlier chapters of this book that God's supremacy—His firstness—was the most significant component of reality. In trouble, we should be looking for ways to show that He is first! It is in this way that Paul said a slave could "adorn the doctrine of God." A mistreated slave could show that God is first if he obeyed his master, "not answering again"—not giving any back talk; if he refrained from "purloining"—refusing to pilfer from his boss though he wasn't getting paid what he deserved; and if he showed "all good fidelity"—faithfully fulfilling his obligations.[9] He must have his eye upon pleasing God above all else.

A wife may ask, "God tells me to obey my husband, but what if I don't trust his decisions?" Fortunately, God never commands a woman to trust her husband. Submission certainly would be easier if her husband were trustworthy, but God tells her to obey her husband and *trust Him*. Notice this in Peter's discussion in his first epistle.

> Likewise, ye wives, be in subjection to your own husbands; that, if any obey not the word [i.e., aren't obedient to God's Word], they also may without the word be won by the [lifestyle] of the wives; while they behold your chaste [lifestyle] coupled with [reverence]. Whose adorning let it not be that outward adorning of [braiding] the hair, and of wearing of gold, or of putting on of apparel; but let it be the hidden [person] of the heart, in that which is not [perishable], even the ornament of a [gentle] and quiet spirit, which is in the sight of God of great price. For after this manner in the old time the holy women also, *who trusted in God*, adorned themselves, *being in subjection unto their own husbands*: even as Sara *obeyed* Abraham, calling him lord: whose daughters ye are, as long as ye do well, and are not [frightened by any fear] (I Peter 3:1-6).

---

[9]Titus 2:9-10.

Never does God call any of us to *trust* our authorities; He merely commands us to obey them *and trust Him.* Now herein is our problem. We may not know God well enough to trust Him.

THE DILEMMA[10]

Bob's Squad Car

A number of years ago one of our graduates who serves on a municipal police force invited me to a certain high-crime area of his city. We approached one intersection in a run-down residential area. A gang of young men were congregating in the middle of the street in front of us. As we approached the group, the men moved out of the way to let us through, scowling at us as we passed. Bob knew most of them by name—and they knew Bob. I am glad I could not hear the comments they made to us as we passed by.

I would never want to drive into that part of that city, even in broad daylight, in my own car. I felt quite safe that afternoon, however, riding in Bob's squad car. I was surrounded by bullet-proof glass and heavy gauge metal. A shotgun was very visible, strapped to the dashboard of the car. Bob had an impressive array of communication radios at his disposal as well as his own personal firearm. An awareness of Bob's resources put my natural fears to rest. . . .

Sometimes people say, "I have a hard time trusting God." The truth may be that they are refusing to trust Him because trusting means giving up control of their lives in some area. We have already seen the danger of our self-centered ways. Another reason they might have a "hard time" trusting God is that they do not know Him very well.

Trusting Strangers

Suppose a man you have never met stops you in a mall. He tells you that if you will loan him $50 and give him your name, address, and phone number, he will gladly pay you back when he gets his paycheck in a couple of days. Even the most compassionate of us will probably not give the stranger $50. And we would all think twice before giving out our name, address, and phone number to someone we did not know. We don't know what he would do with that information. The simple fact is that we don't trust people we don't know.

---

[10]Jim Berg, *When Trouble Comes* (Greenville, S.C.: Bob Jones University Press, 2002), 51-55.

What if, on the other hand, the man who stops you is someone close to you and whom you respect highly—your brother or your father—who has absent-mindedly left his wallet at home. If you have the $50, you will likely loan him the money. He has proven himself trustworthy in your past dealings with him. He has consistently shown in your previous experiences with him that he had your best interests at heart when he dealt with you—hence, your great respect for him. You are very willing to help someone whom you regard so highly.

The Dilemma

The application for many of us is all too pointed and painful. We have to admit that often we have a hard time trusting God because we really don't consider Him trustworthy. To us He looks more like a wolf among the sheep—making life miserable for us—than a Good Shepherd, who is willing to give His life for the sheep. This is our dilemma: Whom will we trust?

We may have formed our view of God from hearsay—what others have told us about Him. Or our view of Him may be skewed by situations that did not turn out the way *we* wanted them resolved, and we have blamed God for our misfortune.

Our sinful natures are clones of Satan's own nature. Our flesh, like Satan, is deceitful.[11] Satan keeps our heart under his rule by scandalizing God. He does everything he can to make God look bad and to make himself look good. Satan is so effective in his strategy that he has temporarily taken over the loyalty of virtually the whole world.

Trust Decisions

The apostle Paul accurately calls Satan "the god of this world," who "hath blinded the minds of them which believe not" (II Corinthians 4:4). In every circumstance of life, we have a trust decision to make. Will we believe what God has said about our situation, or will we believe what *our own heart* tells us about our situation—skewed by its natural bent to mimic Satan?

This is why the Bible speaks so much about faith. We may think that the key factor is the amount of our faith. Scripture indicates that we always have enough faith. Our problems result from placing our faith in the wrong person. When the Bible speaks about our having faith,

---

[11]Jeremiah 17:9; John 8:44.

it refers to having faith *in* God. This is what is meant when the Bible says, "the just [i.e., the ones who are righteous before God because they have experienced God's salvation from sin] shall live by faith" (Romans 1:17).

We cannot make any decisions without believing somebody. The test of our spiritual life is "*whom* are we believing with our faith—God or our own heart?"

So how is it that we can gain this high view of God? How can we believe right—make the right trust decisions—about God? That is what this entire book has been about. We have been looking closely at God's "squad car"—the resources He has at His disposal to use on our behalf. We have seen glimpses of the Grand Reality. We have seen God's supremacy, the Father's sovereignty, the Son's sufficiency, and the Spirit's security. Only by meditation upon these great themes of our great God can we know Him well enough to trust Him. Though others may rule *directly* over us, God rules *ultimately* over all. He is first, and in that fact we find our hope and before His feet we humbly bow.

BUT DO I *ALWAYS* HAVE TO SUBMIT?

Only God's authority is absolute. Governments, citizens, masters, fathers, husbands, and wives have powers limited in scope by God Himself. Consider these principles when facing hard demands from an authority.

If the Authority's Request Is Unreasonable . . .

If the request is unreasonable—as opposed to unbiblical—then I Peter 2:18-23[12] tells us that we are to submit to our authority, committing ourselves to the one who does make righteous decisions.

Basically, if the request is unreasonable, we are to change our desires. Certainly, we can make a respectful appeal. But if the appeal is rejected, we must learn to want what our authorities want—because that is what God wants for us until our authorities change their minds.

This is exactly what Paul was talking about in Philippians 4:11, when he said, "I have *learned*, in whatsoever state I am, therewith to be content." Remember that his "state" was often jail—the result of the de-

---

[12]"Froward" in the Authorized Version means "unreasonable."

cision of a government official. He dealt frequently with "unreasonable" authorities. He went on to say,

> I know both how to be abased, and I know how to abound: every where and in all things I [have *learned* the intimate secret] both to be full and to be hungry, both to abound and to suffer need. I can do all things through Christ which strengtheneth me (Philippians 4:12-13).

It is important that we submit to our authority with God in the picture—in the fear of the Lord—or we will have a hard time learning to be content with the unreasonable demands of our authorities. We basically have only one question to ask, "Am I under this authority in the will of God?" If the answer is yes, then the Bible is clear. We must respectfully submit because God is over that authority. Seeing God in the picture allows us to respond with *humility* and is the source of *hope* for us in our trying situation.

We have to remember that if we are under that authority in God's will and what the authority is asking us to do is merely unreasonable, then we must see that as *God's* will for us. And furthermore, we cannot merely accept the new circumstance as God's will for us and not change our desires to want for ourselves what *He* wants.

We are a bit too "American" when it comes to response to authority. Since we live in a republic, we feel we should have a say in every decision that affects us. But we cannot impose that mindset upon the biblical record. Remember, Paul's admonitions to first-century slaves? These believers often lived and worked under unreasonable masters, and these instructions were given with that in mind.

A believing slave in New Testament times did not have much say in his life. Once his master decided something for him, Paul and Peter commanded him to submit "heartily, as unto the Lord" and in such a way that the gospel was "adorned." Slaves did not have the option of grousing about their situation, complaining to others, or badmouthing their authorities—not if they were submitting in the fear of the Lord. Nothing has changed since then. The commands still stand. They apply to the twenty-first century as well.

If the Authority's Request Is Unbiblical . . .

If the authority's request is in conflict with God's commands, then again, we should respectfully appeal. If the appeal is rejected, then we must respectfully refuse to submit and learn to rejoice in our suffering as the apostles did when they had to "obey God rather than men."[13]

We must be careful, however. It is very easy for us to think something is a biblical command when it is merely our own idea about it. For example, we are not to forsake the "assembling of ourselves together."[14] If, however, the unsaved husband of a believing wife forbids her from going to church except once a week, she cannot disobey him, claiming that she has to be there "every time the church doors are open." His request is simply unreasonable—which means she must submit and change her desires; it is not unbiblical.

If on the other hand, he were to start physically beating her, she has every right to leave the dangerous situation and notify the civil authorities. The Scriptures are full of accounts of God's people running from physical persecution when they had the opportunity.

My point here in these final paragraphs is not to try to cover every nuance of submission to *unbiblical* demands. I want primarily to make the point that most of today's believers have a lot of spiritual work to do in the matter of submitting to *unreasonable* demands. Seldom are we asked to do something unbiblical, though that may change in the days ahead.

I shudder to think of our responses to those days ahead when today we are not dealing biblically with the requests that are simply unreasonable. We will not respond well to either type of request unless we understand very clearly what it means to walk in the fear of the Lord. We will *never* come up with *humble, hope-filled* responses until we see clearly that the sovereign God who is over all is *great* and *good* to all.

I stated in the introduction to this book, "Strong Christian homes cannot be built out of weak Christians." The right response to authority requires strong, vibrant Christians. That is why Paul does not deal with these issues until later in Ephesians. If we have not learned the teach-

---

[13] Acts 5:29, 41-42.
[14] Hebrews 10:25.

ings of Ephesians 1-3, we will have a hard time applying the commands of Ephesians 4-6. In a similar fashion, we will have a hard time "Displaying the Grand Reality," Part Three of this book, if we have not yet been "Rejoicing in the Grand Reality" and "Experiencing the Grand Reality," Parts One and Two of this book.

We have not done well in the modern church with fearing God, so we have had to come up with our own watered-down versions of submission to authority and have succumbed to worldly versions. But if we ever do get this right, the believing church can once again "turn the world upside down" as they did in the first century. God must be *first* and we must live in such a way that His firstness *shows!*

TAKE TIME TO REFLECT

1. List those whom God has placed in your life as your direct authorities.

2. In what ways do you exhibit a self-serving defiance to your authorities (i.e., you disobey them either to their face or behind their back)?

3. In what ways do you exhibit a self-serving deference to your authorities (i.e., you obey them outwardly, but you are doing so not because you see God in the picture but because your obedience gets you what you want)?

4. Think of your last argument or disagreement with an authority. Were you more aware of the issue you disagreed upon or the issues of your own heart responses? Explain your answer.

5. If you had a more mature "fear of the Lord," how would that change the way you relate to your authorities?

A WORD TO DISCIPLE-MAKERS

So Do We Really Need More Self-Esteem?

As individuals in our society have become increasingly self-centered, they have left in their wake a staggering mass of hurting people. My eldest daughter was a student teacher in a public elementary school made up largely of underprivileged children. She told her mother and me story after story of neglected children in her classroom. My heart broke as I pondered their wretched existence and I wept as I prayed for them during her directed teaching experience. Most of them had no encouragement from home and almost no direction for any part of their lives.

They were either fearful and withdrawn or obnoxious and unruly. In either case, the common diagnosis of the world was that they had low self-esteem. The supposed answer was somehow to bolster this mystical component of life so that they could succeed. Because the problem was misdiagnosed, the treatment was also misdirected.

The real problem with these children is that they lacked *humility* and/or *hope*. Those who were "acting up" had not been taught how to subordinate themselves under leadership. They possessed no humility. Those who were withdrawn and self-protective had never received any encouragement or instruction for life. They had no reason to hope in anything.

The solution is the interaction of a "sovereign" in their lives who has both "greatness" and "goodness"—components missing in their experiences.

When a teacher kindly helps a student through a hard problem at his desk, encourages him to try again on the ball field, smiles approvingly when he does raise his hand, and firmly insists that he stay in his seat or he will be asked to leave the room, the teacher is insisting upon humility in an atmosphere of hope.

What society has called low self-esteem, in most cases, is essentially a lack of hope. No one stays at anything long if he has no hope. When hopelessness rules, despair sets in, and people quit trying. They don't need more self-esteem—whatever that is—they need hope!

Hope is built through loving involvement—involvement that says, "I care. Let me help," and involvement that says, "Here's how. Now you try it." This is exactly how God builds hope in *His* children.

When teachers—and parents—are involved in the ways I described above, behavior improves and test scores climb. The secularists confidently announce that the reason is that the teacher's or parent's involvement has built the child's self-esteem. The truth is their involvement has generated *hope*. The child finally has a reason to try and enough instruction and encouragement to finally succeed.

A teacher or parent who leads with firm but loving interaction will be "feared"—in the sense we have been talking about. The child knows that he dare not misbehave in the presence of his teacher or parent because he will be duly humbled if he does. He also knows, however, that his authority loves him dearly and will make personal sacrifices to see him succeed. These are the components of godly fear.

Oh, that God would raise up a generation of believing parents and teachers who would themselves be walking in the fear of the Lord! Their exercise of "biblical sovereignty" would spawn a generation of young people who would learn at a very early age what it is to have proper "fear"—a hope-filled humility. It would be the first step in learning to "fear the Lord."

CHAPTER THIRTEEN

'TIS MYSTERY ALL

Our study in this book began with the statement "What you don't see *can* hurt you." We learned in chapter one that life is more dangerous when you are blind. We also noted that life is more discouraging—sometimes to the point of despair—when you cannot see. That discussion of despair launched us into a survey of the unseen things Paul was "seeing" from his prison cell as he wrote to the Ephesian church.

The core of his Ephesian epistle—truths that fueled his rejoicing in trying times—are three "mysteries." I want to summarize them each as we close out our study together. Before I do that, however, I want us to take another look at despair—this time through the eyes of Solomon.

THE DARK MYSTERIES OF ECCLESIASTES

I want us to see that the answer to the "dark mysteries" of life presented in Ecclesiastes is meditation upon the "divine mysteries" in Ephesians. The Pauline mysteries of God fueled the courage and the steadfastness of the early church in its darkest times of persecution. Most modern believers, unhappily, identify more readily with the mysteries of Ecclesiastes than they do the mysteries of Ephesians. That is the core of the problem. Let's take a look, then, at Solomon's message.

The Old Testament book of Ecclesiastes was written at the end of King Solomon's life, and I believe it is a record of his repentance for pursuing life without God at the center—without acknowledging God as *first!* Solomon for most of his adult years walked "as other Gentiles walk, in the vanity of [his] mind."[1]

---

[1]Ephesians 4:17.

Ecclesiastes is not, as some have taught, the bitter musings of a cynic. It is inspired instruction by an elderly man who had it all, tried it all, and finally saw the emptiness of it all without God at the center. I believe one of the purposes of Ecclesiastes was to demonstrate Solomon's repentance.

This book is not readily understood because its literary form is different from most of the rest of the Old Testament. Its exact form is called a "cultural apologetic."[2] Solomon, as you may know, had distinguished himself in many areas. One of those areas was philosophy. He was one of the "wise men" who readily disputed philosophy and worldviews with other "wise men" of other cultures. The queen of Sheba, for example, made a trip to Jerusalem for this very purpose. She came to "prove him with hard questions."[3]

These philosophers were known to write defenses of their particular worldview—cultural apologetics—to disseminate to interested philosophers of other lands for their consideration and challenge. It is probably this literary exchange that Solomon is referring to when he says, to his philosopher-audience, "of making many books [these cultural apologetics] there is no end; and much study is a weariness of the flesh."[4] He is giving notice to his fellow philosophers that they could continue speculating about worldviews until they wearied themselves with their studies and writings, but they were missing the whole point of life: "fear God, and keep his commandments."[5]

Ecclesiastes does not speak of Abraham, Jehovah, Israel, or the covenants because it is addressed initially to a *Gentile* audience. This "cultural apologetic" may have even had as its audience not only a Gentile world at large but a certain Gentile inquirer in particular—a "youth" perhaps in Solomon's court or a budding "wise man" he met through philosophic interchanges.[6]

---

[2]Walter C. Kaiser Jr. *Ecclesiastes: Total Life* (Chicago: Moody Press, 1979), 32ff.
[3]1 Kings 10:1.
[4]Ecclesiastes 12:12.
[5]Ecclesiastes 12:13.
[6]Ecclesiastes 11:9–12:1ff.

Keep in mind that because of Solomon's many marriages to the princess daughters of Gentile royalty, his court was teeming with the Gentile staff members these royal brides brought with them. In addition, Solomon's worldwide financial enterprises brought many Gentiles to the capital of Jerusalem. He was surrounded with Gentiles with other worldviews.[7]

Ecclesiastes connects with the unbelieving world through one issue: despair. Solomon speaks in a way that is instructive to us as we try to reach our own increasingly godless world with the gospel. He says,

> The words of the wise are as goads, and as nails fastened by the masters of assemblies, which are given from one shepherd (Ecclesiastes 12:11).

Solomon tells us that the conclusions of the thinking man (i.e., "words of the wise") are given for two purposes. Some of the statements in his treatise are "goads" and some are "nails." He further states that all of them come from "one shepherd"—claiming inspiration from God.[8]

WHAT'S THE POINT?

So what are "goads" and "nails"? Goads, as you may know, were those sharp-pointed sticks that Palestinian farmers used to put their oxen into "passing gear." When an ox wasn't moving quickly enough—or not at all—a sharp jab to the flank of the ox with the goad would get him moving again. The ox would "get the point" and do something. Solomon's discussions in Ecclesiastes act like goads to the mind of a searching man *reflecting* upon life's enigmas. He continually prods his audience to consider the futility of some aspect of life. Then he asks,

---

[7]Incidentally, this book presents God to pagan audiences much the same way Paul approached the pagan Gentile philosophers on Mars Hill in Acts 17. The apostle notices their relentless searches in religious matters and introduces them to the living Creator-God. Again, there is no mention of Abraham or other Jewish matters. He starts with God as their Creator, establishes Him as the present Sustainer of life, and then calls them into accountability for their deeds before Him through a resurrected Spokesman.

Paul takes the same approach in Acts 14:15-17, when he and Barnabas are being mistaken for Jupiter and Mercury. Paul declares that they are not gods themselves but do represent the true God, who created all things.

[8]Ecclesiastes 12:11. Who better than the son of the shepherd-king, David, should picture God as the "one shepherd"?

"What's the point?" thereby hoping to "goad" them to "do something"—turn away from their vain speculations and turn to God. *Goads are disturbing reflections about life that lead to the conclusion "What's the point?"* Richard De Haan captures this concept with great insight.

> The fool lives only for the moment. He *refuses to think* about the solemn truths which come to everybody's mind from time to time, and makes short-term pleasure his single reason for living. The wise man, however, observes life carefully. He *thinks* about what he sees and experiences. He asks questions and tries to come to logical conclusions.

> This serious-minded person is a better citizen than the man who lives only for momentary thrills. But in some ways he also suffers more, for he squarely faces painful truths about life and *reflects* upon the meaning of pain, death, and eternity. These *serious thoughts* serve as goads in his life.

> The goads Solomon includes in Ecclesiastes are the recollections, the concerns, the serious thoughts, and the guilt feelings which arise in the consciousness of one who is willing to face things as they are. Their stings are painful, and do not in themselves provide the answer to man's need. But they bring to light a person's sinfulness and helplessness, and thereby may get him started in the right direction.[9]

Solomon observed that men unleash great energy—labor—to overcome the restlessness of the great emptiness—vanity—of life when God is not in the center of their existence. Solomon called the labor expended to make something happen amidst all the brokenness and boredom "sore travail"—better, a "sorry task."[10]

Solomon "goaded" his philosophical audience by thought-provoking questions about the meaning of life. He wanted them to face the emptiness of life when they left God out of their pursuits.

In the opening statements of his book, he said something like this: "What is the profit of all of your efforts? Look at nature around you. The sun goes through her cycles. The winds follow their circuits; the

---

[9]Richard W. De Haan, *The Art of Staying Off Dead-End Streets* (Wheaton: Victor Books, 1974), 9, 12.

[10]Ecclesiastes 1:13.

waters in the rivers return to their source again. And even your desires return upon you again, though you try to satisfy them. There isn't anything new under the sun to try, and you are left the same way you were before. What's worse, even for all your efforts, no one who comes after you even remembers what you have done. What's the point?"

Solomon's exact words are, "What profit hath a man [in] all his labour which he [does] under the sun?"[11] *The point is that all of life is "pointless"—vanity or emptiness—unless something else is involved that transcends the pointlessness.*

Or take another scenario Solomon paints in chapter 3. The opening portion of this chapter contains perhaps the best-known verses of the book. It begins,

> To everything there is a season, and a time to every purpose under the heaven:
>
> A time to be born, and a time to die;
>
> A time to plant, and a time to pluck up that which is planted;
>
> A time to kill, and a time to heal;
>
> A time to break down, and a time to build up (vv. 1-3).

And so it goes for fourteen pairs of "times." Here is a compilation of fourteen positive events and fourteen negative events of life. Solomon ends the list with the same statement we saw in 1:3, "What profit hath he that worketh in that wherein he laboureth?"[12] In effect he says, "Fourteen positive times minus fourteen negative times still equals zero! What's the point?" And the point is that all of this is truly "pointless" unless something else is involved that *transcends* the pointlessness.

Solomon says to his readers, "I have another thought for you to consider. You die, and your dog dies. Both of you lie dead on the ground. What advantage do you have over the dog? You both die the same. What's the point?"[13] Again, the point is that all of life is truly "pointless" unless something else is involved that *transcends* the pointlessness.

---

[11]Ecclesiastes 1:3.
[12]Ecclesiastes 3:9.
[13]Ecclesiastes 3:18-21.

On and on Solomon goes for chapter after chapter, lobbing philosophical grenades into the laps of his heathen philosopher counterparts. He addresses every "dark mystery" of life.

- How are you going to deal with the pointlessness of accumulating wealth when you must leave it all to a fool who will squander it? (2:18-21)

- How are you going to deal with the pointlessness of injustice when the courts let guilty people go and innocent people are condemned? (3:16)

- How are you going to deal with the pointlessness of death itself? (3:18-21)

- How are you going to deal with the pointlessness of political position when the people you try to help turn against you? (4:13-16)

With machine-gun-like staccato Solomon drives home point after point, goading his audience to *think*. And herein is the secret that Solomon wants us to understand: *despair is the inevitable hopelessness of life without light.*

Solomon even shared the testimony of his *own* vain pursuits and their resulting misery. He wore himself out expending wealth in search of meaning and pleasure. He partied,[14] built great palaces,[15] shopped the globe,[16] and ended where he started—in despair.[17]

He then labored at exploring philosophy.[18] He concluded that folly doesn't work,[19] but knowledge doesn't last.[20] He again concluded that when life is lived this way, it is pointless.[21]

He was right. Without God at the center, it is hopeless; it is empty; and *it was designed by God to be so.* The theme of Ecclesiastes could be

---

[14]Ecclesiastes 2:1-3.
[15]Ecclesiastes 2:4-6.
[16]Ecclesiastes 2:7-8.
[17]Ecclesiastes 2:9-11.
[18]Ecclesiastes 2:12-23.
[19]Ecclesiastes 2:12-13.
[20]Ecclesiastes 2:14-19.
[21]Ecclesiastes 2:20-23.

stated, "Life is supposed to taste like cardboard if you insist on eating the box!" God intended for life to be devoid of joy and peace when you ignore the essential eternal aspects of life and consume only its temporal wrappings.

THE EQUATION OF ENJOYMENT

After Solomon drives home with precise, hammerlike blows his point that life apart from God is futile, we brace ourselves for a command to stop having fun. Instead, we find a surprising truth—a nail to anchor our troubled hearts.

The "nails" in Ecclesiastes are the statements of truth that are like the stakes of the tent assembler, anchoring a Bedouin tent against the desert winds. The "nails" of Ecclesiastes anchor the soul against the winds of adversity and trouble. *While goads are the honest reflections that produce despair when God is not in the picture, nails are the statements of biblical revelation that provoke dependency in the man who is in touch with the reality of living on a fallen planet.* Note carefully the "nail" of Ecclesiastes 2:24-26.[22]

> There is no good [inherent] in man that he should be able to eat, drink, or get satisfaction from his work. Even this [i.e., this ability to have satisfaction], I realized, was *from the hand of God.*
>
> *Apart from Him,* who can eat and who can have enjoyment?
>
> For to the man who pleases Him, He *gives* wisdom, knowledge, and joy; but to the sinner [i.e., the one living life his own way] He gives the work of gathering and heaping up in order to give it to the one who pleases God. This also is vanity and a chasing after wind.

These verses give us a "nail"—a divine truth that stabilizes our existence in the midst of the dark mysteries of life. I call this truth "The Equation of Enjoyment." We all learned in elementary school that anything multiplied by zero still equals zero. The equation looks like this.

The Multiplicand		The Multiplier		The Result
50	$\times$	0	$=$	0
(God-given Gifts of Life)		(God-given Satisfaction)		(Joy and Peace)

---

[22]Kaiser, 43 (Kaiser's own translation of 2:24-26).

The message is fairly straightforward. We often labor to pile up posses-sions, positions, and pleasures on the multiplicand side, and God in His common grace may allow us to accumulate much on that side of the equation. Solomon could testify to having all that he could wish on his multiplicand side.

He learned, however, that none of those gifts automatically produced joy and peace because God was the "Multiplier"—the one who gave ability to be satisfied with the gifts. If God chose to withhold satisfac-tion, there would be no joy no matter how many accumulated items were on the multiplicand side.

On the other hand, suppose that a man had almost nothing—little wealth and failing health—and yet had great joy. The reason for that joy is that his "Equation of Enjoyment" looks like this.

$$5 \times 250 = 1250!$$

5	×	250	=	1250!
(God-given Gifts of Life)		(God-given Satisfaction)		(Joy and Peace)

Solomon speaks directly to this at the end of chapter 5, when he says that he has seen something very thrilling.

> Every man also to whom God hath given riches and wealth, and hath given him power to eat thereof, and to take his portion, and to rejoice in his labor, *this is the gift of God* (v. 19).

Don't miss the "nail" here! Riches are a gift from God, but so is the "power" to enjoy them and the ability to "rejoice" in them. If God grants riches but withholds the "rejoicing," riches will bring no satis-faction. Solomon puts God center-stage and spotlights Him as the most important component of life. He is first! The lesson is clear.

> The purpose of life cannot be found in any of the good things found in the world. All the things we call the "goods" of life—health, riches, possessions, position, sensual pleasures, honors, and pres-tige—slip through man's hands unless they are received as a gift from God and *until God gives man the ability to enjoy them and obtain satis-faction from them.*[23]

---

[23]Ibid., 59.

Satisfaction in life is a byproduct of relationship with God—the Muliplier. Listen to how this is expressed elsewhere in Scripture.

> *Thou* hast put gladness in my heart, more than in the time that their corn and their wine increased (Psalm 4:7).

> Ye have sown much, and bring in little; ye eat, but ye have not enough; ye drink, but ye are not filled with drink; ye clothe you, but there is none warm; and he that earneth wages earneth wages to put it into a bag with holes. Thus saith the Lord of hosts; Consider your ways (Haggai 1:6-7).

> The house of the wicked shall be overthrown: but the tabernacle of the upright shall flourish. There is a way which seemeth right unto a man, but the end thereof are the ways of death. Even in laughter the heart is sorrowful; and the end of that mirth is heaviness. The backslider in heart shall be filled with his own ways: and a good man shall be satisfied from himself [i.e., with the results of his ways] (Proverbs 14:11-14).

> Except *the Lord* build the house, they labour in vain that build it: except *the Lord* keep the city, the watchman waketh but in vain (Psalm 127:1).

> Abide in me, and I in you. As the branch cannot bear fruit of itself, except it abide in the vine; no more can ye, except ye abide in *me*. I am the vine, ye are the branches: He that abideth in me, and I in him, the same bringeth forth much fruit: for without *me* ye can do nothing (John 15:4-5).

Walter Kaiser further comments on this Equation of Enjoyment.

> [The] capacity to enjoy, no matter how great or how small, is a gift from God. It is much better to receive wealth as a gift from God, along with the God-given ability to enjoy it, than to see wealth as an end in itself. . . . How sad that men can spend all their days working and sweating to receive the enjoyment that God offers as a gift if men will seek it in the manner that He, in His excellent and beautiful plan, has chosen to give it. Happiness, enjoyment, pleasure, and a knowledge of how the whole substance of life is integrated into a meaningful pattern in the plan of God are all linked in the living God.[24]

---

[24]Ibid., 77.

FEAR GOD

Solomon ends his book with a statement we have already noted but one that warrants a second look as we consider the message of Ecclesiastes.

> Let us hear the conclusion of the whole matter: Fear God, and keep his commandments: for this is the whole duty of man. For God shall bring every work into judgment, with every secret thing, whether it be good, or whether it be evil (Ecclesiastes 12:13-14).

What is Solomon's prescription for the frustrating enigmas—the dark mysteries—of life? What does he say is the answer to the emptiness and the vexation? Does he say, "Solve the dark mysteries! Master life and get your act together if you want a semblance of joy and peace!"?

No. Instead, he says, "Fear God. Learn that there is someone ruling over all the dark mysteries. Rejoice in what He has given you, and above all, rejoice in Him. And remember, there are some things that *are* clear—His commandments. You won't be held responsible for what you don't know about life's mysteries, but you will be held responsible for the light you do have."

When my wife is counseling women who are going through uncertain times, she reminds them of an important truth.

> *When there are things that you do not know about your life's situation, you must focus on the things that you do know about your God.*

That is Solomon's sentiment exactly. "Remember [your] Creator" is his instruction to us.[25] "Remember" here isn't a function of memory, but a function of priority. It means, "Put Him first!" And that brings us back to the message of Ephesians.

THE DIVINE MYSTERIES OF EPHESIANS

The lessons of Ecclesiastes explain why Paul so forcefully commands us to "walk not as other Gentiles walk, in the vanity [emptiness] of their mind."[26] If we walk like an unconverted Gentile, we will experience the emptiness of the unconverted heart. Sadly, many believers *do* ex-

---

[25]Ecclesiastes 12:1.
[26]Ephesians 4:17.

perience that emptiness because they thoughtlessly—and oftentimes, deliberately—adopt the mindset of the unconverted world. The result is predictable: despair.

But Paul not only warns us to forsake the Gentile worldview but he also gives us God's perspective—a view of the divine mysteries that answer the dark mysteries. We looked at them briefly in chapter seven. Let's review them.

- The Mystery of Christ: The divine secret previously unknown at this level of detail is that the *foundation* of all spiritual unity is Jesus Christ (Ephesians 1:1–2:10).

We explored this mystery in Part One of our study. We saw that our redemption is not only about God's forgiveness so that we could be rescued from hell. That certainly is a wonderful byproduct, but our redemption is part of a much bigger program that places Jesus Christ at the center of all things for all time and eternity. Paul called this divine plan the "mystery of his will" in Ephesians 1:9. He follows with the summary of that plan in 1:10.

> That in the dispensation of the fulness of times [i.e., in the management of the divine plan when the time is right] he might gather together in one all things *in Christ*, both which are in heaven, and which are on earth; even in him.

Every knee will bow before Him, and He will receive the glory due to His wonderful name. Paul delighted to speak of His exaltation, just as he marveled at His humiliation. Everything will be restored to its proper position in the universe, and Jesus Christ will be the reigning Head of it all! Lloyd-Jones sums it up. Indeed, Ephesians 1:10

> states what is the central theme of all Scripture. . . . In verse 10 we are taken right up into the heavens and find ourselves looking at God's final purpose with respect to this world. There is nothing higher than this, nothing beyond God's final purpose. It is bigger and greater than our personal salvation. In this verse we are transported above the matter of our personal salvation into the realm of ultimate things—God's grand, comprehensive, final, ultimate purpose. The human mind can never contemplate anything greater.[27]

---

[27]Lloyd-Jones, *God's Ultimate Purpose*, 196.

The old, original harmony [of creation before the Fall] will be restored. Isaiah speaks of it prophetically. . . . (Isaiah 11:6-9).

The perfect harmony that will be restored will be harmony in man, and between men. Harmony on the earth and in the brute creation! Harmony in heaven, and all under this blessed Lord Jesus Christ, who will be the Head of all! Everything will again be united in Him. And wonder of wonders, marvellous beyond compare, when all this happens it will never be undone again.[28]

Though many questions about life and death plague our minds during this earthly pilgrimage, all the answers will be clear when God's plans are fulfilled. Paul likened our incomplete view to dimly seeing our image in a mirror. He confessed that now we know only in part, but in that day we will know God's ways just as clearly as He knows our ways now.[29]

We are too insistent that we know all things now. The increased anxiety, panic, and despair of believers today is a direct result of thinking that we must *have* something else or must *know* something else before our hearts can rest. We think we could be at peace if only we knew . . .

whether we really had cancer.

whether our spouse is really being unfaithful.

whether our teen is really doing drugs.

whether our investments will be there when retirement comes, and so forth.

Consequently, we often go on relentless searches for the answers to those "dark mysteries," seeking rest for our hearts. The trouble with that strategy is that we often cannot find out the answers we want until it is too late to do anything about them.

Though dark mysteries such as these are common, they will not interfere with the peace of a believer who has seen with broader strokes the "Mystery of Christ." *God has injected all of life with mysteries to keep us*

---

[28]Ibid., 206.
[29]I Corinthians 13:12.

dependent—to keep Jesus Christ at the focal point of our attention. As we have seen, this is what it means to "fear the Lord."

- The Mystery of the Church: The divine secret previously unknown at this level of detail is that the *solution* for spiritual unity is the Church (2:11–3:21).

This second mystery of Ephesians was discussed at length in chapter seven. God will unify the universe at the end times by bringing all things under the headship of Jesus Christ. He is doing that on a smaller scale here on the earth through His Bride, the Church. He unites both Jew and Gentile by redeeming them to Himself and making them both into something they had not been before—members of His own Body. The solution to spiritual unity in the church is the accentuating of those elements we have in common—redemption by the blood of Jesus Christ.

- The Mystery of Marriage: The divine secret previously unknown at this level of detail is that the *illustration* of spiritual unity is marriage (5:22-33).

God intended for every home since the creation of Adam and Eve to be a close-up portrait of His overarching plans. God wanted every child born into the world to be able to see how much God has loved His people by watching a God-fearing dad relate to his wife and children.

In addition, God wanted every child born into the world to learn how to properly relate to the God of heaven by watching the God-fearing submission of his mother and older siblings to a godly father.

Tragically, this "parental portrait" is missing in most twenty-first century Christian homes. No wonder the children of our day have such troubles! The church desperately needs more adults who are practicing the vibrant Christianity of the first century. It is much easier to learn something by watching someone else do it well.

A FINAL CHALLENGE

I grew up on the plains of South Dakota. Though we had mammoth blizzards and staggering accumulations of snow, I never learned to snow ski because there were no hills nearby.

I suppose if I were to watch a few videos, take a couple of beginner lessons, and go skiing with a friend who skis well, I might learn to ski. It would have been far simpler, however, if I had grown up in a family of avid skiers. Skiing would be almost instinctive if that had been the case. I would not need so many "catch-up" lessons, nor would I be prone to make serious mistakes on the slopes, as may be the case were I to start skiing now at age fifty.

In the same way, a child who has grown up in a home where Jesus Christ is obviously the delight and passion of his parents will not find it unnatural to give his life totally to the service of such a wonderful Savior. His parents, being expert "skiers" themselves, can help him make the small corrections needed as he grows up so that he is not behind by the time he reaches adulthood.

In addition, he will not need such thorough "lessons" in adult life to make up for his ignorance. Nor will he need to be spending so much time on the "bunny slopes" in his early adult years when he ought to be teaching his own children how to "ski."

This training of the next generation by potent examples is sabotaged when Christian moms and dads do not understand and embrace "The Mystery of Christ." That training is also damaged when moms and dads do not affiliate themselves with a local Bible-preaching church where God's purposes are embraced by other families as well. If their own parents are "skiers," and they meet weekly with other families of veteran "skiers," learning to ski shouldn't be hard for the next generation.

My prayer for this book is that God will use it to raise up a new generation of "Olympian skiers" who are passionate about placing Jesus Christ at the center of all of life! The early church turned the world upside down when they took these matters seriously.

We were *created for His glory*. Let us show the world that our God—and His Son Jesus Christ—is *first!*

TAKE TIME TO REFLECT

1. What perplexing questions of life is God using right now to "goad" you to a greater dependence upon Him?

2. What "nail" of truth has God used recently in your life to stabilize you during a trying time?

3. If you have not experienced any "goads" recently or have not seen any "nails" recently, what do you suppose might be the reason?

4. What components of life have you been trying to accumulate on the "multiplicand" part of "The Equation of Enjoyment," thinking that if you just had enough of those things, life would be satisfying?

5. Describe a time when you had almost nothing on your "multiplicand" side but you had great satisfaction because God—the Multiplier—had decided to give you peace and joy even though from a natural standpoint you had little to rejoice about.

A WORD TO DISCIPLE-MAKERS

The Need for Disciple-Makers

I hope as you have absorbed these studies that your desire to disciple others has increased. Paul's admonition to Timothy is applicable for every believer. Its most potent application is in the family, but it ought to be the norm for every church.

> And the things that thou hast heard of me among many witnesses, the same commit thou to faithful men, who shall be able to teach others also (II Timothy 2:2).

I want to close with the following testimony of Richard Baxter. His book *The Reformed Pastor*, written in 1656, is a call for his fellow pastors to "reform" their practice and begin discipling their congregations. He chides them for thinking that their pulpit ministry is enough to see the full development of their people.

I submit it as a challenge to every believer to get on with the work of discipling others towards likeness to Jesus Christ. I have addressed this at some length in *Changed into His Image*[30] but present it here again—this time in the words of a Puritan pastor.

---

[30]Chapters one and ten.

The *first*, and main point, which I have to propound to you, is this, Whether it be not the unquestionable duty of the generality of ministers . . . to set themselves presently to the work of catechizing, and instructing individually, all that are committed to their care, who will be persuaded to submit thereto?[31]

I find the benefits and comforts of the work [of personal discipleship] to be such, that I would not wish I had forborne it, for all the riches in the world. We [i.e., Baxter and his associate] spend Monday and Tuesday, from morning almost to night, in the work, taking about fifteen or sixteen families in a week, that we may go through the parish, in which there are upwards of eight hundred families, in a year.[32]

When answering the objection, "But to what purpose is all this, when most of the people will not submit," Baxter replies:

It is not to be denied that too many people are obstinate in their wickedness, that the "simple ones love simplicity, and the scorners delight in scorning, and fools hate knowledge." But the worse they are, the sadder is their case, and the more to be pitied, and the more diligent should we be for their recovery.

I would it were not the blame of ministers, that a great part of the people are so obstinate and contemptuous. If we did but burn and shine before them as we ought; had we convincing sermons and convincing lives; did we set ourselves to do all the good we could, whatever it might cost us; were we more meek and humble, more loving and charitable, and let them see that we set light by all worldly things, in comparison of their salvation; much more might be done by us than is done, and the mouths of many would be stopped; and though the wicked will still do wickedly, yet more would be tractable, and the wicked would be fewer and calmer than they are. If you say that some of the ablest and godliest ministers in the country have had as untractable and scornful parishioners as others, I answer, that some able godly men have been too lordly, and strange [distant from their people], and some of them too uncharitable and worldly, and backward to costly though necessary good works, and some of them have done but little in private, when they have done excellently in public, and so have hindered the fruit of their labours.

---

[31]Richard Baxter, *The Reformed Pastor* (1656; reprint, Carlisle, Pa.: The Banner of Truth Trust, 1974), 41-42.

[32]Ibid., 43.

But where there are not these impediments, experience telleth us that the success is much greater, at least as to the bowing of people to more calmness and teachableness; yet we cannot expect they all will be brought to so much reason.[33]

Here Baxter lays the blame for much of the laziness and stubbornness of God's people upon the head of their spiritual leaders, who themselves can be lazy, heavy-handed, distant, and worldly. When a minister attends carefully to these issues in his own life, he will find his people far more teachable and responsive.

He answers a further objection: "But what likelihood is there that men will be [changed] by this means [of personal discipleship], who are not [changed] by the preaching of the Word, when that is God's chief ordinance for that end?"

> ANSWER (1): It will be an excellent means of helping you in preaching. For as the physician's work is half done when he understands the disease, so, when you are well acquainted with your people's case, you will know what to preach on; and it will furnish you with useful matter for your sermons, to talk an hour with an ignorant or obstinate sinner, as much as an hour's study will do, for you will learn what you have need to insist on, and what objections of theirs to repel.

> (2) I hope there are none so silly as to think this [personal] conference is not preaching. What? Doth the number we speak to make it preaching? Or doth interlocution make it none? Surely a man may as truly preach to one, as to a thousand.[34]

And though I know that we have a knotty generation to deal with, and that it is past the power of any of us to change a carnal heart without the effectual operation of the Holy Ghost; yet it is so usual with God to work by means, and to bless the right endeavours of his servants, that I cannot fear but great things will be accomplished, and a wonderful blow will be given to the kingdom of darkness by this work, if it do not miscarry through the fault of the ministers themselves. The main danger arises from the want of either diligence, or of skill.[35]

---

[33]Ibid., 226-27.
[34]Ibid., 228.
[35]Ibid., 231.

So let us take up the challenge. Let us live so that others will know that God is *first!* Let us disciple others so they, too, will show that God is *first!*

Displaying His "firstness" is the purpose for which He redeemed us. Indeed, we were *created for* His *glory!*

APPENDIX A
REPRODUCIBLE STUDY SHEETS

Five Significant Statements
Take Time to Reflect

Chapter _____

A. Write out five significant statements from this chapter.

1.

_____

_____

_____

_____

2.

_____

_____

_____

_____

3.

_____

_____

_____

_____

4.

_____

_____

_____

_____

5.

_____

_____

_____

_____

_____

B. Write out your answers to the Take Time to Reflect questions for
   this chapter.

_____

_____

_____

_____

_____

_____

_____

_____

_____

_____

_____

_____

_____

_____

_____

_____

_____

_____

SUPPLEMENTAL ARTICLE

Salvation: Divine Determination or Human Responsibility[1]

by Layton Talbert

Through the centuries this battle has raged like a theological holy war. Crusaders for both sides have attacked their doctrinal enemies too often with an unholy zeal. Brothers have parted, churches have split, fellowships have divided, denominations have formed, and labels have been devised (some descriptive, some defamatory) as a result of this question and its practical ramifications.

After all these centuries, the debate remains at an impasse. How is it to be resolved? One cannot argue the superiority of the men on either side of the issue. Both positions have had their share of good, godly, able advocates (as well as the other kind). Nor can either side claim a monopoly on clear and unequivocal Scripture. Each side of the debate has its favorite proof texts that allegedly undermine the other's position. Likewise, each side is baffled by certain passages and squirms at the prick of certain scriptural thorns in their theological flesh. Yet both sides have their own answers to such problem passages—answers that often involve some subtle adjustment of the wording, some rational re-definition of the terms, some leap of logic, however large or small, to make all the passages fit more comfortably within the logical confines of their systematic theology.

What, then, is the solution? A genuine impasse is, by nature and definition, unresolvable. If we insist on devising a complete answer to every question and fitting every verse into a system that we find logically comfortable and easily explicable, the impasse will always remain. Our only choice will be to side with one view or the other—accepting all the strengths and rationalizing all the weaknesses of whatever position

---

[1]Layton Talbert, *Not by Chance: Learning to Trust a Sovereign God* (Greenville, S.C.: BJU Press, 2001), 250-64. All emphasis in this article are those of the author, Dr. Talbert.

we choose. But there is another startlingly uncomplicated alternative. It may sound simplistic; in fact, it is merely simple. Let the Bible say what it says—plainly, unadorned by logic and rationalization, without removing its teeth, without tinkering with the terminology—even if you cannot fully understand or explain it. There, it seems, is the rub.

The Limitations of Logic

Shakespeare's *Henry V* opens with an apology to the audience for imposing upon their imagination because of the limitations of the theater. "Can this cockpit [this small stage] hold the vasty fields of France?" the narrator asks rhetorically. The task of theology, properly approached, faces this same limitation. Can any systematic theology, however thick or multi-volumed, adequately display the immeasurable vistas of an infinite and eternal God? "But pardon, gentles all," the bard continues, "the flat unraiséd spirit that hath dared, on this unworthy scaffold, to bring forth so great an object." Necessary and helpful as they are, the constructs of systematic theology and human reason are an insufficient scaffold for the presentation of so great an object as the thoughts and actions of the unfathomable Godhead.

Where biblical theology leaves off, with its explicit focus on what has been revealed, systematic theology often attempts to carry the investigation further through logic and deduction. Sound systematic theology takes the statements of biblical revelation and applies logic, both to organize the data into a kind of theological textbook and to deduce answers not directly addressed in Scripture.

Logic is, of course, a God-given tool, essential for understanding human and divine communication. Drawing logical inferences from Scripture is perfectly legitimate and, indeed, necessary. Jesus (e.g., Matthew 22:31-32), Paul (e.g., Romans 9-11), and others (e.g., James 2:20-26) exemplify this method in their handling of Scripture. At the same time, Paul flatly declares when an apparently logical path leads to a theological cul-de-sac (e.g., Romans 9:18-20). Everyone admits that there are limits to logic—at least in theory.

The assertion that human logic has limitations, however, does not mean merely that logic can carry us along only so far and then stops. There are numerous false turns down which apparent logic can take us and still be logical. In other words, it is possible for something to be

298

both "logical" and wrong. If a deduction is based on a false premise, a seemingly reasonable assumption, or an inadequate or inaccurate knowledge of the facts, that deduction may appear to be perfectly logical and yet be dead wrong. Paul is the most vocal in drawing the line between legitimate logical conclusions and deductions that are as wrong as they are reasonable. Each "God forbid" from the pen of Paul warns the reader against arriving at some apparently logical but erroneous, even damnable, conclusion. We are not at liberty to draw inferences that contradict other explicit statements of Scripture. And we must be tentative about defending apparently logical inferences that carry us beyond explicit statements of Scripture.

One of the challenges to logic is the paradox. Someone has defined a paradox as truth standing on its head to get attention. A paradox is not a contradiction but an apparent contradiction—truth presented in terms of polarities. God is three persons yet one being. Jesus is fully God and fully man. These are not contradictions but paradoxes. It is just as heretical to say that the truth lies somewhere between the two poles as is it to deny either pole of the truth. Within the confines of human logic, the finite categories in which we are accustomed to think, they appear to conflict. Yet, we are willing to suspend our logic in deference to what God says is so, in the face of biblical revelation that clearly asserts the reality of apparently contradictory truths.

This suspension of logic, this acting on the basis of what God says is so (rather than on our own understanding of what seems to make sense or our perception of what seems to be the case) has a very common name: faith—taking God at His word. This is not to say that faith is illogical. Belief in apparently illogical propositions (such as the Trinity or the twofold nature of Christ) is an entirely logical human response to propositions that God affirms are true. Faith acknowledges that revelation may transcend the limitations of human logic.

Logic is a persuasive thing. Paradoxical as it may sound, logic can also be an intoxicating influence, clouding our ability to walk the narrow path between explicit biblical statement and the tenuous extensions of apparent logic that branch off from that path in both directions. At some point in the debate over virtually every major Bible doctrine, two roads diverge in the theological wood. It is vital to learn to detect where reason veers off from the road of explicit biblical statement.

Once you step off the edge of the cliff of clear revelation, trusting in the power of logic to levitate your position, the fact is you are still standing out in thin air with nothing under you.

Getting to the Point

Few dispute the limitations of logic and the necessity of simple faith when it comes to theological issues that clearly transcend our comprehension (such as the nature of the God-Man). Once the debate shifts to the mechanics of salvation, however, we are strangely less inclined to accept by faith paradoxical affirmations as equally true. We insist on hammering out a comprehensive, logical, systematic theology that can answer questions that the Bible, frankly, leaves unanswered.

Is it not illogical to suppose that we can fully understand and explain the doings of a God we readily admit is utterly beyond our comprehension? Is it not unreasonable to insist on theologically psychoanalyzing the works of a God whose infinite nature we freely acknowledge bursts all the boundaries of finite understanding?

The answer to the question raised in the title of this essay—"Is salvation a matter of divine determination or human responsibility?"—is not divine determination *or* human responsibility. The only thoroughly biblical answer is yes. Scripturally, it is not an "either-or" but a "both-and" proposition. Why is this so hard?

For one thing, it is logically unsatisfactory and apparently contradictory. Our insatiable appetite for order and answers makes it difficult to admit—not just in theory but in our practice and in our theology—that God's ways are not our ways, and leave it at that. "For as the heavens are higher than the earth, so are my ways higher than your ways, and my thoughts than your thoughts" (Isaiah 55:9). We don't mind applying this principle in a general, hypothetical way to God's wisdom or methods. But we balk when it interferes with our theological system, our obsession with pigeonholing every Bible fact into a neat, orderly arrangement that leaves no questions unanswered.

But God's point in Isaiah 55:9 is essentially that He is not logical. That does not mean He is illogical. It means He transcends our logic. He is *supra*logical. His thinking, His design, His way, His "theology" is infinitely above our intellect, beyond the grasp of our comprehension, out of the reach of our clever rationalizations. Someone has expressed it cleverly and succinctly: God is *theo*-logical. Man is *anthropo*-logical. The extent of our logic is inherently deficient and inadequate, primarily because our information and comprehension is so limited. Like a two-dimensional square compared to a three-dimensional cube (or to four-dimensional reality), we are merely a finite reflection of an infinite God in this respect.

C. S. Lewis offers a superb illustration of our limitations from the field of geometry. If you are operating in a one-dimensional realm, he explains, you can draw a straight line. Move into two-dimensions and you can draw a square—which consists of four straight lines. In a three-dimensional world you can construct a cube which, in turn, is made of six squares.

> Do you see the point? . . . In other words, as you advance to more real and more complicated levels, you do not leave behind you the things you found on the simpler levels: you still have them, but combined in new ways—*in ways you could not imagine if you knew only the simpler levels.*[2]

"Those things which are revealed belong unto us and to our children forever" but "the secret things belong unto the Lord" (Deuteronomy 29:29). So why do we insist that profound and eternal issues must make complete sense to us? We betray our folly when we presume to discover His secret things and proceed to press them into the limited dimensional realm of a humanly devised systematic theology. Easier to fit the ocean into a test tube, or gather all the mountains into a petri dish, than to press the thoughts and methods of an infinite God into

---

[2]*Mere Christianity* (Nashville: Broadman & Holman, 1996), p. 142. Lewis applies this illustration brilliantly to the paradox of the nature of God, to which I have already alluded. "On the human level one person is one being, and any two persons are two separate beings—just as, in two dimensions (say on a flat sheet of paper) one square is one figure and any two squares are two separate figures. On the Divine level you still find personalities; but up there you find them combined in new ways which we, who do not live on that level, cannot imagine. In God's dimension, you find a being who is three Persons while remaining one being, just as a cube is six squares while remaining one cube. Of course we cannot fully conceive a Being like that: just as, if we were so made that we perceived only two dimensions in space we could never properly imagine a cube. But we can get a sort of faint notion of it. . . . It is something we could never have guessed, and yet, once we have been told, one almost feels one ought to have been able to guess it because it fits so well with all the things we know already" (pp. 142-43).

the Lilliputian cage of human logic. If the Bible contains no clear answer or explanation to a given question, isn't it foolish to plug our limited logic into problem passages in order to manufacture "truths"—and then call them biblical and argue over them?

We serve a precise God. Virtually every major biblical doctrine demands knife-edge precision as we work our way back and forth balanced on the tightwire stretched between two unambiguous and equally valid poles of truth. One footfall too far, one step—however reasonable—beyond the biblical data in either direction, topples one toward heresy. The effort to reconcile the issues of election and free will, of divine determination and human responsibility, is no different. It is a "quest [that] stands upon the edge of a knife."[3] There is little room to stray.

The key to not overstepping the boundary is not easy but it is relatively simple. Learn to see and accept where the Bible draws a line. Distinguish between express statements of Scripture and logical leaps—extensions that may make sense but do not enjoy the "luxury" of explicit biblical affirmation. Trace the branches to the limbs to the trunk of the tree of biblical revelation; but where the trunk disappears below the surface of the ground (into the realm of the unrevealed "secret things"), it is both idle and dangerous to dig with the spade of human logic. It may make for interesting speculative debates. But it does not make for sound theology.

It is no accident that Paul concludes what is arguably his most logically and theologically profound (and, consequently, his most difficult and debated) passage with this exclamation: "O the depth of the riches both of the wisdom and knowledge of God! how *unsearchable* are his judgments, and his ways *past finding out!*" (Romans 11:33).

Terms of the Debate
In the debate over the mechanics of soteriology, problems arise when we fail to observe and consistently maintain precise, scripturally accurate definitions for the terms involved. We ought not be gun-shy about explicitly biblical terms. Are believers actually elected (chosen) by

---

[3]The allusion is to J. R. R. Tolkien, *The Fellowship of the Ring*, Part One of *The Lord of the Rings* (Boston: Houghton Mifflin, 1965), p. 372.

God? There is no question about that (II Thessalonians 2:13). Were believers actually chosen (elected) by God even before He ever created the world? Yes (Ephesians 1:4). Did God predestinate all whom He foreknew to be conformed to the image of His Son? Without question (Romans 8:28-29).

On the other side, if divine election is a fact, are we still responsible to communicate the message of the gospel? Of course (Matthew 28:18-20). Are individuals responsible to respond to the gospel in order to be saved? Certainly (John 3:16, 36). Are we incapable of responding to the gospel without the previous drawing of God? Jesus said so (John 6:44). Are those who fail to respond to the gospel accountable for their damnation? Undoubtedly (II Thessalonians 1:7-9).

Do these truths wreak havoc on our logical systems of theology or undercut our pet explanations of God's actions and our responsibility? Probably. How could it be otherwise? We are time-bound, earth-bound creatures wrestling with eternal truths about an infinite God. We are in the realm of the secret things. Why, then, are we afraid to say, "I don't really comprehend this, but God says it. I don't understand how this command fits with this truth, but I'll believe the truth and obey the command, and leave the understanding to God." There is something, after all, to the old bumper sticker mentality that "God said it. I believe it. That settles it"—although it might be better turned, "God says it. That settles it. So I believe it."

The moment we insist—in order for a passage to fit the context of our theological system—that "world" does not really mean "world" but "world of the elect," or that if God elects some to believe then He obviously must elect others to damnation, or that election "according to foreknowledge" must refer to God's foreknowledge of who would respond,[4] we have just stepped off the foundation of explicit biblical

---

[4]"But," some will protest, "I Peter 1:2 explicitly says 'elect according to the foreknowledge of God.' See? He chose on the basis of whom He foreknew would accept." Check the text again. (1) It does not say "elect according to God's foreknowledge of response." Any such explanatory insertion is the encroachment of logical assumption into the text. "But what else could it possibly refer to?" It need refer to nothing more than God's election based on His foreknowledge of His own sovereign purposes and intentions. The point is, the text itself does not explain foreknowledge here; only theologians do. (2) The literal reading of the text makes the above assumption even more remote: "To the elect strangers scattered throughout

statement and into the realm of systematic theological logic. "But it must be this way," someone protests, "or it just doesn't make sense." Make sense to whom?

Several illustrations have been suggested in an attempt to resolve the tension. Some pose the analogy of a railroad track. Two distinct tracks run parallel into the distance where, to the naked eye, the tracks appear to run together and become one; yet they remain distinct and parallel. Others note that every coin has two sides. You may examine one side fully and carefully, then turn the coin over and inspect the other side in great detail. But, hold it at whatever angle you will, you will never be able to see completely or focus fully on both sides at once. Many biblical truths fit such analogies. The question of divine determination and human responsibility in salvation is no different, giving rise to a popular soteriologically specific illustration: an individual voluntarily enters a banquet hall under a banner that reads, "Whosoever will, let him come"; upon entering, however, he looks over the inside doorway and reads a different banner: "Chosen in Christ before the foundation of the world." How does this work? I don't know, and neither does anyone else. But there are passages that address this very dynamic of polarity in the context of soteriology.

Examples of Textual Tension

Many of the standard proof texts have been badly battered and buffeted from centuries of debate. We all have our rational ripostes to those texts at the ready, hands hovering over our theological holsters. In His wisdom, however, God has given to us a surprising and gratifying array of verses that incorporate, within a single verse, both facets of the theological debate. Note the Spirit-inspired juxtaposition of di-

---

Pontus, Galatia, Cappadocia, Asia and Bithynia, according to the foreknowledge of God." The syntax may even suggest that their scattering was not accidental but providential, "according to the foreknowledge of God." (3) If God is omniscient, He must foreknow all responses—not only who will accept but who will reject. Yet Romans 8:29 indicates that all those "whom he did foreknow, he also did predestinate to be conformed to the image of his Son." It is difficult to assert that "foreknowledge" means foreknowledge of response, since He foreknows both positive and negative responses, yet Paul asserts here that those whom He foreknew He also predestined to conformity to Christ. That cannot be true of those whose rejection He foreknew. This alone suggests that "foreknowledge" must mean something beyond mere prescience.

vine will (**bold**) and human responsibility (*italics*) in the verses below. Most are self-explanatory. Some merit an additional observation.

Matthew 11:20-28. "Then began he to upbraid the cities wherein most of his mighty works were done, because they repented not. . . . At that time Jesus answered and said, I thank thee, O Father, Lord of heaven and earth, because **thou hast hid these things** from the wise and prudent, **and hast revealed them** unto babes. Even so, Father: for so it seemed good in thy sight. All things are delivered unto me of my Father: and no man knoweth the Son, but the Father; **neither knoweth any man the Father, save the Son, and he to whomsoever the Son will reveal him.** *Come unto me, all ye that labour and are heavy laden,* and I will give you rest."

Luke 22:22. "And truly the Son of man goeth, **as it was determined**: but *woe unto that man by whom he is betrayed!*"

Matthew 23:37. "O Jerusalem, Jerusalem . . . **how often would I have gathered** thy children together, even as a hen gathereth her chickens under her wings, and *ye would not!*"

John 6:37. "**All that the Father giveth me shall come** [ηκω, to arrive] to me; and *him that cometh* [ερχομαι, to come] to me I will in no wise cast out." This is quite startling. To argue that the explicit change in verbs is capricious or insignificant is to dismiss the deliberate word choice of the Son of God and the superintending inspiration of the Holy Spirit. All those whom the Father gives to the Son will arrive; whoever comes voluntarily will not be cast out.

John 6:44, 45, 64-65. "**No man can come to me except the Father . . . draw him**. . . . Every man therefore that hath heard, and hath learned of the Father, *cometh* unto me. . . . But there are *some of you that believe not*. . . . Therefore said I unto you that **no man can come unto me, except it were given unto him of my Father**." And yet Jesus only a little earlier said, "*Ye will not come unto me* [lit., "*You are not willing to come to me*"], that ye might have life" (John 5:40).

Acts 13:48.[5] "**And as many as were ordained to eternal life** *believed*"— an inscrutable echo of Jesus' words from the preceding passages in John 6.

---

[5]While they are not soteriologically oriented, the implications of two passages in

Acts 16:14. "And a certain woman named Lydia, . . . heard us: **whose heart the Lord opened,** [so] that *she attended unto the things which were spoken of* [by] *Paul.*" The latter phrase literally reads, "**whose heart the Lord opened** *to heed the things spoken by Paul.*"

I Corinthians 3:6. "*I have planted, Apollos watered;* but **God gave the increase.**" The same principle applies to both evangelistic ministry and the individual experience of salvation.

I Thessalonians 1:3-4. "Remembering without ceasing *your work of faith, and labour of love, and patience of hope* in our Lord Jesus Christ; in the sight of God and our Father; knowing, brethren beloved, **your election of God.**" How could Paul possibly "know" their election? By observing their response to the Word. Note verse 6, "And *ye became followers* of us, and of the Lord." In other words, Paul's "knowledge of their election was an intuitive conviction based upon known and observed facts."[6]

II Thessalonians 2:13-14. "But we are bound to give thanks always to God for you, brethren beloved of the Lord, because **God hath from the beginning chosen you to salvation** THROUGH **sanctification of the Spirit** AND *belief of the truth:* whereunto he called you by our gospel, to the obtaining of the glory of our Lord Jesus Christ." This remarkable passage juxtaposes the two poles of the soteriological paradox. "The salvation of believers rests on the divine choice, not on human effort";[7] yet there are "two aspects or sides of the element in which the divine choice realizes itself—the divine or objective aspect, sanctification by the Spirit; and the human or subjective aspect, believing reception of the truth."[8]

Acts previously discussed in chapter 10 of this book are worth pointing out here. (1) Acts 2:23—Christ, "being delivered **by the determinate counsel and forekowledge of God,** *ye have taken, and by wicked hands have crucified and slain.*" (2) Acts 4:27-28—"For truly *against Your holy Servant Jesus, whom You anointed, both Herod and Pontius Pilate, with the Gentiles and the people of Israel, were gathered together to do* **whatever Your hand and Your purpose determined before to be done.**"

[6]D. Edmond Hiebert, *The Thessalonian Epistles* (Chicago: Moody, 1971), p. 52.

[7]Leon Morris, *The First and Second Epistles to the Thessalonians* (Grand Rapids: Eerdmans, 1959), p. 237.

[8]John Eadie, *Commentary on the Epistles to the Thessalonians* (1877; reprint, Grand Rapids: Baker, 1979), p. 294.

Do any of these, as they stand, do damage to the neat logic of our theological system? Let them. To do otherwise—to redefine the words, to tinker with the terminology, to run the verses through the sieve of a theological system—is to make human logic the line by which we gauge whether God's explicit statements are completely true and plumb as they stand or whether they need a little adjustment here, a little refinement there. We dare not construct a system of theology that helps the Holy Spirit by refining or redefining the words He selected or by interposing words He chose to omit so as to tweak out of it, ever so gently, a slightly modified meaning that better fits the system.

Noteworthy Remarks

Some theologians, willing to set aside the stringent logical demands of a theological system (even their own), have understood the limitations of logic, the need for balance, and the necessity of sticking with the explicit statements of Scripture. Reflecting on the John 6 passages cited above, Scottish Presbyterian David Brown remarked:

> Pity that, in the attempts to reconcile these [the divine drawing and the human coming], so much vain and unsavory controversy has been spent, and that one of them is so often sacrificed to the other; for then they are not what Jesus says they are, but rather a caricature of them. The link of connection between divine and human operation will probably never be reached on earth—if even in heaven. Let us then implicitly receive and reverently hold both; remembering, however, that the divine in this case ever precedes, and is the cause of, the human—the 'drawing' on God's part of the 'coming' on ours; while yet our coming is as purely spontaneous, and the result of rational considerations presenting themselves to our minds, as if there were no supernatural operation in the matter at all.[9]

The theological balance is beautiful, allowing every passage to say precisely and fully what it says—no more and no less.

No one could doubt the fervent evangelistic tenor of the ministry of Charles Haddon Spurgeon, a staunch Baptist Calvinist. In a sermon on Esther, he observes that "the divine will is accomplished, and yet men are perfectly free agents." Logic rebels. How can that be? Spurgeon answers the objection:

---

[9]Jamieson, Robert, A. R. Faussett, and David Brown, *A Commentary Critical, Experimental and Practical*, vol. 3 (reprint, Grand Rapids: Eerdmans, 1976), p. 393.

"I cannot understand it," says one. My dear friend, I am compelled to say the same—I do not understand it either. . . . Certain of my brethren deny free agency, and so get out of the difficulty; others assert that there is no predestination, and so cut the knot. As I do not wish to get out of the difficulty, and have no wish to shut my eyes to any part of the truth, I believe both predestination and free agency to be facts. How they can be made to agree I do not know, or care to know; I am satisfied to know anything which God chooses to reveal to me, and equally content not to know what he does not reveal. . . . Believe these two truths and you will see them in practical agreement in daily life, though you will not be able to devise a theory for harmonizing them on paper.[10]

The scriptural poise is perfect, permitting paradoxical truths to stand in tension to one another without subjecting the declarations of an infinite God to the scrutiny of my finite understanding.

This approach is not novel. We have all sung John Newton's words about this mysterious balance many times:

> 'Twas grace that taught my heart to fear, and grace
>   my fears relieved;
> How precious did that grace appear the hour I first
>   believed.

Daniel Whittle captures the balance even more explicitly in this well-known hymn:

> I know not how this saving faith to me He did impart,
> Nor how believing in His Word wrought peace within my
>   heart.
> I know not how the Spirit moves, convincing men of sin,
> Revealing Jesus through the Word, creating faith in Him.

Earlier in this essay I used the analogy of a tensioned tightwire of truth stretched between two paradoxical poles. Here is another someone has suggested. Theology is structured like an arch. One side does not make an arch. It takes the tension of both sides pressing against each other in opposite directions to hold the keystone in place. In the final analysis, does the arch hold up the keystone, or does the keystone hold up the arch? Yes.

---

[10]"Esther: The Hand of Providence" in Men and Women of the Old Testament (Chattanooga, Tenn.: AMG, 1995), pp. 409-10.

Drawing Conclusions

Carefully consider the following questions and, more importantly, the explicit wording of the accompanying references. Is election sovereign and unconditional or is it activated in accordance with human response? The answer is yes (II Thessalonians 2:13). Does salvation involve effectual grace or the exercise of free will? Yes (I Thessalonians 2:13). Did Christ die for the sins of the world or for the elect? Yes (John 1:29; 3:16; 10:11). Will the elect be certainly, sovereignly, and graciously converted or are we obligated to proclaim the gospel to all men? Yes (John 6:37; Matthew 28:18-20). Are the events of human history orchestrated by divine decree or is there a genuine element of human responsibility which affects circumstances? Yes (Acts 2:23).

Does all this sit well with our natural curiosity and human logic? The answer is no. So what? The bottom line, the final court of appeal, must be the explicit statement of Scripture—not our satisfaction that all bases have been covered and all questions answered, not our sense of logical harmony, and not our theological comfort with where the chips seem to fall. Can the emphasis on one side of the truth be blown out of proportion, leading to the abuse of the other side? Certainly. What, then, is the solution? Side with the half of the truth with which we are more comfortable? But that is to deny the other half of the truth. Should we insist that the "real" truth must lie somewhere in the middle? But that is to deny both halves, both poles of the truth in the fullness of their scriptural presentation. May we not, must we not, fully hold both truths in balanced tension?

The profound insight of Charles Simeon on the paradoxical terminology of Scripture is equally convicting to all sides of the debate and deserves both sober reflection and personal application.

> The author is disposed to think that the Scripture system is of a broader and more comprehensive character than some very dogmatic theologians are inclined to avow; and that, as wheels in a complicated machine may move in opposite directions and yet subserve one common end, so may truths apparently opposite be perfectly reconcilable with each other and equally subserve the purposes of God in the accomplishment of man's salvation. The author feels it impossible to avow too distinctly that it is an invariable rule with him to endeavor to give every portion of the Word of God its full and proper force, without considering what scheme it

favors, or whose system it is likely to advance. Of this he is sure, that there is not a decided Calvinist or Arminian in the world who equally approves of the whole of Scripture . . . who, if he had been in the company of St. Paul whilst he was writing his Epistles, would not have recommended him to alter one or other of his expressions.

But the author would not wish one of them altered; he finds as much satisfaction in one class of passages as in another; and employs the one, he believes, as freely as the other. Where the inspired Writers speak in unqualified terms, he thinks himself at liberty to do the same; judging that they needed no instruction from him how to propagate the truth. He is content to sit as a learner at the feet of the holy Apostles, and has no ambition to teach them how they ought to have spoken. I love the simplicity of the Scriptures; and I wish to receive and inculcate every truth precisely in the way, and to the extent, that it is set forth in the inspired Volume. Were this the habit of all divines, there would soon be an end of most of the controversies that have agitated and divided the Church of Christ. My endeavour is to bring out of Scripture what is there, and not to thrust in what I think might be there. I have a great jealousy on this head; never to speak more or less than I believe to be the mind of the Spirit in the passage I am expounding.[11]

This is not theological schizophrenia; this is respect for the biblical text in the form in which it was inspired (we are verbal inspirationists, are we not?) over respect for a humanly devised system of arranging it. Some have emphasized the biblical assertion of God's election to the neglect of evangelism and the necessity of a personal profession of faith. Logical? Perhaps, but dead wrong. Is the solution, then, to throw out or redefine the explicit biblical assertion of election? Is not the solution to insist that the same God who sovereignly elects also sovereignly commands us to evangelize? And that the gospel we are commanded to declare demands obedience and personal profession?[12] We must hold both simultaneously, since both are explicitly asserted.

---

[11]Excerpt from Handley C. G. Moule, *Charles Simeon* (1892; reprint, London: Inter-Varsity Fellowship, 1956), p. 79. Simeon was the godly pastor of the Church of the Holy Trinity in Cambridge for over half a century spanning the late 1700s and early 1800s.

[12]The NT consistently presents the gospel as a message that demands a response; that response is described not only as belief but obedience. See Romans 10:16; II Thessalonians 1:8; I Peter 2:7; 4:17; and John 3:36 (where "believe not" is not απιστευω but απειθεω).

Rightly and biblically understood, election does not hinder evangelism; it encourages it by insuring that some *will* respond.

Again, some become so protective of human freedom and responsibility that the very thought of election is regarded as a heretical threat to an evangelistic ministry. Logical, maybe, but wrong. The comfort, encouragement and humbling wonder of election—identified by Paul in Ephesians 1 as one of the "spiritual blessings" for which we are to bless God—is forfeited. We diminish God's glory when we forget that it was solely God's initiative that secured and effected our salvation.[13] Is the solution, then, to rationalize away the explicit "whosoever wills" of the Bible and reject real free will as a farce? Is not the only genuinely biblical solution to acknowledge the explicit revelation that God chose before the foundation of the world and calls all men everywhere to repent and to believe and obey the gospel? Each of us is responsible to compel our logic to bow submissively at the altar of divine revelation. Rightly and biblically understood, free will does not contradict divine election; God's Spirit effectually *persuades* the elect to become *voluntary* participants in His saving grace. David Brown captured this tension in his quotation already cited above.

Our ultimate allegiance must not be to human logic or systems of theology. Our consciences and our theology must be held captive by the explicit statements of the Word of God—whether or not it answers all our questions, whether or not the results appear to fit together logically. The truth of Isaiah 55:8-9 must be free to govern our theology as much as it governs our acceptance of circumstances.

---

[13]Read carefully through the phraseology of Ephesians 1—predestined "according to the good pleasure of His will," redemption and forgiveness "according to the riches of his grace," the revelation of his will "according to his good pleasure," predestined "according to the purpose of him who worketh all things after the counsel of his own will." The piling up of these qualifying phrases, one on top of another, gives the inescapable impression of God's absolute initiative in salvation. This is a needed corrective to a prevalent anthropocentric view of the gospel. "Unless we begin with God in this way, when the gospel comes to us, we will inevitably put ourselves at the center of it. We will feel that our value rather than God's value is the driving force in the gospel. We will trace the gospel back to God's need for us instead of tracing it back to the sovereign grace that rescues sinners who need God. . . . He was not coerced or constrained by our value. He is the center of the gospel. The exaltation of his glory is the driving force of the gospel" (John Piper, *The Pleasures of God* [Portland, Ore.: Multnomah, 1991], p. 19).

The Lord's interrogation of Job dramatically demonstrates the deficiency of our knowledge of God and His ways. With our wealth of translations, commentaries, and theologies, there is a tendency to think that we can systematize God, explain all His past actions, pigeonhole His present doings, and predict His future plans in minute detail. There is, to be sure, a foundational body of truth in the Scriptures of which we can be certain. Nevertheless, even when we speak what we know is true and right and in accordance with clear revelation, we must confess with Job that we are speaking of things we do not understand, things too wonderful for us to know (Job 42:3).

In short, we do not know as much as we think we know, and only an infinitesimal fraction of what there is to know. This does not deny our possession of absolute, objective truth. But it is a candid acknowledgment that there is a vast amount of truth about God to which we do not have access and which we are simply not big enough to comprehend. The secret things still belong to the Lord.

In the difficult questions of theology that have been debated for centuries by wise and godly men in the church, our attitude should be humbly instructed by the response of Job to God. We must acknowledge and remember our smallness (40:4), our ignorance (42:3), and God's undiluted freedom to do what He pleases, when and how He chooses (42:2)—and to reveal it in whatever way He sees fit. Accepting all of God's Word as it stands and waiting till we see Him to have all our questions answered is the essence of theological humility (42:5-6).

May God help us to discern the often thin line between scriptural statement and human logic, to herald the former with confidence, to hold the latter with deference, and to be governed in creed and conduct by the whole counsel of God.

How to Use This Book When Working with Others

How to Use This Book When Working with Others

Those wanting a more thorough study of this book can use it along with its study guide, *Taking Time to Rejoice*. This study guide examines one chapter per week and is broken down into five daily assignments for the week.

Churches and small groups can benefit as well from the video version of *Created for His Glory*. Its thirteen 30- to 35-minute segments can be viewed by the group the week before they study the next chapter individually.

More information about these resources, as well as a *Leader's Guide for Created for His Glory*, are available on the BJU Press website at www.bjup.com .

The suggestions below are applicable when using *Created for His Glory* by itself.

Individual Discipleship

If you are working with an individual, have him read each chapter and then write out the answers to the questions in the Take Time to Reflect section at the end of each chapter. You might also want to have him write out Five Significant Statements for the chapter he just read. Ask him to find and write down the five statements in the chapter that had the most significance to him. Tell him you do not want him to write out three or six, but five. Having to search for the five most significant statements will force him to concentrate on the material as he is reading it. If he has more than five, he will have to sift through the ones he previously selected to narrow them down to five. If he has fewer than five, he will be forced to return to the text to add to his list. This process causes him to think carefully about what he is reading. Writing them down will reinforce them in his mind one more time. Sharing them with you the next time you meet will further cement them in his thinking. At the same time, the significant statements he chose and his answers to the Take Time to Reflect section will show you where God is working in his life right now. Duplicate the work-sheet entitled Five Significant Statements/Take Time to Reflect in Appendix A and have him record his answers for each chapter on the worksheet. If you are having him read one chapter each week, encourage him to read the chapter early in the week so that he has time to reflect on what he has read and to see how his life either measures up to or falls short of what he has just learned.

Small Group Study
Small groups within the local church or Christian school that could benefit from studying this book together include Sunday school classes, deacons, church and Christian school staff members, men's or women's Bible studies, church or Christian school teen leadership councils, church Bible institute classes, and Christian counselor training programs. Organizations that serve the local church, such as Christian camps, can use the book for staff training as well.

If you are working with a small group of people reading through this book, you can ask them to follow the same process described above and then have them share with the group what statements were significant to them and why those statements had an impact upon them. Sharing with others reinforces the truth they have seen while encouraging others who saw the same ideas. It also highlights that truth for others who missed it in their reading.

Family Bible Study
The small group process described above is a wonderful way for a father to go through this book with his family if the children are of junior or senior high age and can grasp the material—in fact, this was the initial intent of this book. If there is a wide range of ages and abilities to understand, he can study the book with his wife alone or individually with each child who is old enough to understand it. If he is working with one family member at a time this way, he can follow the helps explained earlier in the section entitled Individual Discipleship.

Premarital and Early Marriage Growth
Engaged couples and newlyweds can study through the book following the process described in the Individual Discipleship section above. Individually answering the questions in the Take Time to Reflect sec-

tions, writing out the Five Most Significant Statements for that chapter, and then discussing the results together will pay huge dividends in a relationship. Couples will find out a great deal about each other while at the same time learning God's ways of handling the problems of living. If there are areas that seem to puzzle them or points of disagreement between them about something they studied, they can seek out the help of their pastor or other mature Christian friend to clarify the issue. Growing together spiritually in this way will help them launch their marriage with a biblical "like-mindedness" that forms the bedrock of a solid Christian marriage.

Bibliography

Adams, Jay E. *Handbook of Church Discipline*. Grand Rapids: Zondervan, 1986.

Arndt, William, and F. Wilbur Gingrich. *A Greek-English Lexicon of the New Testament and Other Early Christian Literature*. Chicago: University of Chicago Press, 1979.

Baxter, Richard. *The Reformed Pastor*. 1656. Reprint, Carlisle, Pa.: The Banner of Truth Trust, 1974.

Berg, Jim. *Changed into His Image*. Greenville, S.C.: Bob Jones University Press, 1999.

Bork, Robert H. *Slouching Towards Gomorrah*. New York: ReganBooks, 1996.

Bridges, Jerry. *The Joy of Fearing God*. Colorado Springs: WaterBrook, 1997.

Bruce, A. B. *The Training of the Twelve*. 1871. Reprint, Grand Rapids: Kregel Publications, 1971.

Bunyan, John. *The Fear of God*. 1679. Reprint, Morgan, Pa.: Soli Deo Gloria Publications, 1999.

Burroughs, Jeremiah. *Gospel Fear*. 1647. Reprint, Morgan, Pa.: Soli Deo Gloria Publications, 1991.

Chafer, Lewis Sperry. *He That Is Spiritual*. Grand Rapids: Zondervan, 1967.

Cheney, Lynne V. *Telling the Truth*. New York: Simon and Schuster, 1995.

Choy, Leona. *Powerlines: What Great Evangelicals Believed About the Holy Spirit 1850-1930*. Camp Hill, Pa.: Christian Publications, 1990.

De Haan, Richard W. *The Art of Staying Off Dead-End Streets*. Wheaton: Victor Books, 1974.

Eaton, Michael A. *Ecclesiastes: An Introduction and Commentary*. Downers Grove, Ill.: Inter-Varsity Press, 1983.

Edwards, Jonathan. *Religious Affections: A Christian's Character Before God*. Edited by James M. Houston. Minneapolis: Bethany House Publishers, 1996.

_____. *The Works of Jonathan Edwards*, 2 vols. 1834. Reprint, Peabody, Mass.: Hendrickson Publishers, 2000.

Ferguson, Sinclair B. *John Owen on the Christian Life*. Carlisle, Pa.: The Banner of Truth Trust, 1987.

Gaebelein, Frank E. *The Christian, the Arts, and Truth*. Portland, Oreg.: Multnomah Press, 1985.

Henry, Matthew. *A Commentary on the Holy Bible*, 6 vols. New York: Funk & Wagnalls Company, n.d.

Hodge, Charles. *A Commentary on Ephesians*. 1856. Reprint, Carlisle, Pa.: The Banner of Truth Trust, 1964.

Horton, Ron, ed. *Christian Education: Its Mandate and Mission*. Greenville, S.C.: Bob Jones University Press, 1992.

Kaiser, Walter C. Jr. *Ecclesiastes: Total Life*. Chicago: Moody Press, 1979.

Kidner, Derek. *A Time to Mourn and a Time to Dance: The Message of Ecclesiastes*. Downer Grove, Ill.: Inter-Varsity Press, 1976.

Lloyd-Jones, D. Martyn. *God's Ultimate Purpose: An Exposition of Ephesians 1*. Grand Rapids: Baker Books, 1978.

_____. *God's Way of Reconciliation: An Exposition of Ephesians 2*. Grand Rapids: Baker Books, 1972.

_____. *The Unsearchable Riches of Christ: An Exposition of Ephesians 3*. Grand Rapids: Baker Books, 1979.

_____. *Christian Unity: An Exposition of Ephesians 4:1-16*. Grand Rapids: Baker Books, 1980.

_____. *Darkness and Light: An Exposition of Ephesians 4:17–5:17*. Grand Rapids: Baker Books, 1982.

_____. *Life in the Spirit: An Exposition of Ephesians 5:18–6:9*. Grand Rapids: Baker Books, 1973.

_____. *The Christian Warfare: An Exposition of Ephesians 6:10-13*. Grand Rapids: Baker Books, 1976.

_____. *The Christian Soldier: An Exposition of Ephesians 6:10-20*. Grand Rapids: Baker Books, 1977.

_____. *Spiritual Depression: Its Causes and Cure*. Grand Rapids: Wm. B. Eerdmans Publishing Company, 1965.

Morgan, G. Campbell. *The Corinthian Letters of Paul*. Old Tappan, N.J.: Fleming H. Revell Company, 1946.

Moule, H. C. G. *Ephesian Studies*. Fort Washington, Pa.: Christian Literature Crusade, 1937.

Myers, Kenneth A. *All God's Children and Blue Suede Shoes: Christians and Popular Culture*. Wheaton: Crossway Books, 1989.

Owen, John. *The Glory of Christ*. 1683. Reprint, Carlisle, Pa.: The Banner of Truth Trust, 1994.

Packer, J. I. *A Quest for Godliness: The Puritan Vision of the Christian Life*. Wheaton: Crossway Books, 1990.

_____. *Keep in Step with the Spirit*. Grand Rapids: Fleming H. Revell, 1984.

Pentecost, J. Dwight. *The Divine Comforter: The Person and Work of the Holy Spirit*. Grand Rapids: Kregel Publications, 1963.

_____. *Things Which Become Sound Doctrine*. Grand Rapids: Zondervan Publishing House, 1965.

Phillips, John. *Exploring Ephesians*. Neptune, N.J.: Loizeaux Brothers, 1993.

Rookmaaker, H. R. *Modern Art and the Death of a Culture*. Wheaton: Crossway, 1994.

Ryrie, Charles C. *Transformed by His Glory*. Wheaton: Victor Books, 1990.

Schaeffer, Francis A. *Art and the Bible*. Downers Grove, Ill.: InterVarsity Press, 1973.

Spurgeon, Charles Haddon. *Morning and Evening*. Peabody, Mass.: Hendrickson Publishers, 1991.

Tagliapietra, Ron. *Great Adventurers of the Twentieth Century*. Greenville, S.C.: Bob Jones University Press, 1998.

Talbert, Layton. *Not by Chance: Learning to Trust a Sovereign God*. Greenville, S.C.: Bob Jones University Press, 2001.

Torrey, R. A. *The Person and Work of the Holy Spirit*. Grand Rapids: Zondervan Publishing House, 1910.

Tozer, A. W. *How to Be Filled with the Holy Spirit*. Camp Hill, Pa.: Christian Publications, n.d.

_____. *That Incredible Christian*. Camp Hill, Pa.: Christian Publications, 1964.

_____. *The Attributes of God*. Camp Hill, Pa.: Christian Publications, 1997.

_____. *The Pursuit of God*. Camp Hill, Pa.: Christian Publications, 1982.

_____. *The Pursuit of Man*. Camp Hill, Pa.: Christian Publications, 1950.

_____. *The Root of the Righteous*. Camp Hill, Pa.: Christian Publications, 1955.

Warfield, Benjamin B. *Biblical and Theological Studies*. Grand Rapids: Baker Book House, 1968.

_____. *The Person and Work of the Holy Spirit*. Amityville, N.Y.: Calvary Press Publishing, 1997.

Scriptural Index

Genesis
1:1 . . . . 28, 52
1:27 206
1:31 140
2:16-17 35
43:18 240

Exodus
15:11 30
18:21 221
19:9-16 214
20:2-3 28
20:3 . . . . 7, 36

Leviticus
25:14-17, 36, 43 239

Deuteronomy
4:39 . . . . 7, 28, 32
6:5 7
6:5-13 122
10:12-13 223
29:29 . . . . 44, 301

I Samuel
2:22 248
3:13 248
14:23-45 246
18:10-11 246
20:30-34 246
22-24 246

II Samuel
23:1-5 236
23:3 . . . . 221, 249
23:3-4 . . . . 236, 240, 247

I Kings
10:1 274

II Kings
6:15-17 2

I Chronicles
29:11 36

Nehemiah
5:9 251
5:15 . . . . 240, 251

Job
2:3 221
40:4 312
42:2 312
42:3 312
42:5-6 312

Psalms
4:7 281
19:1 32
21:13 38
23:3 203
23:6 34
36:9 190
42 63
42:1-2 10
89:27 87
96:3-10 37
96:10 158
103:19 52
112:1 . . . . 221, 222
115:3 . . . . 51, 54
119:18 100
127:1 281
128:1 222
128:4 223
139:23-24 74
145:9 206
145:17 58

Proverbs
2:1 102
2:1-11 179
2:2 102
2:3 102
2:4 102
2:5 102
4:18-19 170
4:19 166
4:23 257
7 3
7:1-3 69
7:22-23 4
9:10 231
10:14 16
13:10 148
14:11-14 281
14:12 3
14:27 223
16:9 51
17:24 . . . . 175, 177
19:21 51
19:23 223
22:3, 5 3
22:4 223
29:25 229

Ecclesiastes
1:3 277
1:13 276
2:1-3 278
2:4-6 278
2:7-8 278
2:9-11 278
2:12-13 278
2:12-23 278
2:14-19 278
2:18-21 278
2:20-23 278
2:24-26 279

3 277
3:1-3 277
3:9 277
3:11 40
3:16 278
3:18-21 . . . . 277, 278
4:13-16 278
5 280
5:19 280
11:9–12:1ff 274
12:1 282
12:11 275
12:12 274
12:13 274
12:13-14 . . . . 220, 282

Isaiah
1:2 122
6 216
6:1-8 217
11:2 . . . . 221, 245
11:6-9 284
14:12-14 35
40 52
40:15-17 53
40:25 30
40:26 52
41:10 . . . . 229, 232
43:1-5 197
46:9-10 51
46:10 54
53 86
53:6 . . . . 122, 256
55:8-9 311
55:9 300
66:2 230

Jeremiah
6:16 176
9:23-24 153

10:6-7 212
17:9 265
30:10 232
32:38-41 217
46:28 232

Ezekiel
18:4 78
37:3 61

Daniel
5:4 213
5:5-6 213

Zephaniah
3:16-17 232

Haggai
1:6-7 281

Matthew
5:1-12 207
5:8 16
5:16 30
5:23-26 151
5:45 206
6:24 10
7:24-27 . . . . 171, 194
8:5-10 255
11:20-28 305
11:28-30 230
13:36 136
13:51 136
15:14 28
16:13 189
16:15 190
16:16 190
16:17 190
18 251
18:6 244
18:15-20 151
22:31-32 298
22:37-38 36

23:37 305
26:37-38 17
28:18 51
28:18-20 . . . . 303, 309
28:20 196

Luke
8:9 136
8:10 136
10:27 9
12:42-47 244
15:11-32 85
15:12 256
17:3-4 151
22:22 305
22:24 148
22:25-27 158
24:45 192

John
1:10-11 245
1:12 . . . . 78, 126
1:14 . . . . 79, 87
1:29 . . . . 86, 309
3 135
3:16 . . . . 26, 168, 309
3:16, 36 303
3:19-21 166
3:36 . . . . 77, 310
5:40 305
6 . . . . 305, 307
6:37 . . . . 305, 309
6:44 303
6:44, 45, 64-65 305
8:12 166
8:44 265
10:10 ix
10:11 309
12:24 10
13-16 185
13:34-35 121

14:9 87
14:12 204
14:16-18 186
14:25-27 186
15 203
15:4-5 . . . . 208, 281
15:8 30
15:19 170
15:26 . . . . 188, 191
15:26-27 186
16:7 94
16:7-16 187
16:13-14 . . . . 96, 128
16:13-16 188
17:14-16 170

Acts
2:23 309
4-5 49
4:27-28 306
5:5 214
5:11 214
5:29, 41-42 268
5:41 49
6:3-5 204
7:55 204
9:5 207
9:6 193
9:31 222
11:24 204
13:48 305
14:15-17 275
15:14 198
16:14 306
16:25 1
17 275
18:10 56
19:17 215
26:18 166

Romans
1 . . . . 167, 256
1:4 80
1:17 266
1:18, 20 77
1:25 19
3:10-18 78
3:18 . . . . 215, 220
3:23 . . . . 30, 32, 36, 62
3:26 . . . . 67, 80
4:25 80
5:5 120
5:8 120
6-8 202
6:23 . . . . 37, 77
8:9 94
8:14 . . . . 105, 202
8:15-16 125
8:16 126
8:22-23 . . . . 17, 45
8:28-29 303
8:28-30 59
8:29 . . . . 60, 304
8:30-32 104
8:32 . . . . 83, 88
8:33 56
9-11 . . . . 58, 298
9:14, 19-20 58
9:18-20 298
10:14 56
10:16 310
11:33 . . . . 144, 302
11:33-34 58
11:36 28
13:1-8 258
15:6 30
16:25-27 44

I Corinthians
1:10-13 149

1:20-23 152
1:25 153
1:26-29 147
1:27-28 170
2:2 89
2:6-8 170
2:8 152
2:9-10 96
2:9-14 105
2:12 169
2:14 110
3 149
3:1-4 149
3:6 306
6:20 30
10:31 . . . . 30, 42
12-14 187
13:4-8 207
13:12 . . . . 61, 106, 284
15 86
15:5-8 198
15:17-28 80
15:20-28, 51-58 48

II Corinthians
3:18 . . . . 131, 188
4:3-4 166
4:3-6 87
4:4 265
4:7 147
4:7-11 25
4:16-18 25
4:17-18 19
5:4 . . . . 17, 45
5:14-15 37
6:4-10 25
7:1 . . . . 215, 222
11:23-30 25

Galatians
1:4 . . . . x, 169
4:4-5 79
5:16 203
5:16-17 187
5:22-23 . . . . 202, 207, 245
5:22-26 187
5:23 105
5:25 203
6:1 . . . . 247, 249
6:7-8 123
6:14 . . . . 90, 169

Ephesians
1 . . . . . . 13, 14, 43, 49, 57, 66,
68, 69, 115, 311
1-3 . . . . 13, 14, 27, 157,
198, 199, 269
1:1 81
1:1-14 102
1:1–2:10 . . . . 156, 283
1:3 . . . . 27, 81
1:3-14 . . . . 43, 68
1:4 . . . . 49, 56, 57, 81, 86, 303
1:4-5 60
1:4-6 31
1:4-6a 43
1:5 . . . . 50, 54, 60
1:6 81
1:6b-12 43
1:7 81
1:7-8 80
1:7-12 31
1:8 50
1:9 . . . . 45, 50, 54, 283
1:9-10 46
1:10 . . . . 81, 283
1:11 . . . . 50, 81
1:12 83
1:12-14 43

1:13 81
1:13-14 . . . . . . 31, 68, 94, 104
1:13-14, 17 198
1:13-23 93
1:14 107
1:15-23 94
1:17-18 102
1:18 . . . . 102, 105, 128
1:18-19 108
1:19-21 . . . . 90, 108
2 . . . . 69, 142, 151, 153
2:1 . . . . 70, 141, 228
2:1-3 70
2:1-10 . . . . 70, 154
2:2 72
2:2-3 . . . . 75, 228
2:3 75
2:4-7 78
2:5 81
2:6 81
2:7 . . . . 46, 67, 83, 140
2:10 . . . . 82, 227
2:11-22 143
2:11–3:11 141
2:11–3:13 70
2:11–3:21 . . . . 156, 285
2:12 150
2:16 151
2:18, 22 198
2:19-22 156
2:21 82
2:22 82
3 . . . . 115, 142
3:3, 5 44
3:4 45
3:5, 16 198
3:6 . . . . 82, 156
3:11 . . . . 50, 82
3:11-10, 21 46

3:14-21 115
3:16-17 204
3:17 . . . . 116, 123
3:18-19 . . . . 123, 130
3:19 . . . . 85, 129, 131
3:20-21 . . . . 48, 133
3:21 31
4 . . . . 151, 155
4-6 . . . . . 13, 14, 157, 199, 269
4:1-6 155
4:13 131
4:17 . . . . 7, 164, 199, 273, 282
4:17-18 . . . . 11, 165
4:17-19 262
4:18 164
4:18-19 71
4:18ff 74
4:19 167
4:20-21 199
4:20-24 199
4:25 135
4:30 199
4:30-32 151
5 ix
5:3-17 167
5:18 . . . . 199, 201
5:21 215
5:22 259
5:22-33 . . . . 156, 285
5:25, 33 259
5:25-29 243
5:26-27 103
6:1 259
6:4 . . . . 243, 259
6:5 . . . . 215, 258
6:5-8 261
6:9 . . . . 241, 260
6:19 45

Philippians
1:6 104
1:21-23 89
2:5-11 79
2:8 84
2:13 104
3:8 . . . . 10, 89
4:6 229
4:8 178
4:11 266
4:12-13 267
4:13 224

Colossians
1:15 87
1:25-27 45
2:10 81
2:18 96
3:1-2 107
3:1-3 180
3:12 56
3:18 259
3:19 259
3:20 259
3:21 260
3:22 259
3:22-25 261
4:1 . . . . 241, 260

I Thessalonians
1:3-4 306
2:13 309

II Thessalonians
1:7-9 . . . . 77, 303
1:8 310
2:13 . . . . 303, 309
2:13-14 306

I Timothy
1:19-20 149

4:15-16 . . . . 102, 247
6:3-5 149

II Timothy
2:2 287
2:10 56
3:1 15
3:14 16
4:10 169

Titus
1:1 56
1:10-16 149
2:9-10 . . . . 259, 263
2:11-12 169
2:13 103

Hebrews
1:1-3 87
2:6-8 87
2:14-15 85
4:1 215
10:25 . . . . 135, 268
11:7 215
11:27 . . . . 3, 104
12:11 246
12:21 215
12:28 215
13:5 196
13:17 262

James
1:5 179
1:8 10
1:14-15 171
1:23-24 134
1:25 134
1:27 169
2:15-16 250
2:20-26 298
3:1 . . . . 241, 260

3:9 206
3:17-18 207
4:1-3 148
4:1-4 172
4:4 169
4:13-15 51
4:13-16 174

I Peter
1:2 . . . . 56, 60, 303
1:6 19
1:8 . . . . 80, 129
1:13 16
1:17 215
2:7 310
2:17 215
2:18 . . . . 215, 259
2:18-23 . . . . 261, 266
2:24 88
3:1-2 259
3:1-6 263
3:2 215
3:7 260
3:15 . . . . 15, 215
4:17 310
5:1-4 241

II Peter
1:3. 2
1:3-11 207
1:9 6
2:5 168
2:22 76

I John
1:9 62
2:10-11 123
2:15 . . . . 135, 168
2:15-16 169
2:16 182
2:27 188
3:2 106
3:16 85
5:4 170
5:20 196

II John
9-11 90

Revelation
1:5 85
1:8 28
2-3 205
2:1-7 89
2:2-3 14
2:4-5 85
3:15-20 10
3:20 118
4:11 33
5:9 . . . . 70, 91
5:12 144
6:15-17 77
15:3-4 58
22:17 57

Topical Index

Abraham, 151, 274
Adam, 32, 35-36, 37, 140, 285
adoption, 15
alienation, 164, 166
anxiety, 284
anxiety disorders, 229
Arndt, William, 203
assurance, 103, 115-33
   levels of, 125-28
   Spirit-taught, 128
atonement, 15
attributes of God, 54, 88
authoritarianism, 246
authority, 73, 161, 267

Babcock, Maltbie D., 55
Baxter, Richard, 287-89
beauty, 178
Belshazzar, 212
Bennett, William, 205
BJU Museum and Gallery, 65
"blessed assurance," 104, 123-28
blindness, 6, 273
   spiritual, 3-14, 27
boredom, 98-99
Bork, Robert H., 160
Bride of Christ, 70, 83
Bridges, Jerry, 53
Brooks, Thomas, 124, 126
Brown, David, 307, 311
Bruce, A. B., 204
Bunyan, John, 14, 218, 221, 225, 239, 261
Burroughs, Jeremiah, 192, 230
Byron, Lord, 41

Calvary, 71, 88, 89
Chafer, Lewis Sperry, 96
Chalmers, Thomas, 184
Changed into His Image, 101-2, 122, 134, 170, 171, 189-91, 192-93, 194, 201-2, 228, 256-57, 287
character, 171, 197, 205
Cheney, Lynne V., 160
children of disobedience, 70, 75
children of God, 78-86, 154
children of wrath, 75-76, 78, 154
Choy, Leona Frances, 129
Christian battlegrounds, 148
Christian Education: Its Mandate and Mission, 179, 181
Christian liberty, 4
Christlikeness, 105, 207-8
Church, the, 70, 139-58
   formation of, 140-58
   triumphant, 69
Comforter, the, 93, 186-87, 188, 191
conformity to the world, 181
"created for His glory," 33-39, 227, 290
creation, 52, 56
Creator-God, 29, 33, 36
Crosby, Fanny, 127-28
cross, 79, 88
cultural weightlessness, 183
culture, worldly, 5, 15, 42. *See also* popular culture

dark mysteries, 273, 278, 279, 282, 283, 284

darkness, 6, 166
David, 10, 32, 36, 236, 246
De Haan, Richard, 276 ·
deference, 260-62
defiance, 256-60, 262
dependence, 18-20
depression, 9, 18, 63
desire, 172, 177, 180
"desire" and "indulge," 172
desire-oriented life of a fool, 175
despair, 6-14, 17-20, 164, 167,
    273, 275, 278, 283
    definition of, 278
Devil, 72. See also Lucifer, Satan
Disciple-Makers, 17, 40, 62, 87,
    110, 134, 158, 182, 205, 229,
    249, 269, 287
    need for, 287
discipleship themes, 182
disobedience, 73, 74, 75
    to God, 73-75
disorders, 37, 94. See also anxiety
    disorders
diversion, 175
divine mystery. See mysteries
down payment, 107
doxology, 27
drug therapies, 11
dwell, meaning of, 116

Eadie, John, 306
earnest of the Spirit, 94, 107-8
Ecclesiastes, 220, 273
    dark mysteries of, 273
Edwards, Jonathan, 50-51, 99,
    218
elect, the, 56
election, 56-62, 127
Elisha, 2

emotion vs. emotionalism, 130
emptiness, 7, 11, 164, 175
end-time demonstration, 48
end-time universal demonstra-
    tion, 49
Ephesians, divine mysteries of,
    282
Equation of Enjoyment, 279-81
essence of man, 220
eternal security, 109
evangelism, 33-38
    responsibility of, 56
Eve, 35, 285
externalism, 199-200
extreme sports, 12

faith, 18, 126
Fall, the, 32, 35, 140, 164, 180
false teachers, 96
farm, 176
"Fascination ≠ Illumination,"
    100
fathers, directives to, 243-45
fear, cure for, 229
fear of the Lord, 15, 211-28, 230,
    232, 233-52, 253-69, 271
    definition of, 216
    trademark of, 239-40
feminism, 159-61
Ferguson, Sinclair B., 74
filled with the Spirit, 201-4
First One, 33, 36, 74
"firstness" of God, 31-38, 290
flesh, 170, 187
fleshly headship, 245
fool, 171, 175, 180-81, 276
foreknowledge, 59, 61
fruit of the Spirit, 207
fullness of God, 131-32

Gabriel, Charles H., 131
"Gallery of the Heavenlies," 66-68, 87, 93
Gentiles, 141, 145, 148, 150, 152, 154, 156, 167, 197
gifts, 147, 187
Gingrich, F. Wilbur, 203
glory, 48, 49
glory of God, 25, 29-39, 42, 48, 49, 87
   definition of, 29
goads, 275-76
God
   as supreme, 36
   at the center, 7, 273
   His decisions, 58
   His glory. See glory of God
   His holiness, 30
   His plan for the ages, 143, 145
   His wisdom, 59
   ordained authority, 73
   the Father, 83
godliness, 221, 228
Goodwin, Thomas, 126, 127
grand demonstration, 62
grand reality, 28, 37, 238, 241, 266
Grand Reality Principle, 238, 255
Grand Reality, the, 238, 255
grieving the Holy Spirit, 199-201
groaning, 45
Guest, Christ as, 117

habits of the heart, 171, 177
Havergal, Frances R., 55
"hear" and "do," 172, 204
heavenlies, the, vii, x, 13, 90
Henry, Matthew, 221, 222, 240

hermeneutics, 31
Hiebert, D. Edmond, 306
Hillary, Edmund, 29, 32-33
hippies, 11
Hodge, Charles, 120, 164-65
holiness of God, 30
Holy Spirit, 69, 74, 83, 90, 93-109, 129, 130, 134, 185-205
   filled with, 201-4
   fruit of, 207
   function of, 96
   grieving, 199-201
   indwelling of, 94
   "leading of the Spirit," 105
   ministry, 187-88, 194-95
   mission, 128
   responding to, 185
   seal of, 104-5
   security of, 43, 93-109
   walking in, 159
   work of, 198
hope, 77, 102, 103, 105, 239, 262, 267, 270
Horton, Ron, 179
house-down, 116-17, 123, 124. See also dwell
humility, 41, 101, 150-56, 239, 256, 262, 267, 270, 271
husbands, directives to, 243
Hymn Texts
   Amazing Grace, 308
   And Can It Be That I Should Gain, 84
   At Calvary, 84
   Blessed Assurance, 127
   How Firm a Foundation, 55
   I Am His, and He Is Mine, 132

I Know Whom I Have
Believed, 308
Like a River Glorious, 55
Look, Ye Saints! the Sight Is
Glorious, 144
My Saviour's Love, 131
This Is My Father's World, 55
hymns, 127, 131, 144
suggestions for meditation, 81

illumination, 8, 14, 25, 88, 95,
96, 97-102, 107, 109, 110, 127,
136, 189, 190, 192
content of, 194-98
effects of, 191-94
Illustrations
Badge and a Gun, 241-42
baseball diamond, 60
Blind Man Sees, 97-98
blind students at BJU, 3, 6
BJU Museum and Gallery, 65-
66
Bob's Squad Car, 264
Boy and a Judge, 72-73, 75
Chief Greenhouse Keeper,
243-45
Christian's Interpreter, 195-96
Cleaning the Carpet, 120-21
Dog Show Parable, 46-48
Dog's Life, 99
Dirty Dishes or a Dirty Heart?,
257-58
Equation of Enjoyment, 279
Extreme Everything, 11-12
Fast Farming?, 176-76
Final Challenge, 285-86
Fireworks in the Heavenlies,
68-69
Fixing an Engine, 227

Flower Children, 11
Grief of a Broken Heart, 200-
201
It Depends on Which Side of
the Law You Are On!, 219-
20
Just One of God's Pets, 33
King on the Hill, 148
Lessons from a Medicine Cab-
inet, 4-5
light bulbs, 147-48
Lost in a Cave, 165-66
Loving and Fearing My
Father, 223-25
Man Without an "Engine,"
163-64
Midlife Crisis, 8-9
Mt. Everest, 29, 32-33
Pagan Mythology, 23
Pile on the Firewood and Pray
for the Fire!, 101-2
Pride in Her Parenting, 146-
47
sand sculpture of family pet,
207
Summer Ministry Teams, 116-
17
Ted/Trisha, 12-13
Tinkerbell, the Cat, 231-32
Trusting Strangers, 264-65
Volkswagen bug, 60, 163, 226
What Is Done for the Groom
Is Done for the Bride!, 83-86
What Is He Doing Here?, 82-
83
What Is Your Tolerance of
Vomit?, 76-77
When Dad Comes Home,
172-74

World Trade Center Towers, 211-12
Wounded Hearts, 233-36
impatience, 176
"in Christ," 81
"in the heavenlies," 13, 14
indulgent-oriented life of a fool, 180
indwelling of the Spirit, 94
inheritance, 106, 127
inner man, 116, 118-19, 123, 132
Ironside, H. A., 57
Isaiah, 53

Jesus Christ, 17, 188
  as Guest, 117
  as Master, 119
  center of all things, 283
  central to God's plan, 82
  importance of, 86-91
  "in Christ," 81
Jews, 141, 145, 147, 152, 156
Jews and Gentiles divided, 145
Jews and Gentiles reconciled, 141
Job, 6
John, 110, 185
Jones, Bob, Sr., 173, 183, 200
joy, 19
  in the Lord, 15

Kaiser, Walter C., 220, 274, 281
Kelly, Thomas, 144

last days, 15
leadership, 248
"leading of the Spirit," 105
Lewis, C. S., 301
light, 166, 181

Lloyd-Jones, D. Martyn, 63, 65, 119, 130, 150, 283
logic, 298-99
love, 36
  rooted and grounded in, 120
Lucifer, 35, 67, 69. See also Devil, Satan
lust, 172
  of the flesh, 75

manliness, 221
marriages, hurting, 121
Master, Christ as, 119
meditation, 37, 74, 111, 232
Meyer, F. B., 129
midlife crisis, 8, 10
Minnick, Mark, 48, 60
Moody, Dwight L., 129
moral destruction, 11
Morgan, G. Campbell, 149
Morris, Leon, 306
Moses, 104, 152, 213-14
Moule, H. C. G., 61, 71, 118, 310
Mt. Everest, 29, 32-33
Myers, Kenneth, 41-42, 170, 173
mystery, 48, 59, 156, 282, 284-85
  definition of, 44
  divine, 44
  of Christ, 45-46, 82, 156, 283, 286
  of Ephesians, 45-46, 156
  of the gospel, 45
  of marriage, 156, 285
  of the Church, 156, 285
"mystery of his will," 45
mysticism, 95

nails, 275, 279

Nehemiah, 251-52
New Age Movement, 41
Newell, William R., 84
Not by Chance: Learning to Trust a Sovereign God, 62, 297

Owen, John, 7, 74, 85, 111, 127

Packer, J. I., 124, 126, 195
Paul, x, 10, 13, 14, 17, 19, 25, 26-27, 31, 44, 45, 49-50, 55, 57, 58, 63, 68, 69, 88, 94, 105-9, 133
peace, 153
  with God, 139
  with men, 139
perilous times, 15
permissivism, 248, 256
Peter, 6, 9
Phillips, John, 31, 139, 157
plan of salvation, 78-86
popular culture, 42, 170-71, 172, 183. *See also* culture
pornography, 9
postmodernism, 11
power of God in us, 108
power struggles, 148
preaching, 74
predestination, 59, 60
pressures of life, 173-74
pride, 59, 145, 147, 148, 149, 151-54, 157, 226, 248
primitivism, 41
providence, 52, 56
Puritans, 6, 124, 126, 127, 247

rationalism, 41
real-time demonstrations, 48, 49
reality shows, 12
realm

physical, 25
spiritual, 2
supernatural, 25
rebellion, 180
reconciliation, 151, 153
Redeemer, 81, 83, 84, 86, 90, 140
redemption, 53, 56
  story of, 78-86
reflection, 8, 135, 136
  necessary for illumination, 134
"Reflection − Illumination = Despair," 8-13
relativism, 160, 178, 180
responsibility of man, 57
resurrection, 80, 83
"Revelation − Reflection = Self-Deception," 135-36
"Revelation + Reflection = Illumination," 136-37
Robinson, George Wade, 132
romanticism, 41
Rookmaaker, H. R., 181
Ryrie, Charles, 29

salvation, 46, 56, 59, 62, 68, 69, 71, 128, 297-312
  plan of, 78-86
sanctification, 202, 207, 228, 243
Satan, 35, 75. *See also* Devil, Lucifer
satisfaction, 281
Saul, 246
Schaeffer, Francis A., 181
seal of the Spirit, 94, 104-5
"secret things of God," 61
Securing One, 93
security, 15, 43, 94
security of the Spirit, 43, 93-109

"seeing the invisible," 2, 37
"seeing the unseen," 13
self-centeredness, 121-23
self-deception, 135
self-esteem, 269
self-exaltation, 73
self-expression, 181
servant of God, 34
Shakespeare, William, 298
Short, Royce, viii
Simeon, Charles, 309
"slavish fear," 225, 256, 261
social decline, 11
Solomon, 236, 273-82
Solomon, Jerry, 40
"sonlike fear," 225
sons of disobedience, 75
sonship, 125, 127
sorrow, 17-20
Sovereign One, 67
sovereignty of God, 43-62, 238-
    39, 241, 256, 262
spelunkers, 165
Spirit. See Holy Spirit
spiritual blindness. See blindness
spiritual gifts. See gifts
spiritual strengthening, 115-16
Spurgeon, Charles Haddon, 190,
    307
stress-relief, 174
submission, 253-69
subordination, 239, 256-62
suffering, 268
sufficiency, 15
    of Christ, 43, 65-86
    of God, 68
Sufficient One, 67, 87
supremacy of God, 15, 23-39, 42,
    66-67, 263

Supreme One, 66, 67
surrender, 118

Tagliapietra, Ron, 33
Talbert, Layton, 53, 62, 297
television, 11, 173, 176
temptation, 177
terrorists, relational, 158
Torrey, R. A., 125
Tozer, A. W., ix, 13, 18, 38, 52,
    110, 190
trademark, 240
trademark of the fear of God,
    239-40
transcendence, x, 15, 40-42, 277
Trinity, 79
trust decisions, 265-66
Twelve, the, 204

unity, biblical, 139-58
universalism, 45

video games, 173
virtue, human, 205, 206-7
vulnerability, 15, 211, 219

"Walk and Warfare of the
    Believer," 14
walking in the Spirit, 159
Warfield, B. B., 26
"Wealth of the Believer," 14
Wesley, Charles, 67, 84
When Trouble Comes, 264
wisdom, 176, 179, 230
    of God, 59
wise man, 171
"Witness of Our Own Spirit,"
    125
"Witness of the Spirit Himself
    with Our Spirit," 126

work of the Holy Spirit. *See* Holy
  Spirit
world, the, 168, 169
  definition of, 170
worldliness, 4, 42, 122, 168-74,
  181, 184
  definition of, 176
  remedy for, 184

worldling, 177, 180, 181
  definition of, 175
worldview, 11, 40, 42, 171, 274
  biblical, 182
  supernatural, 25
  transcendent, 40
wrath of God, 76-77, 80, 88